CSR and Sustainability

CSR and Sustainability

The Big Issues of the Day

Michael Hopkins

ANTHEM PRESS

Anthem Press
An imprint of Wimbledon Publishing Company
www.anthempress.com

This edition first published in UK and USA 2022
by ANTHEM PRESS
75–76 Blackfriars Road, London SE1 8HA, UK
or PO Box 9779, London SW19 7ZG, UK

and
244 Madison Ave #116, New York, NY 10016, USA

British Library Cataloguing-in-Publication Data
A catalogue record for this book is available from the British Library.

Library of Congress Control Number: 2022932182

ISBN-13: 978-1-83998-513-3 (Hbk)
ISBN-10: 1-83998-513-5 (Hbk)

ISBN-13: 978-1-83998-516-4 (Pbk)
ISBN-10: 1-83998-516-X (Pbk)

Cover Image: Professional Photographer/Philip Stockton

This title is also available as an e-book.

CONTENTS

PREFACE

For what is a man, what has he got
If not himself, then he has naught
To say the things he truly feels
And not the words of one who kneels
The record shows I took the blows
And did it my way

[Frank Sinatra, 'My Way']

When I first heard the song 'My Way' sung by one of the most brutal dictators I had ever been near – I was in the front row as a special invitee to President Desi Bouterse's 50th birthday celebrations in Paramaribo, Suriname, in October 1995 – I realized that 'my way' might have been successful for the president, but it wasn't necessarily the right way! It was also the time that I started working on issues of social responsibility, and I wondered who I was working for in Suriname that day.

In fact, I was part of an EU structural adjustment mission aimed at stabilizing Suriname, which was a bit out of the ordinary since normally those issues were addressed by the IMF/World Bank, which would place their then – normal austerity regime on the country requesting its help. Suriname rejected the structural adjustment approach of the IMF/World Bank since it thought it would be better served by the more progressive EU.

Yet I was unsure of what would be the big issue to address, especially as I had learned that, as my former mentor and boss Prof. Dudley Seers, the founder of the Institute of Development Studies in Sussex University, told me, 'the problem with many development advisers is simply that they don't know who to be seen drinking with'. I am pretty sure he didn't mean tea, and I am not sure I had absorbed his lesson.

This book aims to promote social responsibility and sustainability and, more particularly, to link them with 'big' social issues. I dream of a world in which science and positive thinking can prevent violations of human rights, global warming, growing income inequality (aka relative poverty), racism, gender discrimination and absolute poverty.

Given the power of the USA, I thought it useful to look at CSR in the US context and compare it with what has been going on in Europe, as well as elsewhere. My focus is the USA – still the world's most powerful nation with most of the largest corporations – especially because I had spent 2007–2013 there, which made me want to see how I could explore more my own vision of CSR as a strategic tool that can help both corporations and society. To that end I joined the bastion of US corporate power – the US Chamber of Commerce – where my job was to promote CSR. Well, perhaps the vaguely pinkish part of it that focused on something called corporate citizenship. Happily, a decade later I see that the US Chamber now has an institute of CSR that works in partnership with Johns Hopkins University to earn a 'Professional Certificate' in Corporate Social Responsibility. And, my name is still there, albeit perhaps of a different Hopkins![1]

The talk of a new 'responsibility' by Obama when I arrived in the USA had further fuelled my hopes of entering a new era and being able to contribute in some way. The striking appearance of President Obama from seemingly nowhere gave hope to many that persuasion, diplomacy and democracy cannot be assigned to the rubbish heap of hope so carefully nourished by the mean Reagan to Thatcher to Bush years. In the emerging market countries, the lack of responsibility has often been the cry from the West. However, the 25 November 2015 announcement by China of its first firm target for limiting greenhouse gas emissions in carbon emissions, coupled with the spread of corporate responsibility mutterings throughout the Third World, has turned the previous scepticism on its head. Then the Trump years took us all into depths we didn't know existed – we were faced with a president who had recorded over 20,000 lies in four years and one who would say and do anything to get his own way. In fact, he was the perfect example of a person with a complete lack of social responsibility. Yet, how did 73 million people vote for him? Did they also accept lies and zero social responsibility as the new normal?

Since the Trump years, I was impressed with the fact that the USA has a huge slice of responsibility by electing Joseph Biden,[2] even though my concerns remain. As stated in an article written by Suzanne Moore in *The Guardian* in the UK,[3]

> in Europe and, as we can see, in the US too … entirely false promises are being made, but this is a fantasy that comforts many. It is a fantasy of withdrawal from a globalised world, stopping the free movement of people and labour. The real challenge … is to counter this, not with some old-school internationalist vision, but with something that is both local and modern, that accepts there is anxiety instead of telling people they are simply wrong and stupid to feel it, or that it is some kind of false consciousness.

Maybe my mind is clouded today because of the false promises Moore refers to as well as the ease with which social media can be accessed, but was the world always such a mess and do we just happen to know more about it now because we have 24-hour news coverage, something that CNN first made a reality just a few decades ago?

This book is about a new era for business. When I wrote my first book on CSR, *The Planetary Bargain*, in 1995, few thought then that if companies had anything to do with corporate social responsibility. Today, it is generally accepted that companies, large or

---

1. https://www.csrwire.com/events/2986-2017-Institute-for-CSR, accessed 20 July 2020.
2. See Hopkins, 'CSR the New Way..was I Wrong?' Linkedin, Pulse, 2016, accessed 19 August 2016. https://www.linkedin.com/pulse/csr-new-waywas-i-wrong-dr-michael-hopkins
3. Suzanne Moore. https://www.theguardian.com/commentisfree/2016/jul/20/world-going-to-hell-in-handcart-but-no-time-to-disengage, accessed 20 July 2016.

small, can no longer ignore major events outside of their immediate sphere of influence – what I refer to as the big issues of the day. Clearly, the rise of COVID-19 has awoken even the most capitalist (some say selfish) companies to move away from solely profit maximization at any cost.

Drawing on the work of Ed Freeman of the Darden School and Donna Wood, I had built my own definition of CSR around the notion of stakeholders. As my thousands of students know over the past two and half decades, I insist the basis of CSR is to *treat all key stakeholders responsibly* – what is meant by treat, key, stakeholder and responsibly was the subject of my work for many decades and can be found in my last book on CSR, *CSR and Sustainability*. It is a text book – there is a summary in this book when I write about the H-CSR-M – on the Hopkins CSR Model of CSR.

The rationale for this book is that I have spent nearly 25 years and written three books advocating for the incorporation of Corporate Social Responsibility and Sustainability (CSR), which I have now extended as will be seen later in this book, into all bodies and institutions, be they private, public or NGO and for these institutions to treat their stakeholders responsibly.

Happily, the world is catching up with me. The USA-based Business Roundtable announced in 2019 the release of a new Statement on the Purpose of a Corporation signed by 181 CEOs, who committed to[4] 'lead their companies for the benefit of all stakeholders – customers, employees, suppliers, communities and shareholders'. Further evidence for such a change was the focus of the 2020 World Economic Forum on stakeholder capitalism followed by a survey by *Forbes*, which interviewed the top Fortune 500 CEOs and found that 48.2 per cent of them thought that the COVID-19 pandemic would accelerate the move towards stakeholder capitalism. In parallel, the single most important thing for the CEOs was that 'leadership and values matter always but especially in a crisis'.

I now see that working with corporations has meant that I (and they and, in general, the private sector) have ignored many big issues in which social responsibility is key. The COVID-19 pandemic has led me to think that now the private sector has been given increasing prominence, and to avoid the collapse of capitalism a la Marx, the new way must be a mixture of public and private economies with a strong dose of responsibility. And since that heady time of progressive Marxist thought what have we seen? Amazingly, CSR has taken root, and every large company and many governments have adopted CSR.

Yet, is the rise of CSR (or whatever we call it) enough? Since that time of rise and promise for CSR we have seen the rise of Islamic fundamentalism, the disastrous Iraq War mistakenly conducted because of 9/11, the collapse of the Middle East and the rise of the most vicious and nasty group of fanatics since the Nazis known as IS. More recently, we have read the stunning analysis of a few greedy American capitalists – whose greed led to the rise of the amazing gibberish of Trump and disastrous Brexit – in Jean Mayer's *Dark Money*.

---

4. https://www.businessroundtable.org/business-roundtable-redefines-the-purpose-of-a-corporation-to-promote-an-economy-that-serves-all-americans, accessed 19 August 2019.

Take Brexit. I voted against it and also organized an anti-Brexit petition over the course of two years (see my book *Brrrexit*[5]). The EU has never been perfect, but the mixture of isolationism, underlying racism and anti-immigration that characterize, to my mind, Brexit goes too far. It also seems to me that the vote against was composed of people worried about their jobs in the North outside London and the racists in the South, also outside London – i.e. mainly political against the naive Cameron and the directionless Corbyn. Such a decent man as Corbyn woefully misdirected the UK into the clutches of Old Etonians, PPE scholars from Oxford, where I wonder what they teach, and imperialist UK upper classes, who wish to keep the nation white (or pink rather!).

Then come all the lies from that awful racist Farage, as well as the even more awful Boris Johnson supported by Dominic Cummings (who said that the EU costs GBP 350 million per week – an out and out lie) – more awful because smart people using racism to win an argument, even though they can easily argue both sides – like Jean-Marie Le Pen in France – totally disgusts me. As does Putin, killing innocent people for his dream, presumably, of greater glory. I see zero social responsibility in any of that.

So, as CSR rises, the world falls apart. Was I wrong to put my life for 25 years into CSR? Is it worth continuing that work, or should I now turn into an activist and try to influence even one person who has fallen into the trap of nihilism and anti-immigration? In fact, I am trying through the world of entertainment and have written and played, with my music teacher Sylvia Delap, a dozen songs during 2021/22.

Global problems abound: worsening income distribution, high unemployment and underemployment, increasing debt, global warming with climate change, terrorism, repression, human rights abuses, financial crisis and so on. Can, therefore, advocates of more responsibility in our societies, such as myself, be optimistic? Or, as some argue, is it the end for us and our planet?

Certainly, half the people on the planet are already in dire straits and the 'end' has come for them. Is the 'end' also to come to most of us in advanced societies as well?

There is one clear sign of optimism. The ultimate indicator of development is life expectancy at birth. Don't just take my word – I follow Dudley Seers, author of the classic study on the meaning of development. Data from the World Bank show that life expectancy on average for the world as a whole has increased steadily, for instance, from 52.7 in 1960 to 69.4 years today.

Yet concerns about the limits to growth have always been with us – from prehistoric times to the times of the classical economists such as Thomas Malthus and to contemporary times when *Limits to Growth* was written by Dennis and Donella Meadows and their MIT team in 1971. Their work stimulated my interest. I was a researcher at the University of Sussex working on crop yields in northern India when Jorgen Randers, one of the MIT authors, blew my mind with a global simulation model that mapped out that economic growth would result in resources running out, pollution that would asphyxiate the earth and the eventual collapse of the planet around 2050. I thought

---

5. https://www.amazon.com/Brrrexit-England-will-left-cold-ebook/dp/B0849ZLN7G (Michael Hopkins, Amazon.com, 2020) accessed 1 July 2020.

I have to get into that! I did. I worked with Dennis and Donella Meadows and their team in Hanover, Germany, thanks to a NATO grant, and became, temporarily, the UK specialist on Dynamo, the software behind the limits to growth. I was then invited to join the ILO, a UN agency specializing in labour and employment issues, to 'do' a world employment model with the objective of doing something about unemployment and underemployment around the world.

My first book on CSR, *The Planetary Bargain*, documented the period to the end of the 1990s when I wanted to find out what the private sector was doing on development after having spent two decades with the UN (ILO) working with governments on employment and development. I stumbled upon CSR. I showed it mattered and had come of age in that first book. My second book, *CSR and International Development*, showed how the concept had spread further afield into emerging economies during the beginning of the second millennium and how companies themselves had come to see the benefits of international development. Frankly speaking, the analysis and prognostics in the second book surprised even me, as I saw the uptake by companies of international development concerns going much, much further than I had originally envisaged. Today, the idea that corporations are concerned about the global natural environment and those at the bottom of the pyramid and are willing to use CSR to mitigate conflicts in areas where they operate is no surprise. I summarize both books in two chapters of this book and update their key ideas a little.

I have always taken the 'S' in CSR to cover the social sciences, especially social phenomena, economics and finance – thereby closely relating the concept to the business case or how to make profits with CSR – and environmental issues. Thus, CSR is a system-wide business strategy which is holistic, innovative and breeds sustainability. Sustainability, on the other hand, is the aim and end result of an effective CSR strategy. Increasingly, too, the three capitals ESG (Environment, Social, Governance) are cropping up in company lexicons as a 'new' guide to companies. In fact, this book also offers guides on what is next in ESG.

I am indebted to Nadine Hawa for showing me the link between CSR, Sustainability and ESG as far back as 2011. Nadine was a brilliant student (Lebanese/Canadian and presenter/producer CNBC Europe) in the course I directed at the University of Geneva. She took time to reflect not only on my original definition of CSR, but also the various strands introduced during one of our course modules where different, and sometimes confusing, definitions were presented by Nestlé (Shared Value), Intel (Corporate Responsibility and Sustainability) and the UN (Global Compact) in May 2011. She also reflected on the link to ESG considerations and thought that this was 'the 3 wider areas of focus of effective CSR' in which CSR effectiveness can be measured in terms of impact/quantity and quality. She also contributed to the idea that I have used in this book as well as in my writings elsewhere,[6] that 'Sustainability is the aim and end result of effective CSR strategy'.

---

6. https://www.researchgate.net/profile/Michael-Hopkins-4/research, accessed 16 November 2021.

Cynics can always point to PR campaigns and lip service to proud, but ineffective, statements. Yet, if we turn our minds to the 1960s, we can see that there have been huge strides in responsibility since then. In the 1960s, smoking was still glamorously advertised, nutrition details on the side of cornflakes packets didn't exist, child labour was what developing countries had to do, corruption was more or less OK, since every donor had a recipient, and our large corporations, such as Shell, ICI and Cadbury, were widely admired as being good for society. This book maps the rise of a new social movement for responsibility, ethics and caring among institutions and business, something that has not been seen since the heady days of Roosevelt, Beveridge and Gandhi.

In particular, the focus is on the new corporation. The days of exploitation by major business entities of labour, environment, women, children and our financial systems have taken a huge jolt as we enter the second decade of the twenty-first century. As the book will outline, exploitation continues wherever uncontrolled greed appears. Human nature is complex, with some believing so much in free enterprise that nothing else matters. On the other hand, many, and a growing number, realize that business as the heart of our freedom must respect the rules of the game – be they legal frameworks or personal rules shaped by evolution over decades. This book will explore these aspects.

The book, therefore, takes stock of the explosion in interest, writings, websites, newsletters, blogs and social media interest in CSR and its offshoots. The book untangles these concepts and shows that increased social responsibility can also increase the chances of achieving sustainability both inside and outside of a corporation or institution. Thus, as noted above, the book will also widen the concept of 'corporate' to include both public and third-sector (NGOs and Social Enterprises) institutions.

The book will also serve as a reader to my present, past and future students, who I have had, and shall continue to do so, the privilege to host in the executive education programmes I direct, and have directed, across the world. It is also addressed to students both in and out of formal institutions wherever they are, including executives who struggle with the often-bewildering array of concepts and actions. It will update, in two chapters, my previous ideas in my first two books on CSR, thereby bringing up to date my earlier literature reviews while focusing on what I see as the key texts in an exploding literature on the subject of CSR. After examining a number of case studies and stories of good and bad examples of CSR, I outline what I see, today, as a strategy for CSR in companies as well as non-private institutions.

This is the fourth book I have written about CSR, stretching over a period of 15 years. In many ways, this book was much harder to write for two main reasons. First, the subject has taken off to the extent that just about all Fortune 500 companies now have social (also known as sustainability) reports. Second, there is so much new material that it is not easy to keep a book to manageable reading length. There are, of course, numerous criticisms of the concept of CSR, and I always thought that this, my fourth book on CSR issues, would be 'CSR a triple oxymoron'. Perhaps that will be my fifth book but what is surprising is that I still maintain my interest in the subject and don't easily fall into a heavy criticism of other theories, which is often the way the peer-review system gives rise to a lot of negativity in the business academic literature.

Thus, this book will update what CSR is all about, as well as the updates mentioned above. I shall also revisit my measurement chapter with suggestions on how to measure the impact of CSR while not ignoring newish ventures into measurement by such bodies as the Global Reporting Initiative (GRI) and explaining the newish field of impact measurement. But the three main thrusts of this new book will be: first, that CSR has a tendency to fragment into easily handleable morsels such as the fashionable use of the word 'sustainability'; second, concerns with the wider social and economic environment are now critical concerns for companies and institutions and we can now talk about CSR as a strategic tool to conduct the affairs of a company; and third, that the methodology and sentiment of CSR can be extended to the non-private sector. This sector includes the public sector, the civil society sector known as NGOs and a relatively new sector known as the third sector, which covers the growing influence of social enterprises.

Eventually, my plan is to ask all companies to state their position on the big issues via a CSR/Sustainability Annual Charter. The charter will be short, so as to be easily read, and cover issues that concern them through a written statement on how they will deal with external stakeholders as part of their CSR/Sustainability Strategy. I give an example for the Nestlé corporation. The key issues are usually obvious and today probably cover at least democracy, global warming and the COVID-19 pandemic. Certainly, this idea has been given a big boost by the awful COVID-19 pandemic and the forthcoming global warming panic (pandemic too?), which have forced companies to reconsider their business models and the need to care far more than they have in the past about the society they work in.

Chapter One

INTRODUCTION TO CSR, THE TURBULENCE TODAY AND WHY SOCIAL RESPONSIBILITY IS NEEDED MORE THAN EVER BEFORE

Introduction

There has been an explosion in interest in CSR (and related subjects such as corporate sustainability, ESG – Environment, Social, Governance etc.). Yet, as the take-up of CSR rises across the world, the concept seems to fragment into sub-issues such as CSR projects and philanthropy. Does this fragmentation mean that corporations and institutions don't take their social responsibilities seriously?

Or is it only a few such as those involved in scandals (News Corporation's press phone hacking; FIFA's continuing avoidance of corruption allowing Manchester City to avoid Financial Fair Play; tax avoidance by many companies and their CEOs[1] – some of the world's biggest companies such as Apple, Facebook and Google avoid paying an estimated $500bn (£358bn) a year in taxes through shifting their profits[2]), the financial collapses (Lehman and Dubai World) and institutional carelessness (rendition to Libya by the USA and the UK, acceptance of torture by the Bush administration, the Afghanistan disaster, violation of the rule of law by a US president as he freed his corrupt ally Roger Stone)?

Yet not all private companies are corrupt and many, especially the smaller ones, behave exceptionally well on widespread CSR right through the company or institution. One I know well – Ngombe in Africa, as I was told by its CEO Manu Shah – had been trading for 72 years, had never fired an employee and, during COVID times, had kept its employees on full salary despite running down its profits to zero. Ngombe is an excellent example of CSR. There are many more as shall be introduced in this book while not ignoring that many large-scale corporations are rotten to the core. Is the glass half full of good CSR or half empty? As I shall show, the movement is gaining pace and, although the glass is far from overflowing, not everything is bad.

---

1. https://www.theguardian.com/inequality/2021/jun/10/wealthiest-americans-tax-report-details?CMP=Share_AndroidApp_Other, accessed 11 June 2021.
2. https://www.theguardian.com/business/2021/jun/02/eu-agrees-to-force-multinationals-to-disclose-tax-piling-pressure-on-uk, accessed 10 June 2021.

These questions will be examined with perhaps the key question being whether CSR, or however it is interpreted as many clone the concept from triple bottom line to ESG to corporate sustainability to corporate citizenship or corporate sustainability, takes us into a new vision of caring societies or are we witnessing the early signs of a collapse of capitalism? Authors such as my close friend Guy Standing[3] see a collapse of capitalism, as the few make billions from what he calls rentier capitalism and as workers get left behind and see their wages stagnate. He cites Oxfam, who noted that two-thirds of the 2043 billionaires in 2017 gained their wealth from a mixture of inheritance, monopoly and cronyism. The richest 1 per cent was worth more than the other 99 per cent. Thus capitalism must change to the new realities since few want a return to state capitalism and its associated loss of freedoms. I shall argue in this book that the best way forward is a combination of strong and democratic government intervention coupled with social responsibility from all parts of the spectrum, especially from large corporations.

Brief History of CSR[4]

We keep hearing that CSR is an old concept and we should now focus on sustainability or social innovation (SI), ethics or corporate responsibility without the 'S'. Through this book, I attempt to prove that there is still life in the 'old dog' even though there is a tendency to search for the 'new', simply to edge ahead of fellow academics and/or to present to the board a unique concept for one's unique company. Arguably, Nestle and Kramer/Porter's 'shared value' concept discussed in Chapter 1 and GE's 'eco-imagination' both fall into these latter categories. My own definition in the next section widens the concept to cover public institutions as well as NGOs.

In fact, the social responsibility of business was not widely considered to be a significant problem from Adam Smith's time to the Great Depression. However, since the 1930s, and increasingly since the 1960s, social responsibility has become 'an important issue not only for business but in the theory and practice of law, politics and economics'. In the early 1930s, Merrick Dodd of Harvard Law School and Adolf Berle of Columbia Law School debated the question, 'For whom are corporate managers trustees?' Dodd advocated that corporations served a social service function as well as a profit-making function, a view repudiated by Berle. This debate simmered for the next 50 years, according to Gary von Stange, before it once again sprang into prominence in the 1980s, in the wake of the 'feeding frenzied atmosphere of numerous hostile takeovers'. This concern for the social responsibility of a business has accelerated since the fall of the Berlin Wall in 1989, which symbolized the collapse of communism and turbocharged globalization.

Further acceleration occurred in the 1990s. Significant was the Ken Saro-Wiwa affair. He was the leader of the impoverished Ogoni tribe in Nigeria who had worked to

---

3. In a speech to Institute for Responsible Leadership and UNITAR via Zoom, 18 June 2020.
4. Draws upon a draft paper by Michael Hopkins and Ron Cambridge, 'Historical Roots of CSR', August 2018.

gain access to more of oil's benefits and less of its negative effects. Oil-related activities in Ogoniland caused (and continue even to this day) grave damages to the environment. On average, one oil spill occurs every week in Nigeria. Approximately 6,000 kilometres of pipelines cover Ogoniland.[5] Ken Saro-Wiwa and his eight fellow MOSOP officers were eventually held on trial for murder and hanged on 10 November 1995. Shell's image suffered badly from this incident resulting from its do-nothing stance. The cause had been strongly supported by Body Shop but was not picked up until too late by the media. Shell also suffered further problems with the Brent Spar fiasco, which was an abandoned attempt to ditch an oil rig in the deep waters of the Atlantic, opposed some-what flashily, but carelessly, by Greenpeace.

One of the first ethical reports of a company was the social statement of Anita Roddick's Body Shop in early 1996. It laid out a threefold 'mission' statement: It (1) believes that business has a moral responsibility to tell the truth; (2) is a high-profile advocate of social and environmental causes, so that, because sometimes this upsets people, if a company wants the licence to campaign on public issues it must demonstrate its own commitment to reflection and self-improvement on issues like environmental protection, animal protection and human rights; and (3) has – if it is to continue to mix business with politics, cosmetics with campaigns – to take its supporters and stakehold-ers (including customers, employees and suppliers) along with it.

As noted previously, if the word 'sustainable' is seemingly everywhere, it was made possible by the team led by Gro Harlem Brundtland. Global concerns were given an additional edge by the awful event of the terrorist attacks on the USA on 11 September 2001 (now known simply as 9/11). The collapse of Enron and World Com, along with their auditor Andersen in 2007 due to dubious accounting practices, then raised the level of examination of large companies as well as their auditors. Moreover, previously quiet CEOs had begun to note the pressure; for instance, in a rare public appearance in June 2002, the chairman and chief executive of Goldman Sachs Henry M. Paulson Jr. stated, after the collapse of the Enron Corporation in late 2001, "I cannot think of a time when business overall has been held in less repute."

Since then, there has been an explosion in the interest of companies (and now even NGOs and governments) on CSR. Too many activities have occurred to cite them all. Perhaps the main occurrences in the 'noughties' were the UN Global Compact, the rise of Sustainability Reporting led by the Global Reporting Initiative and the fact that nearly all Fortune 500 companies issue reports these days covering not only the environment but economic and social concerns as well with strong references to stake-holders. Then COVID-19 led to the increase in investigations on the role of companies, especially those responsible for the manufacture of vaccines. In India, after the country was a key exporter of vaccines, a sudden, huge surge in the virus and many deaths led to a closer look at companies and their roles. India is the first country, after Mauritius, to create a CSR tax of 2 per cent on the profits of its largest companies that originally

---

5. Margaret Onwuka, *Blood, Sweat, Tears and Oil: The Mistreatment of the Ogoni by Royal Dutch Shell and the Nigerian Government* (Poverty and Prejudice, EDGE Spring 2004).

went to CSR projects but now are widening to multi-stakeholder considerations (see Chapter 18).

CSR essentially refers to the manner in which a business corporation integrates social (social, economic, financial and environmental) issues into its business model, and as you will see later in this chapter CSR is defined using the stakeholder concept based on the work of Ed Freeman et al. who in their book stated that

> there are many different ideas, concepts, and practical techniques that have been developed under the umbrella of CSR research, including corporate social performance, corporate social responsiveness, corporate citizenship, corporate governance, corporate accountability, sustainability, triple bottom line, and corporate social entrepreneurship. All these are different nuances of the CSR concept that have been developed in the last fifty years – and beyond. Each of these diverse efforts shares a common aim in the attempt to broaden the obligations of firms to include more than financial considerations. This literature wrestles with and around questions of the broader purpose of the firm and how it can deliver on those goals.

Up until the 1970s, despite regulations and legislation, businesses largely continued along an autonomous path, ignoring its critics and listening only to its shareholders, to whom it felt somewhat responsible. But the 1960s was to be a period of enlightenment for many. The Korean War had ended indecisively, and new conflicts in South East Asia seemed destined to follow the same pattern. Citizens were distrustful of governments, of businesses and of the undefined 'establishment'. Consumers had grown suspicious of adulterants in their food and dangerous defects in the products they bought. People were becoming aware of the fragile nature of the earth's ecology while simultaneously becoming more cognisant of human rights.

Associated with the rise of this new 'child' are the many different names including corporate conscience, corporate sustainability, corporate citizenship, corporate social performance and sustainable responsible business (Wood 1991[6]), and some have even branched out into the field of social innovation (SI). As every designer in the fashion industry attempts to claim originality with every creation, CSR was probably observed before, even if under a somewhat different name. But whatever the label, isn't a rose still a rose?

Yet, Ed Freeman noted[7] that 'the blunt interpretation of Milton Friedman's view that the corporation should care only for profit maximization and do nothing more than comply with the legal requirements' was explicitly rejected by Davis.[8] This argument is not based on philosophical considerations but is developed in managerial (risk management) terms: to ignore social obligations seemed to Davis a very dangerous

---

6. Donna J. Wood, 'Social Issues in Management: Theory and Research in Corporate Social Performance', *Journal of Management* 17 (1991): 389.
7. R. Edward Freeman, *Strategic Management: A Stakeholder Approach* (Boston: Pitman, 1984).
8. K. Davis, 'The Case for and Against Business Assumption of Social Responsibilities', *Academy of Business Management* 16 (1973): 312–22. in Wood, 'Social Issues in Management'.

corporate strategy. This is because of the 'iron law of responsibility', which states that when society grants legitimacy and power to a business, 'in the long run, those who do not use the power in a manner which society considers responsible will tend to lose it.' We can see some seeds of stakeholder theory in Davis's approach to CSR, particularly in the idea that corporations have broader obligations than solely to stockholders.

So returning to the theme of this chapter, CSR has been around for a long time. Without CSR there is no business. It is self-evident that a business which does not engage in CSR, or at least some form of social awareness (and thus creates value), will not survive. From the individual farmer who sells eggs in the local market to the larger businesses, it is the ability to provide an answer to social needs that allows any business enterprise to operate and survive. It is the social added value that creates financial gain for businesses. If there is no social need for the product or the service offered by a business, then no business will survive, not to speak of profit. One does not require models of CSR, sustainability or SI to understand that very simple logic. What is needed, however, is to ensure responsible treatment of stakeholders (company boards, shareholders, employees, managers, customers, contractors, suppliers, government, local communities, environmental champions, etc.). It is no use selling eggs to customers if they are past their sell-buy date and thereby lead to illness. Nor will a business that breaks societal laws be able to hold long onto its retained profits, as so many of our 'trusted' banks have shown us.

This simple business logic was also obvious to those who created the first share-owned organizations. These joint-share-owned businesses were created by social beings to create social value and thus economic profit. The Roman Republic government used private contractors 'publicani', or 'societas publicanorum' for its services.

The oldest company known was Kongō Gumi Co., Ltd., a Japanese construction company that operated for over 1,400 years until it was absorbed as a subsidiary of another larger construction company. Headquartered in Osaka, the once family-owned construction company traced its origins to the year AD 578 when one of the skilled immigrants, whom Prince Shōtoku brought from Baekje to Japan to build the Buddhist temple Shitennō-ji, decided to start his own business. Over the centuries, Kongō Gumi participated in the construction of many famous buildings, including the sixteenth-century Osaka Castle.

It finally succumbed to excess debt and an unfavourable business climate in 2006. But how does one make a family business last for 14 centuries? According to Bloomberg, Kongo Gumi's case suggests that it's a good idea to operate in a stable industry. Few industries could be less flighty than Buddhist temple construction. The belief system has survived for thousands of years and has many millions of adherents. Kongo Gumi also boasted some internal positives that enabled it to survive for centuries. Its last president, Masakazu Kongo, was the 40th member of the family to lead the company. He has cited the company's flexibility in selecting leaders as a key factor in its longevity. Specifically, rather than always handing reins to the oldest son, Kongo Gumi chose the son who best exhibited the health, responsibility and talent for the job, and thus the signs of social responsibility, from the earliest of days.

Other examples around Europe can be observed in the mid-1200s in France at Toulouse, with the Société des Moulins du Bazacle, or Bazacle Milling Company. In the late 1200s, there was 'Stora', the Swedish mining and forestry product's company. But perhaps the earliest acknowledged share-owned company in modern times was the English East India Company, which was granted an English Royal Charter by Queen Elizabeth I at the end of 1600 with the intention of furthering trade privileges in India and providing the company with a monopoly on all trade in the East Indies (Douglas[9] 1991). It is therefore almost offensive that as it acquired more auxiliary governmental and military functions, the company then transmuted from a commercial trading venture to one that virtually controlled India.

As CSR, globalization too is an old term. In early 1600s, the Dutch East India Company was innovative in issuing the first tradable shares on the Amsterdam Stock Exchange, allowing the attraction of more capital as well as creating an ease of share disposition by existing shareholders. This company, the first multinational megacorporation that traded 2.5 million tons of cargo with Asia on 4,785 ships and had sent a million Europeans to work in Asia over two centuries, stands as the very example of a business that responds to the social needs of society and thus creating economic growth for both society and the company itself.

I thus go back to my contention that many aspects of CSR have been around a very long time. It is apparent that the innovation of joint share ownership contributed a great deal to Europe's economic growth, which also illustrates quite clearly that without social concern there is no business enterprise and hence no economic profitability. Of course, more recent changes have happened, such as environmental concerns (hardly of much interest before the Second World War), care for communities (the need to avoid tragedies like the Bhopal-gas disaster), compliance (laws abound like there is no tomorrow), social licence to operate (there is a growing literature on this strange concept), employee motivation (volunteering), reputation (globalization and the internet are still recent phenomena) and so forth.

What Is CSR All About?

I don't want to go too far into this book without providing the definition of CSR that I have used, and taught, over two and a half decades while gradually refining and improving the CSR concept according to the current times.[10] An academic treatise of CSR was given in my first book, *The Planetary Bargain: Corporate Social Responsibility*

---

9. D. Irwin, 'Mercantilism as Strategic Trade Policy: The Anglo-Dutch Rivalry for the East India Trade', *Journal of Political Economy* 99, no. 6 (1991): 1296–314. Retrieved 29 June 2021, from http://www.jstor.org/stable/2937731

10. Some of this section was drawn, and updated, from an earlier article of mine which has proved popular on Research Gate with over 70,000 reads to date; see 'What Is Corporate Social Responsibility All About?' *Journal of Public Affairs* 6, no. 3–4 (August 2006): 298–306 and https://www.researchgate.net/publication/246912286_What_is_corporate_social_responsibility_all_about

Matters, and a dissection of the three words 'corporate', 'social' and 'responsibility' was provided in my second book *Corporate Social Responsibility and International Development*. My own definition of CSR is based on an earlier work by one of the early pioneers in CSR, Donna Wood[11], whom I interviewed in the early 1990s and who has since been the inspiration behind much of my CSR work. Two further major influencers on my work starting in the 1990s have been Gro Brundtland (see 'Caring for the Earth'[12]) and Ed Freeman (Darden School, Virginia), sometimes known as the father of stakeholder analysis and with whom I have interacted. My experience was further enhanced over a number of years through leading the teaching of business executives starting with Middlesex University in the UK in the year 2000, the advanced certificate on CSR at the University of Geneva that I started in 2007, and many other locations where I have been fortunate to continue to teach and discuss. What most teachers know is that if one is fortunate enough to have good students as I have had, one learns as much as one teaches through the feedback and experiences of others. More and more teachers to graduate students share papers and discuss, rather than lecture. Those papers can be found in depth in my third book, *CSR and Sustainability: From the Margins to the Mainstream* (Greenleaf, UK, 2016).

My definition of CSR is presented and discussed below but, first, let's have a quick look at other definitions.[13]

Archie Carroll, [1979; 2008]: 'The social responsibility of business encompasses the economic, legal, ethical and discretionary expectations that a society has of organizations at a given point in time.'

EU: 'A concept whereby companies integrate social and environmental concerns in their business operations and in their interaction with their stakeholders on a voluntary basis.' This changed in the year 2011 to a more limited version as 'the responsibility of enterprises for their impacts on society'[14] i.e., ignores internal stakeholders!

Mallen Baker: 'CSR is about how companies manage the business processes to produce an overall positive impact on society.'

The World Business Council for Sustainable Development (WBCSD): 'Corporate Social Responsibility is the continuing commitment by business to behave ethically and contribute to economic development while improving the quality of life of the workforce and their families as well as of the local community and society at large.'

---

11. Adele Santana and Donna J. Wood, 'Information, Corporate Social Responsibility, and Wikipedia', *Ethics and Information Technology* 11, no. 2 (2009): 133–44.
12. *Our Common Future*, a report by the World Commission on Environment and Development published in April 1987 by a team led by Gro Harlem Brundtland. Now it is known famously as the Brundtland Report.
13. References next section.
14. http://sdg.iisd.org/news/european-commission-proposes-new-csr-strategy/, accessed 29 November 2021.

Some Comments on These Definitions

Carroll: This describes well what society might expect of a business but ignores external stakeholders at that time. Today, Archie is a firm supporter of the multi-stakeholder view of CSR that I advocate and as Caroll writes[15] the 'three imperatives' of great leadership[16]: (1) managing your team – creating a high-performing 'we' out of all the 'I's' over whom you have formal authority; (2) managing your network – building partnerships with *key stakeholders* both inside and outside your organization; and (3) managing yourself (using yourself as an instrument to get things done) – what I call in this book 'personal responsibility'.

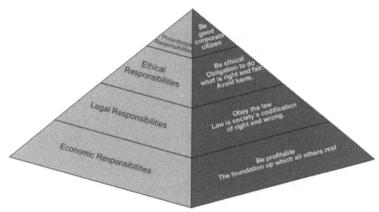

Carroll's CSR Pyramid

Carroll's definition is often pictured in the above CSR pyramid and is where many CSR practitioners and theoreticians start. As can be seen above, he argued that companies should have economic responsibilities. Obviously, without making a profit, a company will cease to exist and eventually CSR dies. Moreover, the key issue is that CSR is not anti-profit but how profits are made, and this theme runs through this book.

Carroll then goes on to mention legal responsibilities but does not consider those countries where the law is ignored (corrupt governments, for instance) or has been modified to support cronyism. No easy guide here, but remember what the heroic Second World War pilot Douglas Bader said, 'Rules are made for the guidance of wise men, and the observance of fools'.[17]

---

15. https://www.linkedin.com/posts/archie-b-carroll-6911117a_being-the-agile-boss-activity-6700023016656515073-iMGj, accessed 15 August 2020.
16. Similar to how we treated in the 'Institute for Responsible Leadership' that I co-founded see https://responsible-leadership.org/, accessed 1 October 2020.
17. http://thinkexist.com/quotation/rules_are_for_the_obedience_of_fools_and_the/13177.html, accessed 2 September 2011.

Ethical responsibilities come next, but it seems that ethical behaviour (see, for instance, *Business Ethics* by Andrew Wicks)[18] is not so easy to define. The best is the golden rule used by many peace lovers, which is 'do unto others as you would wish to be treated yourself' and is my basic mantra on ethics.

At the top of Carroll's pyramid is 'philanthropy'. I shall discuss in a later chapter the link between CSR and philanthropy. Donna Wood has had a fascination with Carroll's pyramid and famously put the pyramid on its head with philanthropy at the bottom – not actually to my liking as will be seen later in this book. In my own model, discussed in detail in Chapter 2, I play down the role of CSR in philanthropy and do not treat any of the levels as superior, or inferior, to any of the remaining other levels in the pyramid.

EU: Here we have a consideration of both internal and external stakeholders. But it does not say how social values are to be addressed, i.e. responsibly or ethically, but simply to interact. This could mean simply reading a newspaper to a full-fledged approach. But, the main issue is the word 'voluntary'. In early discussions of CSR, the fear was that CSR meant that there would be a new set of standards followed by laws on *all* aspects of CSR. Today, there is a concern that too many standards could bring the industry to a halt. What I think is that each law or standard needs to be carefully treated so as to ensure that serious abuses are illegal while others do not interfere with local customs and culture. Clearly, such a statement raises a whole host of questions as to whether, for instance, women should be forced to wear headscarves or forced not to in some countries? What do you think?

Mallen Baker Model: Mallen Baker is included here because of his interesting blog and discussion on CSR definitions.[19] (His definition is limited in only looking at the impact 'on' society. But his graph provides a wider view, as does the text on his website, where he states that 'companies need to answer to two aspects of their operations: (1) the quality of their management – both in terms of people and processes (the inner circle); (2) the nature of, and quantity of their, impact on society in the various areas.' Yet he does not explore further in terms of internal stakeholders, preferring to note that 'outside stakeholders are taking an increasing interest in the activity of the company'. Most look to the outer circle – what the company has actually done, good or bad, in terms of its products and services, in terms of its impact on the environment and on local communities, or in how it treats and develops its workforce. Of the various stakeholders, it is financial analysts who are predominantly focused on the quality of management as an indicator of likely future performance as well as past financial performance.

WBSCD[20]: The World Business Council is a CEO-led, global association of some 200 companies dealing exclusively with business and sustainable development. It simply mentions ethics and contribution to economic development as two key components of CSR. Thus most of its members tend to see CSR as promoting economic development,

---

18. Andrew Wicks, R. Edward Freeman, Patricia H. Werhane, and Kirsten E. Martin, *Business Ethics* (Prentice Hall, Paperback, 2009).
19. see: http://www.mallenbaker.net/csr/definition.php, accessed 31 March 2014.
20. http://www.wbcsd.org, accessed 31 March 2014.

particularly in emerging (developing) countries. Only mentioning economic develop-ment is one of the reasons why CSR tends to be sometimes misunderstood as essentially focusing on development.

Sustainability

Increasingly the notion of sustainability has taken over from CSR. Many use the adjec-tive or the noun as substitutes for CSR or CR. Are they right? If the word 'sustainable' is seemingly everywhere now, it was made possible by the Brundtland Report, *Our Common Future*, discussed earlier. The report was a landmark document that brought environ-mental concerns and their link to social and economic development to the forefront of our understanding of global problems. *Our Common Future* launched the notion of 'sus-tainable development', defining it as 'development which meets the needs of the present without compromising the ability of future generations to meet their own needs'.

Indeed, corporate sustainability is increasingly being taken up by corporations, lead-ing one to wonder what is the relation between corporate social responsibility and cor-porate sustainability. As noted above, the term 'sustainability' first came to widespread acceptance in 1987, and at that time the concept and study of sustainable development had hardly left the domain of environmentalists and ecologists. More recently, the term 'sustainability' has grown to encompass social and economic components as well as its historical work on the environment. Thus the sustainability school has split, rather confusingly, into two: the first being the conservationist school described above (which I denote by 'Sustainability 1') and the second that has moved out into the social and economic field (which I denote by 'Sustainability 2').

PricewaterhouseCoopers define corporate sustainability[21] as 'aligning an organisa-tion's products and services with stakeholder expectations, thereby adding economic, environmental and social value'. And the Global Resources Initiative (GRI), which grew out of environmental work by the Coalition for Environmentally Responsible Economies (CERES) and the United Nations Environment Programme (UNEP), has been producing, since June 2000, the GRI Sustainability Reporting Guidelines that cover economic and social performance as well as the more 'traditional' environmen-tal ones. These are continually upgraded, with the most recent guidelines stating that 'the GRI Standards represent global best practice for reporting publicly on a range of economic, environmental and social impacts. Sustainability reporting based on the Standards provides information about an organization's positive or negative contribu-tions to sustainable development.'[22]

21. https://www.pwc.in/en_IN/in/assets/pdfs/publications/2013/handbook-on-corporate-social-responsibility-in-india.pdf, accessed 17 December 2020.
22. https://www.globalreporting.org/how-to-use-the-gri-standards/gri-standards-english-lan-guage/, accessed 29 November 2021.

Thus, the world of business continues to embrace the notion of sustainability and many are now producing 'sustainability reports'. Yet, Zadek warned[23] that 'it is simply inaccurate and misleading to talk about "sustainable business". The "sustainable" in sustainable development is just not the same as the "sustaining" of a particular business, irrespective of its social and environmental performance.'

The confusion with what is meant by 'sustainability' leads me to prefer the term 'CSR' with its more lofty goals since it talks not only about issues that will sustain a corporation but also those for which a corporation is responsible. Whether there are additional concerns in the CSR toolbox that will, ultimately, provide for longer-term sustainability than those in the sustainability toolbox is a point worthy of further discussion. A useful working approach to CSR and sustainability is to use CSR as the *process* through which *sustainable development* as defined by Gro Brundtland is the goal, especially as many businesses confuse Sustainability 1 (mainly, environmental concerns) with Sustainability 2 (the aim of CSR as defined here). One further comment is that if companies accept sustainability as a goal, then they are moving towards wider society aims of sustainable development. You will find, of course, that companies use terms interchangeably and quite like the term 'corporate sustainability' as interpreted by *sustaining* their company. You will, when working on these concepts, have to be careful that you adopt the full CSR stakeholder model and not assume that a profitable company is aiming at 'sustainable development'. Increasingly, however, in my writings, I use the term 'CSR/sustainability' where I mean Sustainability 2. Nevertheless, what is important is *how* profits are made in a socially responsible manner, not profits at any cost.

My Definition De-constructed into Different Parts

Well, you have seen a number of widely quoted definitions. Let us now return to the definition of choice that I believe fits well to what the early pioneers of CSR advocated.

The definition[24] of CSR is one that I have based upon the original definitions as far back as the 1960s but have steadily improved and changed as time and experience move forward.[25]

---

23. Simon Zadek, *The Civil Corporation: The New Economy of Corporate Citizenship* (London: Earthscan, 2001), 122.
24. Original Source: Michael Hopkins (MHCi), *A Planetary Bargain: Corporate Social Responsibility Comes of Age* (Macmillan 1998, updated and re-printed by Earthscan 2003 and also re-printed by Routledge, UK, 2010). Updated to emphasize materiality on 2 October 2014. Also updated in Michael Hopkins, *CSR/Sustainability – From the Margins to the Mainstream 'A Text Book'* (Sheffield: Greenleaf, 2016). Further updated definition 1 Jan 2017 with clause 6 with thanks to Siemens and also Bob Munro (who worked with Gro Brundtland on 'Caring for the Future' where the idea of sustainability arose) for edits.
25. See for instance Hopkins, 'What Is Corporate Social Responsibility All About?' Special Issue: Corporate Social Responsibility, August–November 2006, (John Wiley) and also see https://onlinelibrary.wiley.com/doi/abs/10.1002/pa.238, accessed November 2010.

Therefore:

1. CSR is a process that is concerned with treating the stakeholders of a company or institution ethically or in a responsible manner. 'Ethically or responsible' means treating key stakeholders in a manner deemed acceptable according to international norms.
2. Social in C'S'R includes economic, financial and environmental responsibility. Stakeholders exist both within a firm or institution and outside. It includes at least an organization's leaders, staff, shareholders and suppliers, as well as the consumers and users of their public goods and services. It may also include media, government and the wider society.
3. The wider aim of social responsibility is to create higher and higher standards of sustainable living while preserving the profitability of the corporation or the integrity of the institution, for peoples both within and outside these entities. The key is how profits are made, not the pursuit of profits at any cost.
4. CSR is a process to achieve the goal of sustainable development in societies. Both CSR and sustainability address multi-stakeholders and their materiality.[26] Thus CSR and sustainability are interchangeable concepts, with the former relating more to the process and the latter more to the goal.
5. Corporate means any body that is private, public or an NGO; thus my definition applies neatly outside the traditional private corporate sphere and covers all institutions, be they public or private.
6. There must be a business case for working with stakeholders. These include the wider society, and, as such, being a responsible company or institution means working in partnership with society and being part of its long-term development. Longer-term 'big' issues are key to prevent collapse and are the responsibility of institutions.

This definition is a bit of a mouthful, so if I meet you in the street I want you to at least remember the essential part, and you won't go far wrong in using and applying it, which is:

CSR Is about Treating Key Stakeholders Responsibly

A good definition essentially defines the conceptual model from which all the elements can easily evolve. I deconstructed the above definition in great detail in my text book *From the Margins to the Mainstream*, but I am confident in the above statement for a number of reasons. First it evolved from the great US thinkers in the twentieth century. Second both the EU and ISO26000 just about use the main thrust of the definition. Third, it

---

26. Discussed more in Chapter 3 Based upon Unilever materiality process, see https://www.unilever.com/sustainable-living/our-approach-to-reporting/defining-our-material-issues/, accessed 31 August 2020.

covers just about every element of what we want to say. Perhaps the key element, and the link to sustainability, is to add the definition of sustainable development which I do in the next section.

Sustainable development

Sustainable development is development that meets the needs of the present without compromising the ability of future generations to meet their own needs as defined by the UN-sponsored report on *Our Common Future* chaired by Gro Brundtland [8].

Thus CSR aims to seek sustainable development as its goal.

In Chapter 4 I use the definition to develop what I call the H-CSR-M, a model that is designed to help companies and organizations implement CSR and sustainability.

Thus CSR is essentially treating key stakeholders responsibly, and sustainability these days is just about the same. In fact CSR is simply business strategy with an eye on the long-term not solely the quarterly financial report. Note, again, from the above definition that CSR and sustainability emphasize profit making with the rider that it is 'how' a company makes profits, not profits at any cost. CSR is also a business strategy that looks more at the longer term than chasing the quarterly financial report or the daily stock market ratings.

CSR (also commonly referred to as corporate responsibility) is a strategic systems approach (see Chapters 4 and 19) that examines and influences the behaviour of a company while preserving its competitive advantage.

Let me deconstruct that sentence:

- CSR means treating the main stakeholders of a company in a responsible manner.
- Corporate means any group of people that work together in a company or organization, whether for profit or non-profit.
- Social means the social system and includes finance, economy, environment and social issues.
- Responsibility is about taking issues that affect the corporate body seriously and about acting within – and even beyond – societal norms.
- Strategic means having a strategy that takes an idea into a working model.
- A systems approach means including all aspects of the system in the decision-making process.
- Competitive advantage is the implementation of a value-creating strategy, not simultaneously being implemented by any current or potential competitors.

What is corporate?

Corporate means any group of people that work together in a company or organization, whether for profit or non-profit. Consequently, interpreted in this way, 'corporate' means any 'body' of individuals and therefore can include NGOs, public institutions and social enterprises (increasingly known as the third sector).

What is a stakeholder?

Stakeholder theory has its roots in the work of Ed Freeman[27] who argued that [...]

> I can revitalize the concept of managerial capitalism by replacing the notion that managers have a duty to stockholders with the concept that managers bear a fiduciary relationship to stakeholders. Stakeholders are those groups who have a stake in or claim on the form. Specifically I include suppliers, customers, employees, stockholders, and the local community, as well as management in its role as agent for these groups. I argue that the legal, economic, political, and moral challenges to the currently received theory of the firm, as a nexus of contracts among the owners of the factors of production and customers, require us to revise this concept. That is each of these stakeholder groups has a right not to be treated as a means to some end, and therefore must participate in determining the future direction of the firm in which they have a stake.

A typical stakeholder map for a company could look like the one displayed in the graph.

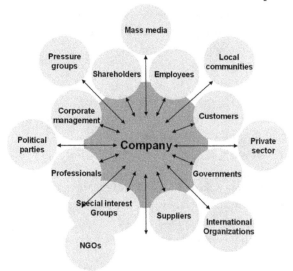

*   Slide Compliments of Klaus Leisinger, Novartis Foundation

Note that stakeholder theory has moved on. Here, and following a more recent custom for instance, the environment is included as a stakeholder and, in that way, the social, economic and environmental model of the firm is complete. Some argue that the

---

27. Freeman, *Strategic Management.*

environment is not a 'person' but that can be side-lined since there are representatives of the 'environment' such as NGOs and/or the communities in which people live.

The choice of stakeholders, and how to consult them, is an art in itself and no one theory covers all aspects. A widely cited article on this is by Mitchell, Agle and Donna Wood[28] who stated that stakeholder identification should be based on three variables: *Power* to influence the firm, *Legitimacy* of the stakeholders' relationships with the firm and the *urgency* of the stakeholders. Of the three the one needing more clarification is the question of legitimacy that is defined[29] as 'a generalized perception or assumption that the actions of an entity are desirable, proper, or appropriate within some socially constructed system of norms, values, beliefs, and definitions'.

You may have noticed by now that I treat the word 'corporate' as any collection of bodies or institutions and not necessarily solely large corporations. Since I was in Nairobi at the time of the Westgate terrorist attack and was struck by the awful reporting of the media, the misleading statements of politicians and the total confusion, I created the following stakeholder diagram.

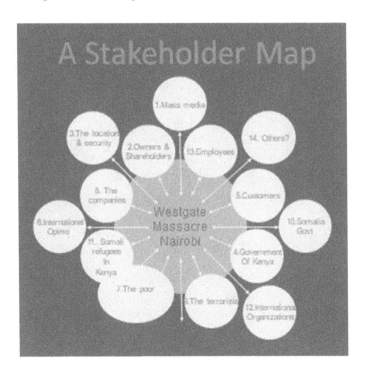

---

28. Ronald K. Mitchell, Bradley R. Agle and Donna J. Wood, 'Toward a Theory of Stakeholder Identification and Salience: Defining the Principle of Who and What Really Counts', *The Academy of Management Review* 22, no. 4 (October 1997): 853–86. Published by: Academy of Management.
29. Source: Stakeholder Salience, https://www.stakeholdermap.com/stakeholder-analysis/stakeholder-salience.html, accessed 15 August 2020.

If you are interested in how I used the above to come to my main conclusion – which was, because terrorists seek glorification of their disgusting deeds and this happens essentially through media, then there is strong case to ban media to report on ongoing events until the event has finished – see Chapter 13 for a full discussion.

These authors argue that the stakeholder theory must account for power and urgency as well as legitimacy, no matter how distasteful or unsettling the results are (the graph below is typical and, again, we use the example from UEFA). Managers must know about entities in their environment that hold power and have the intent to impose their will upon the firm. Power and urgency must be attended to if managers are to serve the legal and moral interests of legitimate stakeholders.

Take account of stakeholder salience – especially media

Level of interest →

Applies to all NFAs, large or small

What is ethical behaviour?

What is meant by business ethics? I had noted above that the easiest way to understand ethics is to apply the golden rule, which is to 'treat others as you would wish to be treated yourself'. Yet easy to further complicate ethics as many others, such as Rosamund Thomas have done,[30] note that there are many definitions of 'business ethics' in the same way that there are numerous different 'Codes of Ethics'. I find that this variety and looseness of terminology, methodology and 'best practices' can cause confusion. Thomas argues that 'business ethics' comprises at least three issues:

30. Rosamund Thomas in Ramon Mullerat (ed.), 'Corporate Social Responsibility – The Corporate Governance of the 21st Century', Kluwer Law International (revised edition, 2010).

1. the *values* underlying the business corporation, such as 'integrity', 'honesty', 'fairness' and others
2. a corporate *Code of Ethics*, which goes beyond separate values to become a set of principles that makes a clear statement of what the business corporation is willing to do or not to do, like forbidding staff to take bribes or other financial incentives
3. *corporate governance*, which is the framework for the policies and procedures that govern the board of directors in a business corporation, including non-executive directors and others who advise the board. Corporate governance is a key part of 'business ethics' since the morality of the board and its individual directors does, or should, underlie these policies and procedures

Thomas believes, for example, the remuneration of directors should reflect the values of 'fairness' and 'honesty'. Where, then, does the current trend for 'corporate social responsibility' fit? Historically, say during the first half of the twentieth century, British writers on 'business ethics', and practitioners, regarded the responsibility of a business company to its local, and the world, community as a key function of 'business ethics'. For example, B. S. Rowntree, Oliver Sheldon and Lyndall Urwick, at the Rowntree Company, York, and Edward Cadbury, who pioneered the model factory in Birmingham, all subscribed to this idealistic view but also put their ideas into practice –what, today, we might call 'best practice' and more.

However, 'business ethics' as a movement faltered to a large extent in Britain, America, and other countries after the Second World War and became intrinsic and less overtly stated as a philosophy, Code of Ethics, or set of practices, or became subservient to quantitative methods, including 'cost benefit analysis' which emerged during the 1950s and onwards.

Business ethics, and ethics in governance, began to resurface following scandals like Watergate in the USA, and others. By the late 1970s/1980s the emphasis was again on *morality*, but with the *social* commitments of business corporations still playing a lesser part. Trust, integrity and ethical dilemmas were thought to be subjects that could be taught to business and government leaders, with new courses developing, particularly in the US post-Watergate, for young students and for practitioners in the professional schools of business, public policy and so on.

Of course, some business corporations had continued throughout the twentieth century to set and uphold 'business ethics', while others disregarded them. But it was not the substance of books or courses on business management after the Second World War until the 1980s and 1990s.

It was nearly a decade later that the modern movement of 'CSR', particularly in Europe, became fashionable – pushed forward by the European Commission[31] and the European Parliament, as well as Scandinavia, Britain and other countries. In contrast

---

31. For example, the European Commission's White Paper *Communication from the Commission Concerning Corporate Social Responsibility: A Business Contribution to Sustainable Development*, Brussels, 2 July 2002, COM (2002) 347 final.

to 'business ethics', CSR focuses more on the *social, environmental* and *sustainability* issues than on 'morality' – although both the 'business ethics' and the 'CSR' movements have converged to an extent – with ever increasing responsibilities being added to both, such as anti-corruption practices, human rights and even the responsibility of directors for 'corporate manslaughter'.

Today, given the complexity and rapid development of globalization, the inter-relationships between developing and the developed nations, the growth of scientific and technological advances that create new ethical dilemmas, such as genetically modified foods, both 'business ethics' emphasizing the *moral* values and 'CSR' focusing on *social* and *environmental* performance, are of prime importance.

Chapter Two

WHERE IS CSR TODAY AND WHERE IS IT GOING?

The COVID pandemic continues to strike across the world as I write, and social responsibility has expanded more than ever before. My brief example in the previous chapter on the actions of Ngombe towards retaining its employees, despite the hardships to the company, have seen parallels right across the world as companies realise that they must value all their stakeholders responsibly and not just their shareholders. Multi-stakeholder capitalism is on the rise as companies need to keep their employees, customers, suppliers, investors, and the government on board. The stop-go of lockdowns, opening and lockdown again, showed the new face of capitalism as all struggle to survive, be it in the private or public sector.

Where Is CSR Going?

It is never easy to know exactly where corporate social responsibility (CSR) has been or is going. Most analyses only look at the partial picture of the multi-stakeholder approach (MSA) I advocate, even as more and more companies follow MSA. Unfortunately, in the absence of system wide surveys to measure MSA, only anecdotal evidence must suffice. For instance, I am often asked whether there is any difference between China and India on CSR, and my response has often been that countries in excess of 1 billion people have a multitude of different systems. On the other hand, CSR needs liberal democracy to survive and flourish. The hierarchical state of China hardly allows responsibility to all stakeholders especially those who even mildly criticise the Xie Government. Moreover, only outside pressure will lead to China observing international climate change rules since domestically the Party dominates and the economy is central whatever the costs may be. Nonetheless, CSR is discussed in China and, as one commentator noted,[1] 'although CSR has seen more than half a century of development in the West, CSR in China is a relatively new concept. With a history of authoritarian regimes largely tackling social challenges, social responsibility was hardly the commission of merchants and traders'.

Social responsibility has been the key word in numerous speeches and debates in the industrialized countries and, increasingly, in emerging markets. After long deliberations in the academic literature dating back to at least the early twentieth century, CSR

---

1. https://www.1421.consulting/2019/08/csr-in-china/, accessed 19 July 2020.

essentially sprang to global consciousness after the fall of the Berlin Wall in 1989. The peace dividend and the end of austere socialism of that time gave freedom and private enterprise an overwhelming victory. Yet, concerns of an over-bearing concentration of capital and power in private hands gave an impetus to how best the private sector could serve society, i.e. CSR.

A number of watershed reports and activities marked the new era. First, the 1987 World Commission on Environment and Development, also known as the Brundtland Commission, led to the largest ever United Nation Conference, known as the Earth Summit in 1992. Then the terms 'sustainable economy' and 'sustainable development' came into usage much before today's notion of a newer term 'Corporate Sustainability'. Second, the publication and activities surrounding Body Shop and its founder, Anita Roddick, led to the first widely read social report for a company.

Since that time, CSR and its closely related offshoots, corporate sustainability, corporate citizenship, corporate ethics, corporate shared value, and so on, have grown to the point that today every major corporation has its own social, CSR, corporate responsibility or sustainability report. Many now produce some form of social report every year.

The impact and implementation of the ideas embedded in these reports have been accelerating, as we can see by the increased use of labelling on consumer products, the rise in so-called organic and green products, the proliferation of global standards for just about every economic activity, the frequent reference to global reporting measuring systems such as the Global Reporting Initiative and the UN Global Compact.

The 'Arab spring' had also furthered our hope that democracy and freedom will flourish, sadly petering out over a decade later. But the recession that started in 2007, which can be attributed to the irresponsibility of our financial institutions and which turned our housing market into a gigantic casino, showed that responsibility was not as obvious as first thought. Our major companies toyed with CSR and loved the idea of corporate sustainability. Many still use the term CSR but others have searched for other expressions, which do not imply a lack of social responsibility previously. Sustainability implies that companies can go on forever, as long as they pay some attention to green products and processes. The sell is easier too.

My CSR Sustainability Rating App available on my website (www.csrfi.com) and also on mobile phones (accessible via Google Play) does provide a multi-stakeholder rating that shows the CSR performance of companies and institutions.[2] However, I have not used it to measure longitudinal performance over time, but if I had there is no doubt that performance would have improved right across the spectrum of companies (small, medium and large), especially in countries with some form of liberal democracy.

But even then, as a glance at any old movie of the 1960s would show, corporate behaviour has, as society itself, changed significantly. Then men were openly casually sexist, just about everyone smoked even in their offices, and alcoholic drinks at lunchtime, late afternoon and early evening were common. The links to health were

---

2. https://www.csrfi.com/rate-your-company, accessed 18 June 2021.

unknown, rubbish was thrown out of car windows, on-the-job training was nonexistent, and impacts on the natural environment, water and air were few unless it was right in your face such as the London smog of that time.

Only recently have companies realized that ethics and stakeholder relationships, both within and outside the company, have affected their competitive positions. Treating employees responsibly, ensuring suppliers don't have health hazards such as lead in petrol, starting to recycle goods as part of a circular economy, ensuring that ethical standards are followed by managers, directors and all staff and treating the environment as a key resource all lead to increased sustainability and profitability. Even the oft-criticised investment community has now embraced socially responsible investment to the tune of trillions of dollars – as much as 34 trillion and one in two out of every dollar invested according to some estimates.

The COVID pandemic, as discussed later in this chapter, has led to much more emphasis on stakeholder capitalism rather than shareholder capitalism, and in the coming decades concepts such as social impact, social capital, stakeholder relationship management and sustainable development will be part and parcel of every organization be it private or public. When I raised all these issues in my book *The Planetary Bargain* in 1995, I assumed it would take a hundred years or more for CSR issues to become mainstream. Maybe we are not quite there as rogue companies continue to survive, but companies are progressing rapidly, and we are still not far in only 25 years since my first book on these issues. The same is not true for public organizations and government bodies; for instance, Shell achieved a score of 80 out of 100 on my CSR Rating App, while my former organization the International Labour Organization (ILO) was much lower with a score of 49. But most are above the worst score achieved, as I shall explain in Chapter 15, where the Trump Organization received a meagre 7 points out of 100 for social responsibility!

In 2007, I joined the US-based Chamber of Commerce as their first-ever adviser on CSR. It was tough going since CSR, known there as corporate citizenship, was then simply seen as an exercise in charity. Today, however, the Chamber has started an Institute for CSR, as noted in the Preface of this book, that, in turn, as they now state, is 'increasingly becoming a discipline for determining where businesses operate, how they operate, and why they do what they do as opposed to other alternatives'. They also now note that companies are increasingly differentiating between assistance (charity, 'giving away fish') and development (investment, 'teaching people how to fish').

I have been teaching my students since the mid-1990s on what advanced responsible corporations should actually do, which, as noted in Chapter 1, is to adopt a systems-wide view of CSR which is, in brief, the responsible treatment of key stakeholders and to ensure that profits are not harmed by the CSR approach. It is how profits are made, not profits per se and that is key. And this increasingly being called 'stakeholder capitalism' as discussed in the next section.

Stakeholder Capitalism

This expression is not new to students of Ed Freeman with whom my main quibble has been that he prefers Corporate Stakeholder Responsibility to Corporate Social

Responsibility. Ed and myself have been putting stakeholders at the core of our push to encourage companies (and all organizations) to be more responsible to their key stakeholders for nearly three decades. The idea is now central to large companies as the Business Roundtable, the association of the largest companies in the USA, announced[3] the release of a new statement on the purpose of a corporation signed by 181 CEOs who committed to leading their companies for the benefit of all stakeholders – customers, employees, suppliers, communities and shareholders.

Since 1978, Business Roundtable has periodically issued the Principles of Corporate Governance. Each version of the document issued since 1997 has endorsed principles of shareholder primacy – that corporations exist principally to serve their shareholders. With its 2020 announcement, the new statement supersedes previous statements and outlines a modern standard for corporate responsibility.

'The American dream is alive, but fraying', said Jamie Dimon, chairman and CEO of JPMorgan Chase & Co. and chairman of the Business Roundtable. 'Major employers are investing in their workers and communities because they know it is the only way to be successful over the long term. These modernized principles reflect the business community's unwavering commitment to continue to push for an economy that serves all Americans.'

'This new statement better reflects the way corporations can and should operate today', added Alex Gorsky, chairman of the board and CEO of Johnson & Johnson and chair of the Business Roundtable Corporate Governance Committee. 'It affirms the essential role corporations can play in improving our society when CEOs are truly committed to meeting the needs of all stakeholders.'

Industry leaders also lent their support for the updated Business Roundtable statement, citing the positive impact this commitment will have on long-term value creation:

'I welcome this thoughtful statement by Business Roundtable CEOs on the Purpose of a Corporation. By taking a broader, more complete view of corporate purpose, boards can focus on creating long-term value, better serving everyone – investors, employees, communities, suppliers and customers', said Bill McNabb, former CEO of Vanguard.

'CEOs work to generate profits and return value to shareholders, but the best-run companies do more. They put the customer first and invest in their employees and communities. In the end, it's the most promising way to build long-term value', said Tricia Griffith, president and CEO of Progressive Corporation.

'This is tremendous news because it is more critical than ever that businesses in the 21st century are focused on generating long-term value for all stakeholders and addressing the challenges we face, which will result in shared prosperity and sustainability for both business and society', said Darren Walker, president of the Ford Foundation.

3. https://www.businessroundtable.org/business-roundtable-redefines-the-purpose-of-a-corporation-to-promote-an-economy-that-serves-all-americans, 19 August 2019 statement.

The statement of the Roundtable was quickly followed by a statement of the World Economic Forum (WEF), which announced in its manifesto for its 2020 Davo's meeting[4] that 'the purpose of a company is to engage all its stakeholders in shared and sustained value creation. In creating such value, a company serves not only its shareholders, but all its stakeholders – employees, customers, suppliers, local communities and society at large. The best way to understand and harmonize the divergent interests of all stakeholders is through a shared commitment to policies and decisions that strengthen the long-term prosperity of a company'. They further emphasized that 'a company is more than an economic unit generating wealth. It fulfils human and societal aspirations as part of the broader social system. Performance must be measured not only on the return to shareholders, but also on how it achieves its environmental, social and good governance objectives. Executive remuneration should reflect stakeholder responsibility'.

Watching Davos 2020 from afar at that time, I noticed only tame references to this new (for them) breakthrough as climate change and economic growth issues dominated. Note too that both the Roundtable and WEF only considered a limited number of stakeholders – customers, employees, suppliers, communities and shareholders – missing the environment, government, media and, more importantly, managers, directors, owners and investors. But a great start, nonetheless!

Of course, in corporate life nothing stays the same for very long. At time of writing,[5] just one year after the Roundtable statement, *Just Capital*, which tracks the impact companies have on society, found that the Roundtable statement had brought mixed results. Companies whose CEOs signed it performed better than others in providing everything from paid sick leave to financial assistance during the COVID crisis, as concluded by *Just Capital's* study of their public statements. Yet it also found, in a poll of 2,000 people, that Americans believe big business is falling short of its responsibilities to workers, customers, communities and the environment.

There is increasing evidence that this is the case as documented by a report by the non-profit investigative journalism organization ProPublica,[6] which exposed just how little the 25 wealthiest people in the USA – including the Amazon founder, Jeff Bezos, the Berkshire Hathaway chairman, Warren Buffett, and the Tesla CEO, Elon Musk – paid in taxes:

- Jeff Bezos, whose net worth was estimated in 2021 to be over $190bn, didn't pay any federal income taxes in 2007. The stock value for his company, Amazon, more than doubled that same year. Bezos also didn't pay federal income taxes in 2011.
- Warren Buffet, one of the world's wealthiest men and a great philanthropist, paid only 0.1 per cent for every $100 he added to his wealth between 2014 and 2018

– while curiously being very vocal in support of raising taxes on wealthy Americans such as himself!

- George Soros, the billionaire investor, is an outspoken supporter of increasing the amount that wealthy Americans like himself are taxed, yet the ProPublica's report showed that he did not pay any federal income tax for three years in a row.
- Michael Bloomberg, the businessman and former mayor of New York City, also did not pay federal income taxes in a recent tax year. He paid $70.7m on his 2018 net income of $1.9bn after claiming numerous deductions.
- In 2018, Elon Musk, the second-richest person in the world, also paid no federal income taxes.

In fact the ProPublica report found that 25 of the richest individuals earned a combined $1.1tn in income in 2018 – the same amount as 14.3 million 'ordinary Americans' put together. The organization also noted that the first group, the wealthy 25, paid $1.9bn in federal income tax that year. The latter group, the 14.3 million ordinary wage earners, paid $143bn. No wonder so many are doubtful of company responsibilities with such vast differences between the rich and the ordinary, i.e. most of the rest of us!

Link to Populism

Did all our work with companies on CSR/Sustainability miss encouraging companies to be involved with the big issues of the day? Particularly, the link to the new wave of populism? In this book I look at a major shift for companies and what they must do given that, as Ricarda McFalls from Canada wrote to me, 'It feels like CSR was for fighting a sneeze, now we are facing cancer stage 3.9'.

Populism is a somewhat ill-defined term. The Oxford English Dictionary's definition is: 'A member or adherent of a political party seeking to represent the interests of ordinary people'. But more recently, it has more narrowly come to mean a leader, member or adherent of a political party who adopts or professes policies and views for the sole purpose of getting elected, e.g. the attributes needed to gain political power are often the opposite of those needed to use it wisely.

But *The Economist*'s analysis on 19 December 2019 went further:[7] Populists can be everything from militarists to libertarians. So what does the word actually mean? It varies. Trump wanted to deport undocumented immigrants and separate migrants from their children when he was president. Podemos, the populist Spanish party, wanted to give immigrants voting rights. Geert Wilders, the populist Dutch politician, wanted to eliminate hate-speech laws. Jaroslaw Kaczynski, the populist Polish politician, pushed for a law making it illegal to use the phrase 'Polish death camps'. Evo Morales, Bolivia's populist president, expanded indigenous farmers' rights to grow coca. Rodrigo Duterte, the Philippines' populist president, ordered his police to execute suspected drug dealers

---

7. https://www.economist.com/the-economist-explains/2016/12/19/what-is-populism, accessed 15 December 2019.

on site. Populists may be militarists, pacifists, admirers of Che Guevara or of Ayn Rand; they may be 'tree-hugging pipeline opponents or drill-baby-drill climate-change deniers'.

In 2004 Cas Mudde, a political scientist at the University of Georgia, offered a definition that has become increasingly influential. In his view, populism is a 'thin ideology', one that merely sets up a framework: that of a pure people versus a corrupt elite. (He contrasts it with pluralism, which accepts the legitimacy of many different groups.)

Today I think it applies to people who are anti-immigrant and/or racist as well as the many millions who hate anyone who doesn't look like them. It also means the end of the liberal consensus on democracy – freedom of speech, a free press, rule of law and human rights. But does it also mean low wages, poor income distribution, anti-vaccination and anti-robotics?

In any case 'it' has led to Trump now happily gone, Brexit, a resurgent Le Pen in France, Wilders in Holland but destroyed the dreams of Ukraine, immigrants and refugees.

Critics of CSR[8]

I remember Allen White, one of the founders of the Global Reporting Initiative (GRI), carefully and dynamically urging members forward on aspects of GRI through various ad hoc working groups in the early years in the 1990s. These working groups numbered from four or five brave souls to several hundred! I have been impressed with the rise and expansion of GRI over the years, and few companies these days are unaware of at least some of its concepts.

However, I was always disappointed that GRI almost never mentioned CSR and, indeed, rarely defined its core concept that unfortunately (or perhaps fortunately) led to hundreds, if not thousands, of indicators.

I think the lack of a clear conceptual definition of CSR in GRI, as for example is outlined here, led Allen White recently to wish to close the CSR movement down,[9] and he suggested instead, yet another, new multilateral organization, the World Corporate Charter Organization (WCCO). The WCCO would set 'requirements for a corporation's purpose statement, multi-stakeholder board structure, and employee ownership. It would mandate integrated reporting that accounts for human, social and ecological as well as financial capital, along with adherence to broadly accepted global norms. With pressure from civil society groups, labour organizations, and kindred multilaterals, a WCCO could be launched as a voluntary program with the aim of evolving mandatory status as it gains legitimacy'. In fact such a standard exists and is known as ISO26000, which I further elaborate in the next chapter on H-CSR-M.

---

8. It is easy for a proponent of CSR to also criticise, but I have done that only once in a publication, of which part is summarized above, in Michael Hopkins, Chapter 4, 'Understanding and Addressing Criticisms of the Corporate Social Responsibility Movement', in *Corporate Social Responsibility – Sustainable Business: Environmental, Social and Governance Frameworks for the 21st Century*, ed. Rae Lindsay and Roger Martella (Amsterdam: Wolters Kluwer, July 2020).
9. https://greattransition.org/gti-forum/corporations-in-the-crosshairs, accessed 20 December 2019.

CSR arose out of the ethical movement of the 1960s, mainly among academics such as Archie Carroll and Donna Wood in the USA. They did little to apply to companies at that time (nor as I have argued elsewhere to extend to both public and NGO institutions). But prompted by Allen White and his colleagues at GRI, although not labelling it as CSR at the time, the rating and certification movement took off in a haphazard way which I described in my first book on the subject *The Planetary Bargain*. The concept of CSR grew into the ethical treatment of stakeholders following the great work of Ed Freeman at Darden School.

I note a despondency in Allen White's last sentence and note that Paul Raskin too, in the same discussion, stated that CSR efforts have had only limited influence. However, this was probably only true in 1995, when I first started working in the area.

The key, of course, is shareholder value followed very closely by stakeholder responsibility – both to stakeholders and from stakeholders. Few companies treat their key stakeholders badly since they would soon be out of business. Thus I define CSR as exactly that – CSR is about <u>treating key stakeholders responsibly</u>. I underline each term to emphasize that each term needs to be defined precisely to proceed and is, thus, the subject of many books and articles as well as my own; see, for instance, 'What Is CSR All About' which I wrote in 2006 and has to date, according to Researchgate, reached 70,500 reads.[10]

Paul Raskin also said that the idea that 'corporations can be nudged toward self-regulation – has had little purchase in a regime of "shareholder primacy"'. Yet only recently the influential body the Business Roundtable, as I noted previously, has rephrased the company rule book in August 2019 from maximizing shareholder value to maximizing stakeholder value. Thus the tide is beginning to change since the Business Roundtable, an influential US business group that is an association of CEOs representing the top corporations in the United States, surprisingly and importantly amended its two decade-old declaration that 'corporations exist principally to serve their shareholders'.

It is increasingly becoming clear that Milton Friedman's influential article published over fifty years ago 'The Social Responsibility of Business Is to Increase Its Profits' gave rise to the simple guiding principle: when in doubt, maximize profits. Thus, that the US Business Roundtable group of executives publicly rejected the primacy of shareholder value in 2019, as noted above, has started to turn the tide and, hopefully as I shall argue in Chapter 8, will lead to less inequality. As noted by Michelle Meagher in the *Financial Times*,[11] 'Business may talk the talk of corporate responsibility, but it is walking a different walk'. She noted as a corporate lawyer that Competition Law was meant to check corporate power, yet markets grew much more concentrated. Citing Stanford University economist Mordecai Kurz, she stated that he had calculated that in 2015, 82 per cent of stock market value in the USA came from the tech sector's 'monopoly wealth'.

She then argued that

---

10. Michael Hopkins, 'What Is CSR All About', onlinelibrary.wiley.com/doi/abs/10.1002/pa.238, accessed 27 July 2020.
11. Michelle Meagher, 'Fifty Years of Shareholder Value have Swollen Monopoly Power'. *Financial Times*, 14 September 2020, https://www.ft.com/content/de8b9a1c-df69-44e5-b571-81f4651de050, accessed 14 September 2020.

'concentrated markets are often linked to growing inequality, disempowerment of workers, hollowing out of communities and environmental harm – all problems that stakeholder capitalists say they are trying to fix. Monopolized industries tend to operate by their own, self-reflexive logic, with the interests of incumbents automatically equated to those of the industry. When regulators do catch up to the titans, the fines levied can be easily absorbed as a cost of doing business. Whether it is DuPont's $671m pay out for poisoning the water in West Virginia or Facebook's $5bn settlement for the Cambridge Analytica scandal, investors barely blink. Consumers have little place to turn.

Returning to Milton Friedman's article that had actually added a caveat to his 'profits first' edict and that although he advocated a focus on maximizing shareholder value, he also argued that businesses should 'stay within the rules of the game, which is to say, engages in open and free competition without deception or fraud'. But, Meagher continued, 'the historic emphasis on shareholder value has led some companies to seek monopoly power by controlling the rules of the game, and even through deception and fraud. That distorts the very idea of competition'.

Therefore, and updating my earlier wish that the rules of the game should be followed voluntarily, Meagher remarked that 'we must disperse economic concentrations, democratize corporate power and dissolve monopolies that are able to distort markets and society. *Voluntary efforts by business will not be enough.* Competition law and corporate law must be used to their full potential' (my italics).

Thus, America gave us both Friedman and Silicon Valley, but now increasing monopoly is not just a US problem leading Meagher to conclude that 'we are all at the mercy of global as well as homegrown monopolies. We need a European movement to rebuild competition, to protect our democracy and the hope of a resilient future. Only then will we leave Friedman's doctrine behind!'

Paul and Allen would probably agree that most companies have heard of sustainability and are doing something about it. Yet word games multiply in company speak, and so corporate citizenship, the ethical corporation, the good corporation, the sustainable company, and so on have all been used to describe various aspects of CSR. Consequently, my view is that CSR is a process to achieve the goal of sustainability via creating stakeholder value through responsibility.

Further, public institutions rarely have a CSR approach and even my old organization, the United Nations, doesn't do a great job with all stakeholders just talk to their employees! Second, I note that CSR has taken an interesting tangent in many emerging market countries where they emphasize philanthropy as CSR projects. India even passed that notion into company law. Originally against the notion, I came around as I noted that at least CSR was getting huge press and discussion in India, and I therefore proposed using the term 'sustainable philanthropy'.[12]

Let me end this section by noting that the issues of declining democracy, increasing income inequalities, climate change and increasing profits by large corporations are

---

12. Michael Hopkins, 'Sustainable Philanthropy', https://www.linkedin.com/pulse/sustainable
    -philanthropy-dr-michael-hopkins/, accessed 27 July 2020.

dominating the news these days. The two major issues that have been affected by the lack of social responsibility in Russia, those of Brexit and Impeachment, coupled with poor and dictatorial leadership worry us all. We have set up the Institute of Responsible Leadership[13] to address these issues, and I hope many readers here will join and some even become fellows.

Tax Behaviour and CSR

The subject of this section often arises. In fact one of my ILO colleagues simply stated that if corporations paid their taxes the CSR issue would be easily resolved. But it is not as easy as that as different countries have different tax regimes. I shall discuss that briefly here while citing a longer article on the subject by Even and Lars Fallan.[14]

The Fallans explore trade-offs between corporate tax behaviour and environmental performance disclosure, both important elements of CSR. They find in an empirical study of Norwegian companies, that 'there are no indications of trade-offs between corporate tax aggressiveness (TAG) and mandatory disclosure, in line with stick-to-the-rules/compliant behaviour for both. However, the positive relationship between TAG and voluntary disclosure indicates that strategic trade-offs exist and ensure an accept-able level of legitimacy from different stakeholders overall. Hence, corporate strategies differ for mandatory and voluntary actions, in line with a multidimensional legitimacy risk and legitimation strategy framework'.

Such a subject has been taken up by the Organization for Economic Cooperation and Development (OECD),[15] which, according to Chris Giles of the *Financial Times*, has organized many of the world's leading economies to sign up to a plan to force multinational companies to pay a global minimum corporate tax rate of at least 15 per cent following intense negotiations in Paris at the OECD. According to Giles, 'the his-toric agreement among 130 countries will ensure the largest companies, including Big Tech, pay at least $100bn a year more in taxes, with more of that money going to the countries where they do most of their business'. The OECD noted that the rules should be put in place next year and implemented in 2023 and, surprisingly, only nine of the 139 countries involved in the talks refused to sign up, including Ireland, Estonia and Hungary. All of the G20 leading nations backed the plan following lobbying by the USA.

Despite such a historic agreement, with Mathias Cormann, the OECD secretary-general, saying the agreement would ensure that 'large multinational companies pay their fair share of tax everywhere', many issues remained. For instance they agreed that

---

13. https://responsible-leadership.org/
14. E. Fallan and L. Fallan, 'Corporate Tax Behaviour and Environmental Disclosure: Strategic Trade-Offs Across Elements of CSR?', *Scandinavian Journal of Management* Elsevier, vol. 35(3). (September 2019).
15. See Chris Giles, 'World's Leading Economies Agree Global Minimum Corporate Tax Rate', *Financial Times*, 1 July 2021, https://www.ft.com/content/d0311794-abcf-4a2a-a8a4-bcabf-c4f71fa, accessed 26 November 2021.

'that countries could still use low taxes to encourage investment that the rules were not designed to impose the same corporate tax regime everywhere'. Further the 'package does not eliminate tax competition…but it does set multilaterally agreed limitations on it', while Cormann stated that 'it also accommodates the various interests across the negotiating table, including those of small economies and developing jurisdictions'. Additional weight came from the USA when US President Joe Biden stated, 'With a global minimum tax in place, multinational corporations will no longer be able to pit countries against one another in a bid to push tax rates down and protect their profits at the expense of public revenue'. Consequently, this was a major step forward to ensure the social responsibility of companies. But clearly much haggling will be left and will continue for many years to come.

Personal Responsibility in CSR

CSR and sustainability are about treating all key stakeholders responsibly. CSR, as argued here, is much more than that and requires companies to be engaged in all the big issues of the day, such as global warming and poverty and leading responsibly in dealing with all stakeholders. Many countries experienced a lack of personal social responsibility during COVID. The main issue was the wearing of face masks which had proved to be the most successful method, other than complete isolation, to reduce the pandemic. But was often ignored by up to 60 per cent of the population (my own figures; see an example from Kenya[16]).

At the time of COVID, the need to open up economies, to prevent climate change disasters and to deal with discontent, such as riots in the USA, were key issues that changed the global scene. The need for increased social responsibility from companies as well as governments was widely accepted. At the time, the onus also fell more than ever on the individual and their personal responsibility. In the future more pandemics are likely and the biggest one will be the pandemic that will, if not already, result from global warming and climate change.

Personal responsibility was, and still is, needed to control violence against others; to prevent the spread of the coronavirus through asymptotically infected persons especially through wearing face masks; to demonstrate peacefully in the face of increasing administrative violence of the sort seen in America, Brazil and Hong Kong; and to respect the natural environment from jettisoned long-lasting rubbish such as plastics.

During my daily 30-minute runs in Nairobi, on a major street, I counted the number of people I passed who wore face masks to prevent the spread of the coronavirus and wrote several articles in leading Kenyan newspapers which also appeared in India and Mauritius on the subject.[17] In Kenya it was clear to me that personal responsibility was

16. Michael Hopkins, 'Corporate Social Responsibility Needs Personal Social Responsibility', 22 June 2020, https://www.the-star.co.ke/opinion/columnists/2020-06-22-corporate-social-responsibility-needs-personal-social-responsibility/, accessed 22 June 2020.
17. Michael Hopkins, https://www.the-star.co.ke/opinion/columnists/2020-06-22-corporate-social-responsibility-needs-personal-social-responsibility/, accessed 22 June 2020.

key for the persons I ran past without masks. Interestingly, my observation showed that of the around 20 to 30 per cent who did wear masks, most were women, and that young men, in particular, were very lax. Why? The issue of personal responsibility was blared out by most major newspapers but was ignored. The reason was difficult to fathom (as in many other countries around the world at that time). For poor people living in slums as much as ten in a one-room shack, social distancing was impossible. Masks even at one fifth of a dollar were too expensive to the poor living on one or two dollars a day at most. Then most poor young men get their news via social media, and mobile phone ownership was surprisingly high among the poor with only around 2 or 3 per cent not having access to a phone.

Consequently, any government strategy of personal responsibility during COVID, I argued, must include the distribution of free masks and free education through social media. A strategy happily taken up in one slum, Mathare in Nairobi, through a donation from the Norwegian Government in conjunction with the NGO Mathare Youth and Sports Association (MYSA).

As Mauritius closed down its airspace and tourist centres, I suggested to the government that CSR could help and, in particular, a strategy of personal responsibility be implemented. In Mauritius, CSR had been narrowly viewed to be a contribution of 2 per cent of large company profits so as to give NGOs the ability to finance projects and families registered under the Social Register of Mauritius, i.e. essentially charity – useful, but mistaken in my opinion, as CSR is much, much wider than that. The aberration that CSR is charity is poor economics as companies should pay their taxes on profits and a democratic government should decide tax allocation.

The proposed strategy for Mauritius could also have been appropriate for just about any country with a large tourist industry.

First, tourists, especially the high-end group that loves Mauritius, would appreciate that everything is being done for their safety and they would flock back to the island.

Second, social responsibility would, of course, have to be matched by private sector responsibility so that airlines would practice COVID safety in the air and on the ground, as would the airport.

Third, hotels and restaurants would have to practice best practice as seen in countries such as New Zealand, Germany, Singapore, South Korea, and so on.

Fourth, the relatively high initial number of cases in Mauritius was probably because of the social responsibility of the government to test which led to fewer and fewer new cases. Such evidence would have delighted potential tourists.

Concluding Remarks

As can be seen, companies were involved in helping reduce the effects of COVID-19. Could they have done more? Yes, there is no doubt that the private sector, which has to be very clear about what their products do and whether they are noninjurious to people, can help the public sector enormously. It depends on the country. The rich countries did not come out of COVID so well at first, with the exception of Australia, New Zealand,

Éire, South Korea and Singapore. And most developing countries were all over the place from Ecuador to Yemen to Venezuela.

Could companies have helped more? Rather difficult, when the host country of many companies was behaving irresponsibility, as was the case, at the time, of USA's rejection of the World Health Organization (WHO), but happily revoked and reworked by the G7 group of countries at their meeting in Cornwall in the UK in mid-2021. There is no doubt that strong responsible leadership has helped, as seen in New Zealand, Canada and even in some developing countries such as Senegal. Kenya, from where I write, saw impressive leadership with its leader wearing a mask in public, although not always applied to large political rallies with, to-date, unknown consequences.

Then, a lack of resources severely hampered virus testing especially, while hospitals struggled due to lack of proper protective clothing, masks and ventilators. Nonetheless, companies through their private association (Kenya Private Sector Alliance) contributed directly to the government's COVID-19 committee and one company, Safaricom, even heeded my plea to include a message emphasizing social distancing and wearing of face masks to their customer message to everyone (especially through their online money transfer MPESA).

Worse is the suffering of the poor, in many countries, who have lost jobs and their livelihoods through curfews and social distancing. Elsewhere I have suggested the strong need for a basic income for the most distressed. But that has been slow going, as resources needed are large and management is poor. In fact, it is a huge space for the private sector to back such an initiative and lend its skills to implement since leads to massive increases in effective demand and, therefore, more business. This I will explore more in Chapter 8.

Chapter Three

CSR/SUSTAINABILITY AND BIG ISSUES: A NEW CHARTER FOR BUSINESS

Introduction

Did all our work with companies on CSR/Sustainability miss encouraging companies to be involved with the big issues of the day? In general, only recently have big companies started to grapple with societal issues that were once played down. COVID-19 has certainly helped to change their understanding, and this is why I argue here for a new reporting structure, a Charter for Business, as I tell in a short narrative how companies have moved to the big societal issues of the day.

The original lack of involvement by companies in the social good has nevertheless hurt companies. For instance, Bill Clinton left a robust economy in the year 2000 that let in George Bush Jr (who brushed aside Al Gore's legitimate claims to the presidency) who then proceeded to enter into expensive and useless wars whose effects we feel until today. Companies may then have benefitted from arms sales but little else. Then in 2008 Obama came to power and managed, despite total resistance by the Republicans, to pull the USA from a disastrous recession into once again a robust economy. Car companies and financial institutions did well but small business and private sector wages stagnated. But Obama's inheritance led, mysteriously, to a president, who was clearly 'unfit to serve', through hacking on a scale that took the election away from Hillary Clinton as I have argued elsewhere.[1]

In the above processes, companies were rarely to be seen at the policy level yet were consistently hurt by the recessionary presidents. Never have the cards of incompetence been revealed so quickly as we saw in the Trump years. Finally, attacking the Muslim world and invoking a travel ban on legitimate visa holders have led to serious action and major US reputational damage that has fed onto lower tourist numbers, fewer foreign students and increased uncertainty in the world. Some companies reacted: 97 major firms in the US[2] – including tech companies like Apple, Airbnb, Facebook, Google, Intel, Microsoft, Netflix, PayPal, Twitter, Uber and Y Combinator – joined hands in filing an *amicus brief* opposing President Trump's travel ban, which he invoked in 2017 through an executive order. The brief, filed with the US Court of Appeals for the

---

1. https://www.linkedin.com/pulse/us-election-hacked-dr-michael-hopkins?trk=prof-post, November 2016.
2. https://thenextweb.com/us/2017/02/06/google-facebook-uber-and-nearly-100-others-team -up-to-take-on-trumps-travel-ban/

9th Circuit, stated that 'the companies believe the order to be unlawful, discriminatory and harmful to business in the US'.

Mark Zuckerberg, Founder of Facebook, had warned[3] of a growing backlash against globalization and urged the public to respond by building a 'global community' instead of 'sitting around being upset'. 'Every year, the world got more connected and this was seen as a positive trend. Yet now, across the world there are people left behind by globalization, and movements for withdrawing from global connection', he wrote. Leaders had failed to foresee the negative consequences of global changes. 'For a couple of decades, maybe longer, people have really sold this idea that as the world comes together everything is going to get better', he said. 'I think the reality is that over the long term that will be true, and there are pieces of infrastructure that we can build to make sure that a global community works for everyone. But I do think there are some ways in which this idea of globalization didn't take into account some of the challenges it was going to create for people, and now I think some of what you see is a reaction to that'.

Yet[4] when a group of four large IT companies were challenged by the US Congress on 28 July 2020, the leaders of Apple, Google, Facebook and Amazon, which included Zuckerberg showed they still had a long way to go. Their performance was characterized by 'ignorance, grandstanding and fawning on these exemplars of the American Way'. 'Our founders would not bow before a king', said the House Antitrust Subcommittee Chairman David Cicilline, in his opening remarks. 'Nor should we bow before the emperors of the online economy.'

According to the *Guardian* article cited, the two who came off worst were Mark Zuckerberg, the Facebook boss, and Sundar Pichai, chief executive of Google. The key issue was that since they were practitioners of one of the most toxic business model in the tech business, known as surveillance capitalism, they seemed to be unaware how they mistreated those who try to earn using their company's products.

Tim Cook of Apple defended the company's monopolistic behaviour in controlling its App Store, but his defence was, apparently, not convincing, when for instance he was asked what would prevent the company from increasing the 30 per cent commission it charges developers, he simply replied that Apple had not increased it since the store's launch.

One key issue was that while existing laws can deal with the anticompetitive antics of the four firms, they are obsolete in relation to their conceptions of 'consumer harm' from monopolistic behaviour by companies that do not directly charge for their services. Further, existing laws in the USA have nothing to say about 'societal' harms, such as undermining democratic elections or polluting the public sphere.

Not all issues are on the other side of the Atlantic. The Brexit vote is disastrous for the UK through its loss of a 600 million market with zero trade barriers.[5] Financial

3. http://www.independent.co.uk/news/business/news/mark-zuckerberg-facebook-globalisation-backlash-essay-social-networks-a7584751.html
4. https://www.theguardian.com/technology/commentisfree/2020/aug/02/at-last-the-tech-titans-nerd-immunity-shows-signs-of-fading, accessed 2 August 2020.
5. https://www.linkedin.com/pulse/why-mps-must-vote-reject-article-50-brexit-dr-michael-hopkins?trk=prof-post, accessed February 2017.

institutions that have done so well under the conservative government are now scattering as the implications of change sets in. While in France the toxic message of the Far Right is shaking previously held values of Liberté, égalité, fraternité!, the French President Macron took a firm hold in France and resisted the many Russian hacking attempts to disrupt the political process.

We are in a crisis in the world right now. A war on Islam from USA started by a president unfit to serve and further shown by his disastrous COVID-19 policy. Consequences are occurring, with one serious issue being the increasing breakdowns between Israel and Palestinians talks, leading to massacres in the Gaza Strip. The Taliban has been given carte blanche to practice their medieval repression in Afghanistan. Followed by great disturbance in Europe as Putin takes Russia down a repressive trail, starting with a war on Ukraine. While the UK is blindly going along the Brexit[6] path without having seriously considered future economic and social disasters. These are still happening as I write with Northern Ireland being just one of the new hotspots, as companies suffer from all sorts of new and changing export and import rules. Why the UK needed to break away from the EU without thinking through the long-term consequences is a continuing tragedy and negatively affects all UK citizens. The 3 million resident UK citizens in Europe including myself were not allowed to vote in the 2016 referendum, and the consequences are still unfolding from the right to drive to crossing borders under COVID.

Few Companies Have Focused Upon 'Big Issues'

To date the response of the CSR community as expressed through a number of standard setting bodies such as Global Reporting Initiative (GRI), ISO26000, UN Global Compact and OECD Multi-National Principles have focused on societal issues. Perhaps the furthest along was the WBSCD with its 'Building the Social Capital Protocol' where, for instance, its 'insights into employment skills and safety provides an insight into the ongoing development of the Social Capital Protocol'. The results of a dialogue between 15 WBCSD member companies, Accenture, AkzoNobel, BASF, BMW Group, DSM, Deloitte, EY, Evonik, KPMG, Lafarge Holcim, Nestlé, PWC, SCA, Siemens and Solvay.[7] The aim of the project was to provide[8] 'a harmonized approach

---

6. The surprising vote for BREXIT has been claimed by most as democratic. Given that over three million UK citizens living in the EU were not given the possibility to vote in the June 2016 referendum, democracy is debatable. I also suspect that, given the surprise of the vote, Russia was involved in some way (see http://cybernewsgroup.co.uk/uk-politician-accuses -russia-of-corrupt-involvement-in-uk-elections-amid-hacking-fears). I have found to date no evidence for my suspicion, although I am surprised that there has been no statement from the UK Secret Services despite several requests, including from myself.
7. http://www.wbcsd.org/Clusters/Social-Impact/Resources/Building-the-Social-Capital -Protocol-Insights-into-employment-skills-and-safety
8. http://www.wbcsd.org/Clusters/Social-Impact/Social-Capital-Protocol

for businesses to measure and value their interactions with society, to bring together the currently fragmented landscape of social measurement and valuation, and to provide the universal processes, principles and tools needed by business to ensure social risks and opportunities are considered alongside financial and environmental issues in corporate strategy and decision-making. It will also lay solid foundations for integrated reporting'.

The WBSCD initiative fits well into expanding the role of companies from focusing upon key stakeholders to enter the wider policy discourse. As Beth Jenkins noted,[9] it was 20 years ago when her colleague Jane Nelson, director of the Corporate Responsibility Initiative at the Harvard Kennedy School, introduced her 'famous "three circles" diagram – suggesting that business could play a positive role in society through core business, social investment, and public advocacy and policy dialogue. In that time, her last circle has received relatively little attention'. This book provides some guidance it is hoped.

The UN's Sustainable Development Goals (SDGs) may provide a pathway for companies. Amazingly companies see that and were active in the preparations of the 17 goals. Even the highly conservative US Chamber of Commerce's Foundation has stated that 'the private sector can get involved … aligning CSR strategies with the SDGs…and raising awareness of the SDGs and efforts to achieve them among staff and the public'.[10] My main quibble with the SDGs is that they list development issues rather than create a system with clear goals and processes. Elsewhere[11] I have argued that the SDGs can actually boil down to one main goal – improving human well-being. But the SDGs do offer a route for companies to become even more involved in big and longer term issues than their usual focus on reducing taxes and regulation. Failed economies are no answer to business progress, and it is surprising they are not more positively involved as suggested in the SDG table in Chapter 9 on the examples of private sector involvement per SDG.

Sustainability and Integrated Reporting[12]

Before suggesting a new path ahead, a Charter for companies on the Big Issues of the day, as a key proposal from this book, I briefly review a number of initiatives that have come up in the past decade. Even more recently has been the burgeoning of 'Sustainability' which is seemingly everywhere and often closely linked to the slogan of ESG – environment, social and governance – as a 'new' guide to companies. In fact this book also

9. By Beth Jenkins, Insights Director, Business Fights Poverty, http://community.businessfig htspoverty.org/profiles/blogs/beth-jenkins-a-new-era-of-corporate-statesmanship; thanks to Martin Summers for drawing my attention to this.
10. See US Chamber of Commerce Foundation, https://www.uschamberfoundation.org/blog/post/corporate-engagement-will-be-critical-sdgs-success/43828
11. https://www.linkedin.com/pulse/csr-uns-sdgs-role-private-sector-profs-michael-hopkins-hopkins/, accessed 15 June 2021.
12. Thanks to an unknown reviewer for Anthem for suggesting much of the content of this section so as to bring this book up-to-date since the first draft was written in 2019.

offers guidance on what's next in the ESG sustainability arena, always following my basic definition of CSR, which you know by now, in its simple form for any corporate body, public or private, which is 'treating key stakeholders responsibily'.

EU nonfinancial reporting directive

In the European Union (EU), the so-called Non-financial Reporting Directive (NFRD) (Directive 2014/95/EU of the European Parliament and of the Council), the communication of the Commission 2017/C 215/01, offered guidance on nonfinancial reporting, and, more recently, the 2021 Corporate Sustainability Reporting Directive (CSRD) was proposed.[13] The EU lays down rules on disclosure of nonfinancial and diversity information by certain large companies. Kinderman (2018, p. 109) considered the Directive 2014/95/EU as 'the most important legacy of the EU's renewed strategy for CSR'.[14]

EU law now requires certain large companies to disclose information on the way they operate and manage social and environmental challenges. As they state, this is to 'help investors, civil society organizations, consumers, policy makers and other stakeholders evaluate the non-financial performance of large companies and encourage these companies to develop a responsible approach to business,' happily replicating my own definition of CSR of 25 plus years ago. They might have also mentioned as key stakeholders suppliers, communities, governance, employees, managers and shareholders as well.

Thus, EU's rules on nonfinancial reporting currently apply to large public interest companies with more than 500 employees. This covers approximately 11,700 large companies and groups across the EU, including listed companies, banks, insurance companies and other companies designated by national authorities as public-interest entities. In fact, Under Directive 2014/95/EU, large companies have to publish information related to environmental matters, social matters and issues related to treatment of employees, respect for human rights, anti-corruption bribery and diversity on company boards (in terms of age, gender, educational and professional background).

In June 2017, the European Commission (EC) published its guidelines to help companies disclose environmental and social information. These guidelines are not mandatory and companies may decide to use international, European or national guidelines according to their own characteristics or business environment. Then, in June 2019 the EC published guidelines on reporting climate-related information, which in practice consist of a new supplement to the existing guidelines on nonfinancial reporting, which remain applicable.

---

13. This section on the EU is drawn from https://ec.europa.eu/info/business-economy-euro/company-reporting-and-auditing/company-reporting/corporate-sustainability-reporting_en, accessed 26 November 2021.
14. D. Kinderman, 'Global and EU-Level Corporate Social Responsibility: Dynamism, Growth, and Conflict', in M. Kunze and S. Nährlich (eds), *Gesellschaftliche Verantwortung von Unternehmen in Deutschland* (Springer VS, Wiesbaden.za, 2018), 101–13.

Even more recently, albeit before the huge climate conference, COP26, on 21 April 2021, the EC adopted a proposal for a CSRD, which would amend the existing reporting requirements of the NFRD. The proposal extended the scope to all large companies and all companies listed on regulated markets (except listed micro-enterprises) and required four key issues: (1) the audit (assurance) of reported information, (2) more detailed reporting requirements, (3) a requirement to report according to mandatory EU sustainability reporting standards and (4) companies to digitally 'tag' the reported information, so it is machine readable and feeds into the European single access point envisaged in the capital markets union action plan.

The EU sustainability reporting standards under its proposed CSRD envisages the adoption of EU sustainability reporting standards. The draft standards would be developed by the European Financial Reporting Advisory Group (EFRAG) and are intended to be tailored to EU policies, while building on and contributing to international standardization initiatives. The first set of standards would, it is hoped, be adopted by October 2022.

World Economic Forum (WEF) and stakeholder capitalism

The WEF was slow to start but has now embraced CSR/Sustainability under what it calls 'stakeholder capitalism'.[15,16] It has been urged by the global challenges of COVID-19 to make ESG issues even more pressing for policymakers, boards and executives. To promote alignment among existing ESG frameworks, the WEF, with partners including Deloitte, EY, KPMG and PwC, has drawn upon existing frameworks and identified a set of universal disclosures – the Stakeholder Capitalism Metrics.

During the Sustainable Development Impact Summit 2021, the Forum announced that over 50 companies have begun including the Stakeholder Capitalism Metrics in their mainstream reporting materials, including annual reports and sustainability reports. The Stakeholder Capitalism Metrics promote alignment among existing ESG frameworks and create a set of data points that can be compared between companies, regardless of their industry or region. The metrics include nonfinancial disclosures centred around four pillars: people, planet, prosperity and principles of governance, and include measurements around greenhouse gas emissions, pay equality and board diversity, among others.

Since January 2021, approximately 120 companies have shown their support for this initiative. Companies which have adopted this approach include: Accenture, Bank of America, Eni, Fidelity International, HSBC Holdings, IBM, Mastercard, Nestlé,

---

15. Drawn from https://www.weforum.org/our-impact/stakeholder-capitalism-50-companies -adopt-esg-reporting-metrics/, accessed 26 November 2021.
16. 'Measuring Stakeholder Capitalism – Towards Common Metrics and Consistent Reporting of Sustainable Value Creation' (in collaboration with Deloitte, EY, KPMG and PWC) and Transparency International UK's (2020) 'Principles and guidance for anti-corruption corporate transparency'.

PayPal, Royal DSM, Salesforce, Schneider Electric, Siemens, Total, UBS, Unilever, Yara International and Zurich Insurance Group.

The WEF analysis of reports from 45 companies shows how enterprises are building skills for the future, with over $1.5tn invested in training. They also indicate that companies are innovating, with over $20tn spent on research and development and $23tn in multi-year innovation investments. Lastly, they are contributing to their communities with nearly $140tn paid in taxes.

In parallel, the WEF has also been collaborating with an Impact Management Project (IMP) to bring together the major standard setters and frameworks and is collaborating with the International Financial Reporting Standards Foundation (IFRSF). By contributing to the Technical Readiness Working Group, the Forum has played a significant role in the establishment of the International Sustainability Standards Board, which was unveiled during the 2021 Climate Change Conference COP26 that started on 13 November 2021. Note that COP stands for Conference of the Parties. In diplomatic parlance, 'the parties' refers to the 197 nations that agreed to a new environmental pact, the United Nations Framework Convention on Climate Change, at a meeting in 1992.

As part of the Forum's continued partnership with the IFRS Foundation, WEF's private sector-led coalition will provide inputs through the appropriate consultation mechanisms of the ISSB as they state[17] 'to ensure the standards are fit for purpose and deliver for all stakeholders in the capital markets'.

At the WEF 2020 Annual Meeting in Davos, 120 of the world's largest companies supported efforts to develop a core set of common metrics and disclosures on nonfinancial factors for their investors and other stakeholders. In September 2020, following a six-month consultation process with over 200 companies, investors and interested parties, the project published a refined set of 21 core and 34 expanded metrics and disclosures in its report Measuring Stakeholder Capitalism: Towards Common Metrics and Consistent Reporting of Sustainable Value Creation.

Since the launch of the Stakeholder Capitalism Metrics, the Forum has been building a coalition of CEOs who are willing to show their commitment to stakeholder capitalism and to reflect these metrics and disclosures in their mainstream reporting. Their aim, reflecting what we CSR people have argued for 30 years, is to bring stakeholders together to simplify and harmonize the various approaches to nonfinancial reporting. Better late than never!

The work is being carried out through three interconnected communities:

1. Business Leaders: Advancing the adoption of the Stakeholder Capital Metrics and offering a collective, private-sector voice to the convergence dialogue
2. ESG Practitioners: Leading the ESG strategy for their organization and implementing the recommendations into the reporting materials of their companies
3. ESG Ecosystem: Harmonizing the global dialogue among standards foundations, private standard setters, regulators and international organizations

---

17. International Sustainability Standards Board, see https://www.ifrs.org/groups/international-sustainability-standards-board/, accessed 27 November 2021.

US Sustainability Accounting Standards Board
(SASB) and Value Reporting Foundation (VRF)

A wide range of constituencies – including investors, companies, policy makers, regulators, NGOs and civil society – use corporate sustainability reporting to inform a wide range of decisions. A dynamic ecosystem of organizations has evolved to meet these various information needs.[18] Disclosure standards and frameworks, including SASBs, are the foundation of this ecosystem. They facilitate the disclosure of comparable, consistent and reliable ESG information.

There is a clear difference between sustainability frameworks and sustainability standards. Frameworks provide principles-based guidance on how information is structured, how it is prepared, and what broad topics are covered. Meanwhile, standards provide specific, detailed and replicable requirements for what should be reported for each topic, including metrics. Standards make frameworks actionable, ensuring comparable, consistent and reliable disclosure. Frameworks and standards are complementary and are designed to be used together.

Happily, there is increasing collaboration among frameworks and standard-setters. For instance, in September 2020, five leading framework and standard-setting organizations – Carbon Disclosure Project (CDP), Climate Disclosure Standards Board (CDSB), Global Reporting Initiative (GRI), International Integrated Reporting Council (IIRC) and Sustainability Accounting Standards Board (SASB) – announced a shared vision for a comprehensive corporate reporting system that includes both financial accounting and sustainability disclosure, connected via integrated reporting. The joint statement outlines how existing sustainability standards and frameworks can complement generally accepted financial accounting principles (also known as financial GAAP).

In December 2020, that 'group of five' published a prototype climate-related financial disclosure standard that illustrated how the concepts from their joint paper could be applied to climate disclosure and consolidated content and metrics into one practical guide. They were designed for unique sets of stakeholders and are based on unique definitions of materiality. Companies can use different frameworks and standards as building blocks to develop a system of disclosure tailored to the unique needs of their stakeholders. Within this system, SASB Standards fill the need for ESG disclosure tailored to investors and other providers of financial capital.

SASB Standards are designed for communication by companies to investors about how sustainability issues impact long-term enterprise value. SASB Standards can be used by companies as a practical tool for implementing the principles-based framework recommended by the Task Force for Climate-related Financial Disclosures (TCFD). Similarly, SASB Standards enable robust implementation of the Integrated Reporting Framework, providing the comparability sought by investors. Other

---

18. See https://www.sasb.org/. The recent creation of the Value Reporting Foundation (https://www.valuereportingfoundation.org/) and the attempt of IASB to become a player in the sustainability reporting standardization arena (https://www.ifrs.org/projects/work-plan/sustainability-reporting/), all accessed 27 November 2021.

sustainability-related disclosure frameworks serve their own unique purposes, and ultimately, companies must evaluate and decide which tools serve their communications objectives and meet the needs of their key stakeholders.

SASB and the VRF were merged, in November 2020, as a unified organization, the Value Reporting Foundation. By integrating the two entities that are focused on enterprise value creation, this merger hopefully will represent significant progress towards simplifying the corporate reporting landscape. Currently, the VRF is a global nonprofit organization that offers a comprehensive suite of resources designed to help businesses and investors develop a shared understanding of enterprise value – how it is created, preserved or eroded. The resources – including Integrated Thinking Principles, the Integrated Reporting Framework and SASB Standards – can be used alone or in combination, depending on business needs.

So you may ask with all the above activity what happened to other activities such as the ILO principles, UN Global Compact, UN Principles on Human Rights, the SDGs, and the first of all of them, the GRI (formed as far back as 1997). In fact collaborative efforts are being formed as quick as the eye can capture. For instance, in July 2020, SASB and GRI announced a collaborative workplan to show how companies can use both sets of standards together.

Now, SASB and the GRI provide complementary standards for sustainability information, which are designed to fulfill different purposes and are based on different approaches to materiality. SASB Standards focus on ESG issues expected to have a financially material impact on the company, aimed at serving the needs of most investors and other providers of financial capital. GRI Standards focus on the economic, environmental and social impacts of a company in relation to sustainable development, which is of interest to a broad range of stakeholders, including investors. Many companies – including ArcelorMittal, PSA Group, Diageo and Nike – use both SASB and GRI standards to meet the needs of their audiences.

The first deliverable of the collaborative workplan is 'A Practical Guide to Sustainability Reporting Using GRI and SASB Standards', which shows how companies are using the two sets of standards together and provides reporters with insights from peer companies to support their sustainability reporting and disclosure journeys.

When formulating accounting metrics for its disclosure topics, SASB considers the existing body of reporting standards and uses existing metrics whenever possible. SASB Standards reference metrics already in use by industry, from more than 200 entities, such as the World Health Organization, CDP, Environmental Protection Agency (EPA), Occupational Safety and Health Agency (OSHA) and industry organizations such as International Civil Aviation Authority (ICAO), International Petroleum Industry Environmental Conservation Association (IPIECA), Electric Power Research Institute (EPRI) and Global Real Estate Sustainability Benchmark (GRESB). Aligning SASB Standards with existing reporting standards avoids additional costs for companies and aligns SASB Standards with global corporate transparency efforts.[19]

---

19. See https://www.sasb.org/about/sasb-and-other-esg-frameworks/, accessed 27 November 2021.

A Charter for Companies on 'Big Issues'

To fill the gap of CSR/Sustainability, and even traditional business strategies, in ignoring the big issues of the day, I propose here a new charter for large companies to map out their progress on 'Big Issues' and these should include some of the issues I list below:

1. Democratic participation (human rights, freedom of the press, rule of law, freedom of association) and the new cybernetic world
2. Poverty (both relative and absolute) and income distribution
3. Illiteracy
4. Appropriate skills and human capital
5. Ethical treatment of stakeholders
6. Key areas of interest to work for the social good with other companies
7. Climate change
8. Anti-terrorism
9. Anti-racism
10. Immigration including international migration and refugees
11. Cybernetic control
12. Robotics
13. Education and skill development
14. Health and life expectancy
15. Anti-corruption
16. Quality of jobs and un-and under-employment
17. Youth alienation
18. Hunger and famine
19. Defence (military, terrorist, drug industrial complexes)
20. Ethical treatment of stakeholders

Should these issues be compulsory for large companies to address or, like GRI, be essentially voluntary but certified. I prefer voluntary for the Charter but some aspects, such as human trafficking, must be supported by the law.

Why this new approach? In my CSR work of the past 20 years, I had stated that CSR should emphasize key stakeholders and also focus on the business case. We have been successful in that approach (ignoring those who still see CSR/Sustainability as merely philanthropy) since it is rare to find a company that does nothing on CSR/Sustainability – well the Trump Organization (lowest score ever on CRITICS[20]) – and that is the problem. My overly limited definition in the first five clauses above allowed companies to ignore bigger issues affecting everyone, such as income distribution, low wages, poverty, unemployment and so on. Now I think it is in their interest to be involved even though you may think democracy might be threatened by business interests. In fact, business is often involved in big issues, mainly secretly and not always for

20. https://www.linkedin.com/pulse/trump-organisation-socially-responsible-sustainable-hop-kins?trk=prof-post, December 2016.

the better as we have seen with the Koch Brothers or Rupert Murdoch's organization. Hence the need for a Charter, which is a statement from each company, on how they currently, or will address, the big issues of the day.

Key Questions to Be Addressed in the 'Charter on the Big Issues of the Day'

So I plan to ask all companies to state their position on big issues that concern them through a written statement on how they will deal with external stakeholders as part of their CSR/Sustainability strategy for each of the following issues both in their headquarters and main countries where they are active.

1. What do you see as the most pressing issue for society today?
2. Do these issues also affect your company and if yes, how?
3. Can your company do anything about these issues?
4. What steps, if any, are you currently taking or plan to take?

Next Steps

You will note that many of these issues are also in the SDGs of the United Nations. So each company may wish to link the two reports into one. I suggest a short annual report of 10 pages maximum with links to the company's activities as discussed on its website. I would also suggest that each company produce such a report toward year end, say 16th November, so that it can be used for reflection and potential action in the following year.

These reports[21] are not just needed in a post-Brexit/Trump world? Indeed, there has been much debate over the past few decades over whether managers (including in the private sector) should be professionalized, with codes of ethics. That is a long way off and, in the end, people have to take responsibility onto their own shoulders. One cannot legislate for everything and that should be reserved for excesses. Without personal responsibility, legislation is anyway ignored.

Some guidance can be gleaned from professional associations which have for long been regulated by codes of ethics and disciplinary procedures. Hence professional service firms in accountancy, law and corporate professional workers can, for instance, be mobilized to work with companies and institutions to draw up the annual Charter.

The envisaged Charter should be both national and international in scope. International law is, in the end, only administered by national law or groups of countries coming together such as the EU. This enforcement is not envisaged again taking the basis of the Charter to be responsibility.

---

21. Thanks to Prof. Mike Saks, former rector Suffolk University, for suggesting many of these points.

So What Now for Companies and CSR/Sustainability?

We are in a crisis in the world right now. As noted earlier, Islamophobia from USA led by a former president unfit to serve; the UK blindly going along the Brexit[22] path without having considered the future economic and social disaster; the Trump's retreat from treaties and institutions such as COP, NAFTA, WTO, Iran peace deal etc. and the embrace of North Korea by formerly liberal USA; the consequent uncertainty in trade, recruitment of immigrants, and the seeming loss of the new world order after the Second World War promoted by NATO, the EU and even the USA, especially after the invasion of Ukraine by Russia in 2022, are all bad news for business.

I was quoted in Kenya Daily Nation's columnist Ritesh Barot (Wed 9 March 2022) on this that "Times are increasingly hard for companies after COVID and now an unnecessary war. Sustainability (aka CSR or ESG) had taken off even before COVID as the private sector saw that being responsible to their key stakeholders was great for business too. But the economic bite of an unnecessary war is having consequences far and wide as inflation, energy and food costs rise rapidly. Belt tightening quickly follows and new ventures, even profitable ones, such as sustainable investment are often the first to suffer. Mistakenly in my view since new opportunities usually present themselves and times of crisis often present new profit centres. So be careful what you cut!"

Yet, companies were given tremendous power after the Fall of the Berlin Wall to conduct business more or less how they wished. Companies are not individuals and, in theory, should have little to do with democratic processes. But the Supreme Court in the USA, through Citizen's United, gave companies untold power, as much as individuals, to sponsor election candidates without revealing their names. The Koch brothers had a field day as detailed in Jane Mayer's book[23] on 'dark money'.

Nonetheless some companies have been amassing huge fortunes for their owners and shareholders in the last two decades, providing a question mark on how far companies have gone in becoming socially responsible. In an address to billionaires cited in a speech to our IRL on 28 June 2020, Guy Standing, the father of universal basic income and rentier capitalism analysis (more on that in Chapter 8) remarked that 'You leaders are the problem. You are taking all the rent, you are exploiting the situation to increase your power and using your power to manipulate politics and corrupt the system. Wealth equals power thereby allowing them to influence government policy simply through their huge wealth that cannot be ignored by mere elected officials.'

In Kenya, for instance, the construction lobby is huge and rail lobby miniscule, hence the proliferation of roads and the almost total absence of rail in its cities, while the previously admired Volkswagen has been caught cheating on its emissions to the detriment of its reputation and the health of people across the world.

Finally, I end this chapter by referring to the Annex at the end of the book, where I give an example of how my Charter can be applied with the example of Nestlé.

---

22. My own take can be found in my book *Brrrexit! Why England Will Be Left Out in the Cold: The UK Decides upon Perpetual Winter* (Amazon.com, January 2020).
23. Jane Mayer, *Dark Money -The Hidden History of the Billionaires Behind the Rise of the Radical Right* (New York: Penguin – Random House, 2017).

Chapter Four

CSR/SUSTAINABILITY MODEL (H-CSR-M) DEFINED

Introduction

In this chapter, I present a methodology to define and measure CSR/Sustainability and some aspects of leadership. The model has been updated from earlier versions that started with my first book, *The Planetary Bargain*, and can also be found on my website www.csrfi.com. It may also be used for rapid CSR/Sustainability Reporting.

There are perhaps four main types of private companies today.

First are those companies that practice responsible leadership in a full-fledged manner.
Second are those that say they do but, in practice, don't always follow responsible leadership.
Third are those that focus on grants to good causes (philanthropy) but not much else.
Fourth are those that are antagonistic to the whole idea of doing anything, and I mean anything, except to maximize profits.

Increasingly, those who fall into my first category often don't maximize their shareholder value as well as others do.

There are a variety of different approaches to measurement, mainly because there is continuing discussion, if not confusion, on what CSR, sustainability, ESG, etc. really mean.

As already noted, CSR is a systems approach to managing a company, i.e. all important aspects of a company (or institution be it public or NGO) are subject to review under the searchlight of CSR. As mentioned in my Preface, I got interested in CSR over 25 years ago because of the rise in the emphasis and power of the private sector and my worry that the UN was losing influence. Yet, until then, myself and many of my colleagues, had been very suspicious of the power and arrogance of large companies and worried that they could cause, following Marx, the collapse of capitalism. But unlike some of my colleagues, I didn't want to live under State control of the means of production and had also seen, while working for a major corporation, both its excesses and its immense power of empathy (now also known as Emotional Intelligence).

I thus mused about whether companies (and later large public organizations) could behave more socially responsibly so as to avoid State control (or public institutions to be more precise, responsible and customer friendly). Twenty-five years after my personal discovery of CSR, I see that CSR along with corporate responsibility, sustainability and many similar concepts have converged into a simple model of CSR and, indeed, companies *are* moving ahead in a responsible manner – sometimes one step forward and two back, but CSR is a process after all.

As seen with Koch Brothers in Chapter 3, and many other companies such as Volkswagen (VW) or Exxon, who have shown that being socially responsible is not a sufficient condition, just look at the mess they have created. A closer examination, and this is true of so many institutions, is that CSR has been examined in the case of many internal and external stakeholders but rarely in the governance of the organization itself. The family structure of VW's Board (including the CEO's inexperienced fourth wife) was never subject to the same level of investigation as were, for instance, the conduct of its lower-level workers. By the way, we also saw this at Enron, Lehman Brothers and more recently at FIFA. My last 25 years of investigation, experience, analysis and teaching as well as the complete details of my CSR model were included in my book *CSR and Sustainability – From the Margins to the Mainstream: A Text Book* (Greenleaf, UK, November 2015).

After a presentation of the book at one of my CSR Meetups in Geneva in September, I emphasized the conceptual CSR model I had been using. One of the audience insisted that it should be called the 'Hopkins CSR Model (H-CSR-M)' since that way it would form a focus for future CSR efforts. At first I was not sure whether such a model should be called after myself, especially as I have stood on the 'shoulders of giants' in the model's development and many of its components have come from such people, albeit adapted to my own view of CSR. Three main academic influences, as already noted, were the work of Archie Carroll and his famous pyramid that I have adapted, Donna Wood and her model of Corporate Social Performance and the work of Ed Freeman on stakeholder dialogue. I believe my own contribution is putting the aforementioned work together, adapting it and applying it in practice.

The Hopkins CSR Model (H-CSR-M) in Summary

So, what is the model? The basic framework of the model is illustrated in Figure 4.1 and is composed essentially of CSR definition, CSR principle processes and products, CSR measurement and CSR strategy.

CSR is a systems approach or model to look at the social responsibility of all key stakeholders of an institution or company, i.e. all aspects of a company or institution that contribute to its business or efficient operation are considered. I also insist that the business case for private companies' use of CSR *must* be maintained, i.e. profits must be targeted (or efficiency in the case of a non-private institution). Further, the model is not against profits per se, but *how* profits are made, i.e. they must be made in a socially responsible manner.

Thus, the CSR systems[1] model I describe consists of four main components: the CSR definition, which is the core of the model and from which the other components

---

1. A line of thought in the management field, which stresses the interactive nature and interdependence of external and internal factors in an organization. A systems approach is commonly

Hopkins C SR Model

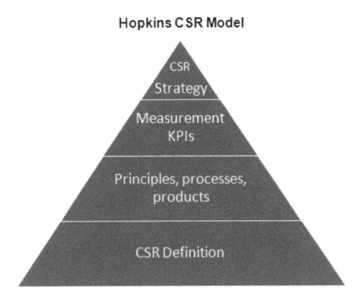

Figure 4.1 Hopkins CSR Model pyramid.

and detail emerge – a process to describe the main components of the model, which are its principles, processes and products.[2]

My model definition leads to a set of components, indicators and measures which allow the measurement of CSR with the Key Performance Indicators that allow one to assess progress and impact. The fourth main component is a 15-point strategy for any company or institution to follow. Like any model, the four points can be taken in the order I propose, but its actual use will be used iteratively to ensure the best practical implementation.

Figure 4.2 shows all the elements of the model and allowed me, in fact, in my teaching to systematically cover all elements of CSR. It also shows the structure of my text book, where each of the main elements has its own chapter.[3]

In Figure 4.3, I show the basic building blocks of any CSR strategy under the H-CSR-M. Links are created pointing in both directions simply to illustrate the iterative process as you create your own CSR strategy.

used to evaluate market elements which affect the profitability of a business. http://www.businessdictionary.com/definition/system-approach.html#ixzz3nP05aekR, accessed 2 October 2015.

2. Based upon Prof. Donna Woods' work and the adaptation of which I call the Hopkins-Wood model in my text book.

3. Michael Hopkins, *CSR/Sustainability – From the Margins to the Mainstream: A Text Book* (Sheffield: Routledge/Greenleaf, 2016).

PUTTING IT ALL TOGETHER

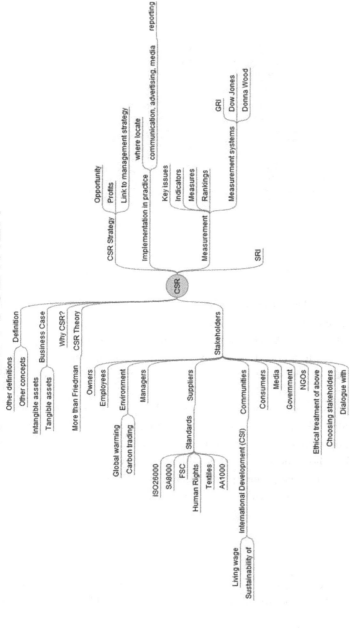

Figure 4.2 The main elements of the Hopkins CSR Model.

CSR Building Blocks

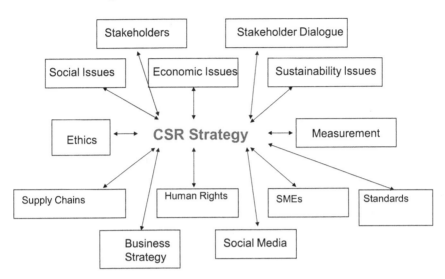

Figure 4.3 CSR basic building blocks.

Four Elements of the H-CSR-M

I shall look briefly at each element of the model next.

The definition[4]

As noted in more detail in Chapter 1, CSR is a process that is concerned with treating the stakeholders of a company or institution ethically and in a responsible manner. Key stakeholders must be treated in a manner deemed acceptable according to international norms.

Social responsibility includes economic and environmental responsibility. Stakeholders exist both inside and outside a firm or institution.

The ultimate aim of corporate social responsibility is to create higher and higher standards of sustainable living while preserving the profitability of the corporation or the integrity of the institution, for peoples both within and outside these entities. The key is how profits are made, not the pursuit of profits at any cost.

CSR and sustainability are closely linked in that they both aim to achieve sustainable development in societies. Both address multi-stakeholders and their materiality.

---

4. Original Source: Hopkins (MHCi), *A Planetary Bargain: Corporate Social Responsibility Comes of Age* (Macmillan, 1998); updated and re-printed by Earthscan, 2003 and re-printed by Routledge, UK, 2010). Updated to emphasise materiality on 2 October 2014.

Corporate is taken to mean any 'body' and as such includes the private corporate sector as well as NGOs, associations and governments.

This definition is a bit of a mouthful, so if I meet you in the street, I want you to at least recite the essential part, and you won't go far wrong in using and applying it, which is:

CSR is about treating key stakeholders responsibly.

A good definition essentially defines the conceptual model from which all the elements can easily evolve. I de-construct the above definition in great detail in my text book, but I am confident in the above statement for a number of reasons. First, it draws on ideas expressed by the great US thinkers of the twentieth century. Second, both the EU and the ISO26000 just about use the main thrust of the definition, although they are much weaker than I am on multi-stakeholders. Third, it covers just about every element of what we want to say. Perhaps the key element, and the link to sustainability, is to add the definition of sustainable development, which is:

Sustainable development, as defined by the UN-sponsored report on Our Common Future chaired by Gro Brundtland, is development that meets the needs of the present without compromising the ability of future generations to meet their own needs.[5]

Thus, CSR aims to seek sustainable development as its goal.

The 3-P model of CSR[6]

The basic elements of the model are threefold:

- Principles of social responsibility
- Processes of social responsiveness
- Products (or outcomes) of social responsibility

Principles of social responsibility		
Legitimacy	Public responsibility	Managerial discretion
Processes of social responsibility		
Environmental scanning	Stakeholder management	Issues management
Products (Outcomes)		
Internal stakeholder effects	External stakeholder effects	External institutional effects

I call this the 3-P model for the measurement of CSR. The three levels of this model are summarized here and based on the work of Donna Wood. In more detail, these are as follows:

---

5. See http://www.un-documents.net/our-common-future.pdf, accessed 2 April 2015.
6. Based, and updated from, my book *The Planetary Bargain*.

Level I: *Principles* of social responsibility

The level of application of this principle is institutional and is based on a firm's basic obligations as a business organization. Its value is that it defines the institutional relationship between business and society and specifies what is expected of any business.[7] This level of the CSP model itself contains three major elements:

Legitimacy. The element of legitimacy concerns business as a social institution and frames the analytical view of the interrelationship of business and society.

Public responsibility. This element concerns the individual firm and its processes and outcomes within the framework of its own principles in terms of what it actually does.

Managerial discretion. Managers and other organizational members are moral actors. Within every domain of CSR, they are obliged to exercise such discretion as is available to them, towards socially responsible outcomes.

Level II: *Processes* of social responsibility

Corporate social responsiveness is a business's capacity to respond to social pressures. This suggests the ability of a business organization to survive through its adaptation to its environment. To do this, a firm must know as much as possible about this environment, be capable of analyzing its data and must react to the results of this analysis. But the environment of business is not static; it is a complex and ever-changing set of circumstances, encompassing complicated interpenetrations of social systems. The ability to successfully scan, interpret and react to the business environment requires equally complex mechanisms. Three such elements have been identified as basic elements of this level of the CSP model: environmental scanning, Stakeholder management and Issues management.

Environmental scanning (assessment) indicates the informational gathering arm of the business and the transmission of the gathered information throughout the organization with its ultimate use in forward planning.

Stakeholder management refers to mapping the relationships of stakeholders to the firm (and among each other) while seeking to balance and meet legitimate concerns as a prerequisite of any measurement process. A stakeholder is defined as any group or individual who can affect or is affected by the achievement of the firm's objectives. For example, owners, suppliers, employees, customers, competitors, domestic and foreign governments, non-profit organizations, environmental and consumer protection groups, and others.

Issues management. The area of issues analysis and management concerns those policies to be developed to address social issues. Having identified the motivating

---

7. K. Davis, 'The Case for and Against Business Assumption of Social Responsibilities', *Academy of Business Management* 16 (1973): 312–22, in Donna J. Wood, 'Social Issues in Management: Theory and Research in Corporate Social Performance', *Journal of Management* 17 (1991): 389.

principles of a firm and having determined the identities, relationships and power of stakeholders, the researcher now turns to the issues that concern stakeholders. The researcher is aware that 'social problems that may exist objectively but may become issues: requiring managerial attention when they are defined as being problematic to society or an institution within society by a group of actors, or stakeholders capable of influencing either governmental action or company policies'.[8]

Level III: *Outcomes or Products*

The issues of measurement are most concerned with the third level of the CSP model. Programmes and the behavioural outcomes of motivating principles can only be significant if they are measured in terms of the stakeholders that they affect. To determine whether CSP makes a difference, all of the stakeholders relevant to an issue or combination of issues must be included in any assessment of performance.

Internal stakeholder effects. This element is concerned with stakeholders within the firm. This might be used to examine how a corporate Code of Ethics affects the day-to-day decision-making of the firm with reference to social responsibility. Similarly, it might be concerned with the positive or negative effects of corporate hiring and employee benefits practices.

External stakeholder effects. This element examines the impact of corporate actions on persons or groups outside the firm. This might concern such things as the negative effects of a product recall, the positive effects of community-related corporate philanthropy or assuming the natural environment as a stakeholder, the effects of toxic waste disposal.

External institutional effects. This final element of the model would examine the effects upon the larger institution of business rather than on any particular stakeholder group. Several environmental disasters have made people aware of the effect of business decisions on the general public, for example. This new awareness has brought about pressure for environmental regulation, which affects the entire institution of business rather than one specific firm.

Applying the model: an example

I offer an example of the way in which the model might be applied by looking more closely at Ben & Jerry's Homemade Ice Cream (now part of Unilever). Ben & Jerry's founder, Ben Cohen, articulated one aspect of the ethical principles of the firm:

> Businesses tend to exploit communities and their workers, and that wasn't the way I thought the game should be played. I thought it should be the opposite—that business had

---

8. J. E. Mahon and S. A. Waddock, 'Strategic Issues Management: An Integration of Issue Life-Cycle Perspectives', *Business and Society* 31, no. 1 (1992): 19–32.

a responsibility to give back to the community, that because the business is allowed to be there in the first place, the business ought to support the community. What we're finding is that when you support the community, the community supports you back (Levering, 1993)[9].

This is a clear statement of principles that belongs in the first level of the CSP model. As stated, the *principle* fulfils both the institutional element (it acts to legitimize the institution of business) and the discretionary element (it directs the firm in a socially responsible path) and goes well beyond any legal requirements, the element of public responsibility.

At the level of *processes* of social responsiveness, scanning of Ben & Jerry's social issues is accomplished through a number of mechanisms ranging from direct community involvement through newsletters to special events sponsored by the company. The effectiveness of the scanning and issues management mechanisms can be seen in its funding of organizations as diverse as the Native American Community Board in South Dakota to the Central Massachusetts Safe Energy Project. We can see clear linkages from the realm of principle towards corporate action.

One specific *outcome* of Ben &Jerry's concern for community welfare is carried out through its purchasing policies. The firm called on the Greystone Bakery in Yonkers, New York, to bake its brownies, a firm that uses its profits to house the homeless and train them as bakers. This outcome is very specific and wholly measurable in a number of ways. One could simply measure the number of homeless people employed by the bakery and the number of trained bakers graduated by the programme. One might also look at how many are still employed at the bakery or somewhere else as bakers. There is a clear causal linkage back through corporate mechanisms to ethical principles and the analytical framework can be seen to function. Further research could be done at Ben & Jerry's to cross-relate different elements and their indicators to determine how, for example, profitability is affected by the 7.5 per cent share of pre-tax earnings given by Ben & Jerry's for philanthropic purposes. Conversely, one might take a proposed indicator such as 'outcomes of community involvement' and examine its statistical relationships with other indicators in other elements (Levering and Moskowitz [10], 1993).

The *stakeholders* in this process are first external to the company and are the homeless who take part in the training programme. A second group of stakeholders can be identified as the community from which the homeless are taken. Clearly, the bakery itself profits as a supplier to Ben & Jerry's and it, in turn, provides benefits to the stakeholders, which are possible because of its business with Ben & Jerry's. As one aspect of a very successful social programme, this also benefits shareholders as the success of the firm grows.

---

9. Robert Levering, *The 100 Best Companies to Work for in America* (Plume Book, 1993).
10. Robert Levering and Milton Moskowitz, *The Best 100 Companies to Work for in America* (New York: Penguin, 1993), 45–7.

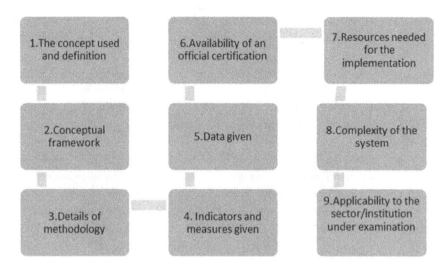

Figure 4.4 Sam Racine's analytical framework.

I have thus defined nine elements of an analytical framework through which to view the dimensions and relationships of a responsible company. This framework has neatly been put into a diagram in Figure 4.4 by Sam Racine.[11]

Measurement

Others have also attempted to look at measurement, the most well-known being the GRI (Global Reporting Initiative), but there is also a 2005 article by Sezekely and Knirsch titled 'Responsible Leadership and Corporate Social Responsibility: Metrics for Sustainable Performance', as well as one of my widely cited articles.[12]

The CSP model, which I now call part of the Hopkins CSR model, is used in Table 4.1 as a basis to develop a set of suggested indicators to measure CSR profiles. As already noted, there are three 'layers' of the model and nine essential elements of measurement. The indicators suggested in the following paragraphs are constructed within these elements and will offer ways to measure and compare outcomes in each element and collectively impact outcomes of the total system.

11. Sam Racine is one of my former students (University of Geneva, Switzerland, 2012).
12. Michael Hopkins, 'Measurement of Corporate Social Responsibility', *International Journal of Management and Decision Making* 6, no. 3/4 (January 2005). DOI: 10.1504/IJMDM.2005.006549, https://www.researchgate.net/publication/247831664_Measurement_of_corporate_social_responsibility, *International Journal of Management and Decision Making* 6, no. 3/4 (January 2005). DOI: 10.1504/IJMDM.2005.006549 50,072 reads on Researchgate as of 28 November 2020.

Table 4.1 CSR measurement: elements, indicators and measures

Indicators and measures		
Elements of CSR model	**Indicator**	**Measure**
Level 1 - Principles of social responsibility		
Legitimacy	• Code of Ethics • Code of Ethics • Code of Ethics	Published? Distributed to employees? Independent group does monitoring?
Public responsibility	• Litigation involving corporate lawbreaking • Fines resulting from illegal activities • Contribution to innovation • Job creation	Amount, size? Amount? R&D expenditure Number of net jobs created
Managerial discretion	• Code of Ethics • Managers convicted of illegal activities	Managers and employees trained? Number, amount?
Level 2 - Processes of social responsibility		
Environmental scanning	• Mechanism to review social issues relevant to firm	Exists?
Stakeholder management	• Analytical body for social issues as integral part of policymaking • Social audit exists? • Ethical accounting statement exists?	Exists?
Issues management	• Policies made on basis of analysis of social issues	Firm's regulations and policies
Level 3 - Outcomes of social responsibility			
Element of SRE model	**Stakeholder groups (assumed)**	**Indicator**	**Indicator**
Internal stakeholder Effects	Owners	• Profitability/value • Corporate Irresponsibility or illegal activity • Community welfare • Corporate philanthropy • Code of Ethics	• Share value, Return on Investment, etc. • Fines, number of product recalls, pollution performance measured against some industry standard • Amount of giving, programmes as per cent of earnings • Amount of pre-tax giving as per cent of earnings • Published, distributed, trained 0 or 1

(Continued)

Table 4.1 (Continued)

Indicators and measures			
	Managers	• Code of Ethics	• Trained in Code of Ethics and apply in demonstrable and measurable ways • Rank of manager responsible for applying code
	Employees	• Union/staff relations • Safety issues • Pay, pensions and benefits • Lay-offs • Employee ownership • Women and minority policies	• Evidence of controversy, good relations • Litigation, fines • Relative ranking to similar firms (measuring per cent spent on employee benefits, programmes, etc.) • Percentage, frequency, individuals chosen • Amount by per cent • Existence, rank with similar firms, litigation and fines, equal pay for equal work?
External stakeholder effects	Customers/ Consumers	• Code of Ethics • Product recalls • Litigation • Public product or service controversy • False advertising	• Evidence of application to products or services • Absolute number, seriousness demonstrated by litigation or fines, percentage of total production • Amount of fraud, price fixing, antitrust suits • Seriousness, frequency • Litigation, fines
	Natural environment	• Pollution • Toxic waste • Recycling and use of recycled products • Use of eco-label on products? • CO_2 emission	• Performance against index, litigation, fines • Performance against index, litigation, fines • Percentages • Yes/No? • daily rate

(Continued)

Table 4.1 (Continued)

Indicators and measures				
	Community	<ul><li>Corporate giving to community programmes</li><li>Direct involvement in community programmes</li><li>Community controversy or litigation</li></ul>	<ul><li>Amount, percentage</li><li>Number, outcomes, costs, benefits</li><li>Number, seriousness, outcomes</li></ul>	
	Suppliers	<ul><li>Firm's Code of Ethics</li><li>Supplier's Code of Ethics</li><li>Litigation/fines</li><li>Public controversy</li></ul>	<ul><li>Applied to all suppliers</li><li>Applied</li><li>Number, amount, outcomes</li><li>Amount, outcome</li></ul>	
External institutional effects	Business as a social institution	<ul><li>Code of Ethics</li><li>Generic litigation</li><li>Class action suits</li><li>Public policy and legislation improved due to pressure from corporation</li></ul>	<ul><li>Published and applied</li><li>Amounts, number, outcomes</li><li>Amounts, type, number, outcomes</li><li>Yes or no</li></ul>	

Simplifying the Number of Required Indicators[13]

Table 4.1 is quite easy to fill in for any company. I am rather concerned at the huge number of indicators expected in other certification systems. For instance, as noted earlier, the three big elephants in the CSR room are GRI, ISO 26000 and International Integrated Reporting Council (IIRC). But therein I think we are in danger of asking too much of companies and institutions. Will the demand for lengthier and lengthier description requirements lead to increased reluctance to incorporate CSR? There is a danger, and I recommend here the need for more limited reporting so that we may encourage more to become socially responsible without increasing their baggage.

In the pursuit of the highest (A+) rating from the GRI, Nestlé produced an impressive web-based 300-page report of indicators and data.[14] Nestlé can surely afford the expense involved, and one doesn't blame them in any way from doing so. But in the

---

13. This section was originally based on Michael Hopkins and Adrian Payne Linchpins of 'CSR performance' or 'Weapons of Mass Description': An argument for orthogonality in reporting standards. http://mhcinternational.com/images/stories/weapons.pdf [RECHECK], accessed 24 August 2015.

14. http://www.nestle.com/csv/Nestle/ourperformance/GRIContentIndex/Pages/GRIContentIndex.aspx, accessed 2 August 2012.

greater scheme of things, this may be the start of a worrying trend when it comes to judging CSR performance on the ground.

Will slavish advocacy of these three complementary voluntary standards mean that companies that simply cannot afford to generate and deliver such a comprehensive report should give up trying to measure and communicate on their CSR performance? Even worse, might they take this as a signal to disinvest in their CSR programmes if they cannot compete on, one might say, the Olympic stage of reporting on social performance?

There is no doubt that trying to satisfy GRI at level A+ did lead to enormous volumes of indicators as Nestlé bravely showed for GRI3.1. The G4 guidelines, which represent the GRI's latest reporting guidance, extend to over 300 pages.[15]

Furthermore, the management complexity of trying to implement the seven aspects of ISO 26000 could lead many companies into despair if they do not have the resources to do so, particularly when it comes to SMEs. But it does not follow that by not being able to do so such companies are necessarily being irresponsible in the way in which they conduct their business operations.

Both GRI and ISO 26000 have been created by committees of well-intentioned and dedicated people drawn from across the spectrum. But, as we know, committees tend to try to satisfy everybody and sometimes end up satisfying nobody. Clearly, we need to promote CSR (and its offshoots sustainability, shared value, etc.), and monitoring and evaluation is crucial to inform the public on where our corporate institutions are leading us to. However, too much complexity in monitoring and auditing means that the metaphorical tail could wag the dog too hard with unintended consequences in the sectors (e.g. SMEs) in which, by number, most businesses exist. Much simpler reporting guidance codes, while not diluting the perceived wisdom of more detailed standards, might help smaller companies embrace CSR and a sustainability agenda.[16]

CSR Strategy

What happens when these ideas are transformed into a strategic framework to enhance the competitive advantage of a company while preserving the values of CSR?

Instigating a CSR programme simply on a 'nice-to-do' or 'wishful thinking' basis just won't wash in today's 'goldfish bowl' business environment. CSR is not just the right thing to do; it has to be the right thing to do for your company or organization. Hence, the first step is to identify and pin down the key business or organizational goals. Having

---

15. https://www.globalreporting.org/resourcelibrary/G4/G4-Exposure-Draft.pdf, accessed 1 August 2012.
16. In fact, an attempt has been made by GRI, although we have not managed to find the document online since the one given to us was 'Le cycle GRI du reporting developpement durable – Un manuel pour les petites et moins petites organisations', GRI, 2008. A reduced set of indicators were suggested but not the notion of orthogonality suggested here.

done so, the purpose of a strategic CSR programme in terms of how it will align with and hopefully advance these goals can be clearly stated. Hopefully, this will be self-evident to those who will have to sign off on the programme. As such, the aims and objectives of any CSR programme have to be aligned with the corporate or organizational goals and also be congruent with the corporate or organizational values. If not, they will simply bounce off, and it will be back to square one!

I have worked out such a strategy and applied these points in over 50 companies around the world.[17] Based on the aforementioned experiences, this strategy has been converted into 15 key steps in creating a corporate CSR strategy. Here I present the 15 steps of the strategy.

1. Identify business goals and decide on the purpose of the social responsibility programme. Is the president, CEO or similar, demonstrably involved?
2. Define the values statement and mission of the company or institution. Are these well-known to management and employees? How does the long-term vision match up with business goals?
3. What are your competitors doing on CSR? (benchmarking)
4. Decide on the overall budget. Is there a steering group or some other kind of structure identified to implement and monitor CSR?
5. Identify the key stakeholders. Does a report exist that includes input/responses to, and feedback from, these stakeholders?
6. Do some research. What are the latest business standards? Check out SA8000, AA1000, GRI, International Labour Organization (ILO) conventions, World Trade Organization (WTO) discussions, Caux principles, UN Global Compact, Integrated Reporting and so on. Have the key issues for the company or institution in the social, economic and environmental area been identified and addressed?
7. Has a CSR strategy for each key stakeholder been developed after consultation with them?
8. Revise budget accordingly and embed CSR into all key non-financial asset functions.
9. Carry out stakeholder dialogue and ensure it is being done in a systematic way and on a regular basis.
10. Identify the key indicators to measure progress as a socially responsible enterprise and ensure they are appropriate and measurable.
11. Identify the costs and benefits of the proposals to ensure they are realistic.
12. Implement the activity or programme, ensuring that it relates well to other proposals in the pipeline.
13. Research and develop a series of advertisements to show what is being done in the area of CSR and market the programme accordingly. Ensure that the advertising

---

17. Thanks to Adrian Payne, former Manager of BAT's award winning CSR programme for working with me on these 15 points and drawing upon his vast experience.

can be backed up with internal consistent practices since this is a dangerous pitfall if that is not the case.

14. Evaluate the social responsibility proposals against cost/benefits on an ongoing basis.
15. Ensure CSR policies are operating and truly embedded to the extent that no CSR exit strategy is required.

The Hopkins CSR Model: 15-Point Strategy Applied

What happens when we apply these 15 points to a specific situation? This is presented here, and the examples given are drawn from many sectors. The model has been applied in many situations in the private sector, and also in some public institutions.

Is the purpose of the CSR/Sustainability programme (or similar) clearly stated? Are they consistent with business goals? Is the president, general secretary or CEO demonstrably involved?

A good place to start on this step is to check carefully what the stated goals of your company or organization are. It is helpful that these days many entities state these quite succinctly on their websites in the context of their overall mission. A good example is provided by Unilever, who are perhaps unique in incorporating their various commitments to CSR/sustainability as pictorial elements in their corporate logo. On its website (https://www.unilever.com/about/who-we-are/our-vision/) it states quite clearly: 'We work to create a better future every day'.

Then, how it sees itself doing this is captured in three short paragraphs, namely[18]:

We help people feel good, look good and get more out of life with brands and services that are good for them and good for others.

We will inspire people to take small actions every day that can add up to a big difference for the world.

We will develop new ways of doing business with the aim of doubling the size of our company while reducing our environmental impact.

One example of purpose is shown by the company Manpower Inc., which has a deep heritage of operating at the highest level of integrity. It states[19]:

Our strong commitment to responsible business practices is reflected in everything we do, from the transparency of our communications with shareholders to the unparalleled benefits that we offer to our temporary employees and contractors. We strive to provide a great work environment for our employees and to be a beacon of integrity for our clients.

---

18. http://www.unilever.co.uk/sustainable-living-2015/
19. http://www.manpowergroup.com/sustainability/inside-manpowergroup.html

Table 4.2 Example: Manpower business goals[i]

Manpower stands for	Manpower stands against
Creating a bridge to employment for disadvantaged individuals around the world	Labour practices that exploit individuals, particularly those who are vulnerable
Our focus is on providing jobs and job training for the following groups, working in partnership with governments and NGOs, as appropriate:	Our focus is on increasing awareness of, and opposition to, these practices, until such time as we can provide a bridge to employment for these individuals:
Long-term unemployed/ underemployed	Human trafficking
People with disabilities	Child labour
Disenfranchised individuals	Illegally low wages paid to vulnerable individuals
Victims of disaster	Exploitation of disadvantaged individuals
Victims of exploitation	Unsafe working conditions
Refugees	
Youth	

[i] http://www.manpowergroup.ae/SocialResponsibility.aspx

What is particularly interesting and informative about their business goals (Table 4.2) is that they state what they stand for and what they stand against. Indeed, one could almost transpose many of these statements directly into the goals of a strategic CSR programme in terms of a combined 'offensive' and 'defensive' strategy (see below).

Once you have defined the corporate/organizational goals, you can start to sketch out and refine as necessary the core elements of a strategic CSR programme that will align with these goals. As Werther and Chandler recommend,[20] these core elements comprise: (1) why the strategy should be implemented, (2) where it should be implemented, (3) how it should be implemented, and (4) who should oversee the process. It is also important to take account of the industry context as this will vary, and to obtain a clear understanding (and agreement) as to whether the programme is being initiated for offensive or defensive reasons. In practice, it is often a mixture of the two reasons so as to be both proactive and reactive to stakeholder expectations of responsible behaviour. At the same time, it is important to realize that these expectations evolve, which is why regular stakeholder dialogue is essential.

Offensive CSR, if it genuinely enhances the corporate or organizational brand, can be a game-changer for obtaining competitive advantage over rivals. This is especially so if one of the goals of the CSR programme is the stated aim of being the sector leader in setting responsibility standards others would aspire to. On the other hand, defensive CSR is primarily designed to avoid criticism, especially in controversial sectors, and therefore go some way to protecting the brand. Both require an upfront investment, and

---

20. David Chandler and William B. Werther, Jr., *Strategic Corporate Social Responsibility, Stakeholders, Globalization, and Sustainable Value Creation*, 3rd edn (SAGE Publications, Inc., 2455 Teller Road, Thousand Oaks, California 9132 © 2014), 664 pp.

in either case don't guarantee that some kind of reputational crisis might arise, but they might mitigate the consequences of such a crisis.

As McElhaney has stated,[21] the higher in the organization that CSR reports, the more closely linked it is to providing value. This is true from both an internal and an external perspective. Hence, it is vital to get the CEO involved as a sponsor for, and the execution of, a strategic CSR programme. Such a programme might well require changes in business practices, and if one meets any resistance in effecting these changes, it is immensely useful to have the CEO's endorsement and support in your back pocket as what might be described as executive 'air cover'. CSR champions are first and foremost 'change agents', and to some people, of course, change can be quite threatening.

Furthermore, if you are trying to put into practice a CSR programme in a large organization, it is useful to carry out some targeted internal lobbying of those in the management who have the responsibility and expertise for forward strategic planning. In other words, identify and engage with those who have their hands on the 'organizational rudder', small changes in the direction of which can have dramatic changes in the overall direction of corporate strategy. This is another reason why it is so important to have at minimum the CEO on board from the word go.

Can you see the value statement and mission?

Are these well-known to management and employees? Does the long-term mission match up with the company or institution's purpose?

In defining a values statement, what one is really doing is trying to capture the ethos of how a corporation or organization conducts its day-to-day operations on the ground. A good example here is again that provided by Unilever.[22] It is particularly helpful to have a clearly defined code of business standards that employees can be held accountable for.

Thus, it is key to be able to see a value statement and a clearly defined mission of the company. Questions one would ask include whether these elements are well-known to the management and employees. Furthermore, does the long-term mission match up with the companies' purpose?

However, everything is not as straightforward as it seems, for instance, Patrice Caine, the boss of the French defence and technology company Thales, made a dismal announcement[23] on its statement of its purpose. 'It is a statement that took six months to write', even though there had been six months of consultations with nearly half of the group's 83,000 employees. The result was just seven words: 'Building a future we can

21. K. McElhaney, 'A Strategic Approach to CSR', *Leader to Leader*, Issue 52 (2009): 30–36. First published online 13 March 2009. DOI: 10.1002/ltl.327, http://responsiblebusiness.haas.berkeley.edu/documents/Strategic%20CSR%20%28Leader%20to%20Leader, %20McElhaney%29.pdf, accessed 14 June 2014.
22. http://www.unilever.co.uk/aboutus/purposeandprinciples/, accessed 9 September 2015.
23. https://www.ft.com/content/f1dc0001-384a-4acb-b881-b4ade85689a8, accessed 13 September 2020.

all trust'. The FT article further noted that 'the purpose statement, which supposedly spells out why a company exists, is a younger relative of the decades-old mission statement which supposedly defines what an outfit does. The two are regularly confused with each other and with the "vision statement", which allegedly alerts the world to what a company will do in future'.

Other statements revealed that '[w]e remain focused on our enduring values of safety, quality, and integrity in all that we do', Boeing's chief executive, Dennis Muilenburg, said last year – five months before he was fired in the crisis over two fatal crashes of the company's 737 Max jets. Rio Tinto, the mining group whose CEO just quit after an outcry over the destruction of two ancient Aboriginal sites in Australia, stated on its website that '[b]usiness integrity underpins everything we do'.

Consequently, there is some cynicism about the idea that statements of corporate values, be they purpose, mission or otherwise, can have any effect on performance. The FT also quoted that Chris Bart concluded in 1997 after asking senior managers from 88 large North American companies about their companies' statements that 'the vast majority are not worth the paper they are written on'. Indeed, a study of nearly 700 companies published in the MIT Sloan Management Review in July 2020 looked at how well employees thought their companies walked their talk on values. The result? Not much, or as the researchers drily put it: 'Data shows no correlation between official values and corporate culture'. Clearly, there is much more to do for companies to ensure they walk the talk!!

What are other organizations doing? Benchmarking and scoping study

Another key initial step is to benchmark your company's or your organization's current or planned CSR performance against either competitors or similar organizations. A benchmarking exercise carried out by MHCi for companies in the oil sector is shown in Figure 4.5.

Having carried out the benchmarking exercise you can carry out a scoping study to determine the following:

Why the programme should be implemented in the context of social and industry trends, which can change rapidly?
Where it should be implemented, for example, in the organization, its supply chains, marketing, etc?

How it should be implemented, for example, all at once or gradually? Obviously, circumstances will vary, but our experience leads us to believe that when it comes to putting in place a CSR strategy, 'evolution' often works better than 'revolution'. This strategy can lead to better acceptance and, ultimately, better embedding, as many companies and organizations often tend to be conservative in terms of their operating practices.

Thus, you would first of all check if benchmarking has been done, and, if so, against what other similar companies in your own country and/or internationally. Then

3:Example of Benchmarking from the Oil sector

Benchmarking of web sites and annual reports

Key CSR Issues	Comp any X	Tullow Oil	Premier Oil	Wood side	Burren	Nexen	Shell
Have a Foundation?	4	1	1	1	1	1	4
Governance Policy?	2	4	4	1	4	4	4
Code of Conduct?	3	1	4	1	1	4	4
UN Global Compact?	1	1	4	1	1	4	4
GRI?	1	1	4	1	1	3	4
Have CSR report?	1	4	4	1	1	4	4
Human Rights?	1	1	4	1	1	4	4
Stakeholder Dialog?	1	1	4	1	1	4	4

1 = Little or Nothing
2 = Some (some statements)
3 = Good (taken seriously but no monitoring)
4 = Excellent (implement and monitor)

Figure 4.5 Example of benchmarking from the oil sector. *Source:* Created by Michael Hopkins.

you would check if a scoping study has been done to try to capture CSR and CSR-related activities that might already be ongoing but not defined as being part of a CSR programme.

Is the overall budget for CSR disclosed?

Is there a steering group, or some other kind of structure, to implement and monitor CSR? Putting in place a strategic CSR programme will probably require a financial investment in that the requisite management infrastructure may have to be put into place, and when carrying out a scoping study and doing benchmarking, it is sometimes prudent to hire consultants. Furthermore, publishing social/sustainability reports can be expensive when considering the cost of social auditors for verification of the content. On the other hand, it may be possible to offset these expenses by identifying short-term wins, for example instigating eco-efficiency initiatives to save costs on energy and water consumption.

If you are dealing with a large company or organization – and especially if the concept of CSR is new to senior management, it may be useful to set up a CSR steering group. This group can review the results of any scoping study and help frame subsequent recommendations accordingly. It is helpful in this regard to ensure cross-functional representation on this group. We would recommend at least three functional directors: one responsible for corporate affairs, one responsible for operations and one responsible for human resources functions. The last of these directors is particularly important as the development and roll-out of a CSR programme may well involve behavioural changes. The knock-on effect of this may necessitate a realignment of pay and bonus policies. It is also a good move to have the head of audit (if there is one) on the group as this may help convince the finance director and other board members of the accuracy of budget proposals. From a governance perspective, the steering group can usefully be tasked with setting up a board CSR committee and signing off the appointment of an internal CSR champion who may be (but not necessarily) the individual who was charged with getting the CSR programme up and running in its conceptual phase.

Driving and embedding a CSR programme throughout the organization can be a complex and challenging task. Hence, whoever is selected to have organizational responsibility for doing this must at minimum understand and be committed to the principles of CSR. He or she must be fairly senior (although not necessarily a board member) and be respected by their superiors and peers by setting an excellent personal example. Internal respect offers a good platform on which to build external credibility. Critically, whoever is selected must be persuasive at executive and high-value-stakeholder level. It could be you!

Questions that should be considered at this stage are the following: Has a CSR budget been set? Note that few, if any, companies seem to publish externally their budgets for CSR, but they will have internal figures for this. Is there a steering group, or some other kind of structure, to oversee the implementation and monitoring of CSR? Companies vary in how they incorporate a CSR department in their organizational structure. Sometimes it can be found in either the regulatory compliance or in the communications function. Preferably, it should be a stand-alone unit, at least in the initial stages, so that its importance is clear to the rest of the organization. Once the CSR programme is up and running, it may be possible to shrink the department and place it under an appropriate alternative function. This assumes, of course, that the principles of CSR and the elements of the CSR programme have been successfully embedded in the various functions.

Have the key stakeholders and their expectations been identified?

Does a report exist that includes input/responses to, and feedback from, these stakeholders?[24]

The identification and interviewing of key stakeholders are essential prerequisites before embarking on future full-fledged stakeholder dialogues. It is particularly important that CSR programmes are developed on an iterative basis rather than by generating a package of initiatives in isolation. Hence, interview a selection of stakeholders

---

24. For further reading on stakeholder selection, see Ronald K. Mitchell, Bradley R. Agle, Donna J. Wood, 'Toward a Theory of Stakeholder Identification and Salience: Defining the Principle of Who and What Really Counts', *The Academy of Management Review* 22, no. 4 (October 1997): 853–86.

in each category depending on the complexity of your organization and the external environment in which it operates. For corporations we would consider that it is crucial to attach importance to investors, suppliers and employees in the first instance. You can make use of standard KPIs for social, economic and environmental issues as per the GRI as a basis for discussions on performance as perceived internally versus external perceptions. Be prepared for variations in these perceptions, perhaps resulting from lack of external communication. As appropriate, you can also map these KPIs against the UN Global Compact Principles and the UN Millennium Goals.

A typical stakeholder map for an institution is shown in Figure 4.6, created by me. So what does this mean for NFAs? Obviously, one has to ask if the key stakeholders have been identified. If not, they could be something like owners at club level, managers, employees, leagues, clubs, players, referees and referee associations.

Other stakeholders would probably include governing bodies such as the Fédération Internationale de Football Association (FIFA), the Union of European Football Associations (UEFA), sports ministries, fans, spectators (the millions who watch football on TV, but may not be active fans), local communities (including schools), media and individual commentators, suppliers, sponsors, representatives of national and local government and those providing security at the grounds (the police and other agencies). It would be good to know whether or not a report exists that includes inputs to and responses (including feedback) from some of these stakeholders.

For each one could think of a CSR strategy (see some examples in Section 4.7.7).

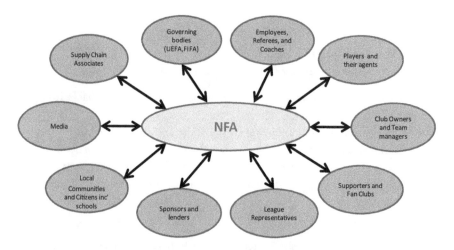

NFA – National Football Association

Figure 4.6 A typical stakeholder diagram.

Research: has the company or institution considered the latest CSR/Sustainability standards?

Typical standards are SA8000, AA1000, GRI, ILO conventions, WTO discussions, UN Global Compact, UN SDGs, B-Corp, ISO 26000, Integrated Reporting, etc. The best of the bunch is probably ISO26000, but you will go a long way by going through my H-CSR-M, which has been applied around the world for decades.

Have the key issues in the social, economic and environmental areas been identified and addressed?

CSR is an ever-evolving discipline, so it is always advisable to 'keep one's eye on the ball' (if you will forgive the intended pun). For example, recent years have seen the development of new GRI guidelines, the launch of ISO 26000 and the growing interest in Integrated Reporting.

Des Tomlinson of the Football Association of Ireland (FAI) wrote this very illuminating comment that I think helps elaborate illustrate this section well:

> From my reflections and learning as I progressed through the recent EU preparatory action project I was involved with, I believe that FA's, dependant on a range of factors, including whether they view the wider social function of sport as a core objective of their work, could use football to strategically complement policy area of focus with respect to the social function of sport (e.g. Health, Integration/Inclusion, Informal Education and Training, Active Ageing etc.). This could (and does for some FA's already) take the form of joint programmes with relevant departments or companies, for example ground level programmes in schools targeted at health. To more social marketing type activity using the high media profile of football/footballers to support and convey key social or health messages via public campaigns/awareness raising initiatives. The possibilities for creative CSR work probably remain endless, and should be about real impact not simply about showing an organisation's commitment, and here a coordinated approach is underscored (The social issue/challenge, the stakeholders, the football intervention, the outcome and the impact assessment).

Has a CSR strategy for each key stakeholder been developed after consultation with them?

Apart from having varying expectations in terms of CSR performance, different groups of stakeholders may well have their own ideas about taking part in the dialogue process. Some may be happy to take part in multi-stakeholder dialogues, others might prefer a more one-to-one approach. In 'controversial' industries, for example, tobacco, alcohol and oil, certain stakeholders, such as NGO pressure groups, may decline to take part at all; the justification being that participation adds credibility to the process. The important thing to realize is that you may have to develop the CSR programme and the engagement process to suit the stakeholder(s) in question.

You also have to take account of 'stakeholder salience' on a matrix of 'level of interest' plotted against 'level of power' of the various stakeholders, as shown in Table 4.3.

In my experience, even though sometimes the views and perceptions of the organization and some of its stakeholders may at first glance seem poles apart, in almost

Table 4.3 Level and interest and power

Level of interest	Level of power	Action
Low	Low	
Low	High	Keep satisfied
High	Low	Keep informed
High	High	Manage closely

Source: Author, based on Mitchell et al. (1997) op.cit.

all instances there will be some common ground. If this can be identified at an early stage, it is possible to develop potential synergies and sell them to the organization and 'hesitant stakeholders'. Indeed, there are more and more instances of NGOs working in partnership with big corporations on projects that would not have seemed possible a decade or so ago. This also underlines why it is so important to keep an eye on changing societal expectations as these change over time. It also reinforces the need to restart the stakeholder engagement process at regular intervals; we would recommend at least every two years.

You do though have to guard against 'stakeholder fatigue' in that some stakeholder groups, particularly charities, may not have the resources to accept all the invitations they get from organizations. And do not be surprised if some stakeholder expectations are either simply unrealistic or outside the organization's control and sphere of influence. An example would be where governments are perceived to be failing to live up to their own responsibilities and companies are expected to step into their shoes. Note also that combinations of stakeholders can be quite powerful, as Shell found on the Brent Spa issue when Greenpeace, an NGO, joined the media to harass Shell[25] – wrongly as it turned out.

Finally, it is important to realize that many stakeholders have their own stakeholders too. As such they may not be 'free agents' and so cannot make commitments without consultation with their own stakeholders.

Comment. One example, the UEFA Respect programme,[26] is clearly linked to almost all the stakeholder groups. But other than the brilliant use of the word 'Respect', how is it interpreted by all the stakeholders listed, for instance, in point 5 above? What does it mean in practice? As avid TV football fans, we have not noticed any of the football commentators ever discussing the issue during games, which would suggest more work to be done between the governing bodies and the media.

Another area to tackle is players as role models. Other than avoiding yellow cards, what additional incentives could be thought of? For instance, UEFA already has a fair play ranking for teams and player of the year awards and project to build up respect ambassadors.

---

25. http://priceofoil.org/2015/02/03/ghost-brent-spar-haunts-shell/, accessed 26 August 2020.
26. I was fortunate to be an adviser to this programme as well as Football for Social Responsibility for UEFA over 2012--2020.

The community level has seen many innovations in NFAs. To take just one example, in my research for this article, I was much impressed by one NFA's involvement in conflict resolution. A divided community was encouraged to cross physical walls simply by organizing a game of football. We all know that ugly areas such as racism, hooliganism and many aspects of conflict are caused by poor education and ignorance of others. NFAs have certainly shown innovative measures through using football to get people together and work on reducing ignorance. Great stuff to build on!

Regarding the natural environment, the Montréal Alouettes, Montreal's American football club, employed 180 people. The club has reduced energy use and waste, in part through collaboration with its partners: Montreal's public transportation company, venue owners and cleaning services providers. As a result of these collaborations, a free shuttle between a metro stop and the stadium reduces vehicle traffic, more efficient lighting at the stadium reduces energy consumption during matches and better waste management after the matches has led to 14 tons of waste reduction per season. The team is actually 'carbon-neutral', producing no net greenhouse gas emissions, because of its energy efficiency efforts and purchase of carbon credits. The club is also active in the community. Players tour schools, raising awareness of environmental issues and encouraging students to stay in school.

Other short examples

In your association's pension plan, are the pension funds invested in a sustainable way? Is there a sustainable investment policy ruling out some industries?

For the environment: Does a ticket to a home game of your national team systematically include a free ride with public transport?

For health: Does your association apply a 'no smoking' policy in the football stadiums?

For fans: Does your association have a programme to accommodate disabled fans? Have you thought about the free speech rights of fans?[27] Do you aim at implementing the good practice proposals in the guide 'Access for all' to create accessible stadium and match experience?[28]

How does your association promote football for the disabled?

How does your association management structure stand up to scrutiny in terms of 'institutional discrimination'? How many women, if any, are on your NFA (National Football Association) Board? How many at executive or middle-management level?

For business air travel: Does your NFA take out CO_2 compensation?

---

27. Mentioned to me by Tim Rich, author of *The Extraordinary World of The Football Fan* (London: Virgin Books, 2000).

28. See http://www.cafefootball.eu/en/access-all, access for All -- UEFA and CAFE Good Practice Guide to Creating an Accessible Stadium and Matchday Experience.

Revise budget and embed CSR into all company (or organization) functions

Once the initial series of dialogues has been completed and stakeholder input used to hone the evolving internal CSR strategy, it will probably be necessary to revise the budget (which is where the steering group can be helpful) and also embark on embedding CSR into all functions. Far better functions, such as human resources, procurement and marketing, are able to apply CSR principles to policies and operational decisions than the CSR team being asked to sign off on every new initiative. This is where it is important to get functional directors involved, with the assistance of, if necessary, the CEO, in what should be a 'top-down' process. Monitoring of the functional embedding should be a key action standard for a CSR committee if there is one.

Tangible evidence of budgets is normally not given in the public domain and, clearly, actions speak louder than words. For instance, in your NFA's supply chain, does your NFA order footballs according to CSR terms: 'child-labour-free certified' products? For instance, many may remember the use of footballs being sewn together by child labour in Pakistan. Such incidents lead to reputation being damaged. And as the corporate magnate Warren Buffet once said: *reputation takes 20 years to make and 2 minutes to destroy!*

Further stakeholder dialogue

The next step is to carry out more in-depth stakeholder dialogues to help refine the ongoing CSR programme. This can involve tailoring and managing the resulting message on progress to the differing stakeholder groups. Depending on the size of the organization and the environment in which it operates, it may also entail strengthening corporate governance, policies and procedures, including working up codes for suppliers. Now is a good opportunity to focus on corporate social investment programmes, exploring (if not done already) collaborative partnerships and developing a 'sustainability agenda'. The latter is twofold. First the sustainable part of the environment, and second, the sustainability of actions taken. Some may also include sustainable development and SDGs, to be discussed in Chapter 9.

Coming back to the CSR committee mentioned above, arguably the true mark of a company that takes CSR seriously is not just that they have such a committee, but that it is given equal status to the audit committee. In other words, social performance and stakeholder dialogue is accorded the same importance as financial performance and dialogue with analysts in the pursuance of profit.

A good example of a portfolio of corporate policies that reflect an investment in strategic CSR is provided by Hewlett Packard in, for example, their 2014 Living Progress Report (http://www8.hp.com/us/en/hp-information/global-citizenship/reporting.html).

As far as corporate social investment is concerned, it is worth taking a look at the strategy taken by BHP Billiton (http://www.bhpbilliton.com/society/ourcontribution/our-approach).

For a description of the various types of collaborative partnerships that exist these days, readers are directed to the recent report on this from Globescan/Sustainability (www.sustainability.com/library/attachment/397.)

This report, 'Collaborating for a Sustainable Future', describes and gives examples of single industry collaborations, multi-industry collaborations, company/NGO collaborations and company/company collaborations.

When it comes to developing a sustainability agenda, a good example is provided by the Ford Motor Company (http://corporate.ford.com/microsites/sustainability-report -2014-15/strategy-sustainability.html), who have mapped out quite a comprehensive blueprint, informed by stakeholder engagement during an early phase in its development (http://corporate.ford.com/microsites/sustainability-report-2014-15/strategy -stakeholder.html). However, to do this, you will probably have to do some more work on generating a set of KPIs that are material to the long-term sustainability of the organization (see below).

Comment. Companies often report on their stakeholder dialogues. UEFA, for instance, has a stakeholder page on its website[29] where it also displays its latest FSR (Football for Social Responsibility Report), which happily is led by one of my former students!

Identify the key indicators to measure progress as a socially responsible enterprise

By now you should have a good grasp of the KPIs (Key Performance Indicators) that are perceived as being important both internally and externally to the organization, and hopefully they coincide! As such, you should try to provide data for as many of these KPIs as possible in the short term and suggest methodologies for calculating or harmonizing those currently missing over the long term.

Comment. As noted above, the main guidance on indicators, these days, comes from the GRI - they have many supplements to guide you, see for instance, their sports events sector supplement.[30] But some of us are uneasy at the large coverage and details required in GRI reporting and the consequent certification. I have stated elsewhere that more work is required to ensure that the 'data tail does not wag the dog', and I have argued for a reduced set of orthogonal indicators. A quick method to assess whether your association is socially responsible is to carry out MHCi's short questionnaire of 20 questions.[31]

Identify costs and benefits of the programme

In the early stages of developing a strategic CSR programme, some of the costs and benefits may seem rather nebulous in the absence of scoping study and stakeholder input. However, by this stage it would have become clearer, and one can make projections

---

29. See http://www.uefa.com/uefa/stakeholders/index.html, accessed 17 August 2015.
30. See University of British Columbia Centre for Sport and Sustainability GRI Releases Event Sector Supplement, http://css.ubc.ca/2012/01/31/gri-releases-event-sector-supplement/, accessed 17 August 2015.
31. MHC International Rate Your Company! See http://mhcinternational.com/csr-services/ rate-your-company, accessed 17 August 2015.

based on real data and firm information. For example, it would have become evident that internally superior CSR performance could lead to increased profits through lowering operating costs by more eco-efficient practices and a reduced risk of non-compliance with regulatory requirements.

Comment. Again, few do these types of calculations, but it is possible to carry out return-on-investment calculations for individual projects.

Has the activity or programme been implemented?

External recognition is an important element of deriving benefits from the CSR programme; hence, it is essential to get the word out by communicating on progress. Many companies produce reports under various titles: social reports, corporate responsibility reports and sustainability reports. However, as already mentioned, there is increasing interest in Integrated Reporting. Whichever method is chosen, for external credibility it is essential to have the information, provided it is verified independently by social auditors. Unilever has already been flagged up in this chapter as an example of best practice in setting out corporate goals, etc. It is also unique in the top 10 FTSE 100 group of companies in producing a corporate 'sustainable development' report, which at the end of the day is arguably what CSR is all about. Rio Tinto deserves a mention too, as while it provides CSR date in its annual report, it also produces local sustainable development reports.

Is CSR publicity in its social report, website or other medium really focused on its CSR profile and performance, or is it just PR? What do independent observers think?

The words 'greenwash' or 'whitewash' are sometimes used by independent observers when looking at publicity for CSR activities. The main point is to walk the talk. Believe it or not, many PR companies/departments would prefer the truth in advertising than what is now sometimes called in derogative terms 'PR'!

Are the social responsibility proposals evaluated against cost/benefits on an ongoing basis?

How is this done, e.g. by employee surveys, supplier surveys, member surveys, carbon offsets? CSR is not a 'fire and forget' initiative, nor is it a 'one-hit wonder'. Proposals for superior CSR performance will constantly evolve and need to be evaluated in terms of cost versus benefits. If there is greater external recognition of superior CSR performance, an improved reputation should follow. In this case, given the increasing trend towards ethical purchasing, market share might increase, thus generating increased profits. It might also lead to new market opportunities, and thus also increase profits. Economies of scale may also play an important part.

Importantly, an improved reputation also directly influences regulation, especially today. Demonstrating the societal and political legitimacy to justify being part of the debate will hopefully enable your voice to be heard by policymakers. As an example, for a growing number of industry sectors, 'responsible marketing' is becoming an increasing concern when it comes to children. This is where the development of marketing codes in conjunction with external stakeholders such as NGOs can play a key role in demonstrating superior CSR performance. A

Comment. It is better to incur a cost that is in line with what the company is trying to do rather than something that sounds nice but is not especially relevant to the company's mission, for example, an oil company financially supporting a horse show.

Exit strategy

The true measure of success in embedding CSR is that CSR management systems and governance sit at the heart of the alignment of company values and principles with societal values and expectations and the adaption of company policies, common platforms and best practices in concert. Providing this is so, CSR in the organization should become self-sustaining without the need for a large CSR team. However, because CSR constantly evolves, it is still advisable to keep a small team to continue to monitor this evolution and refine/revise such policies and best practices as necessary, especially if the organization concerned has taken it upon itself to be the sector leader. So, ensure embedding is exemplified by the management and behaviour of the enterprise or institution.

Here we have given some examples of practical CSR activities that could be carried out by companies. Some, or even many of these, are already being carried out by the company. The main advantage of a focused CSR programme would be to bring these activities together in a systematic manner and under one organizational umbrella.

Certification

The final stage of the above is certification, and I have a questionnaire that you can fill out; and on completion of the form, we will examine and issue a certificate accordingly (for Part III H-CSR-M, see details on https://www.csrfi.com/hopkinscsrmodel). The CSR Rating App may also give you a guide on how well you will perform.[32]

---

32. https://www.csrfi.com/rate-your-company, accessed 13 September 2020.

Chapter Five

MY OWN EXPERIENCE IN APPLYING CSR[1]

What Are the Different Ways/Forms through which CSR Manifests?

The definition I use that CSR is all about treating stakeholders responsibly is easier to criticize than to revise. Indeed, I am not sure that any definition of social phenomena ever reaches widespread agreement and I would be surprised if my lengthy definition in the previous chapter would, anyway, be the definition of choice, especially because of its length. Wordiness aside, the definition still does not cover all the key issues, and there are many concerns that are not elaborated in my definition. For instance, CSR manifests itself in a variety of ways, and today we see corporate citizenship, corporate sustainability, the ethical company, corporate responsibility (without the 'social'), the social enterprise, even the misguided shared value made famous by Michael Porter.[2]

Businesses struggle to find the right concept to hold the attention of their managers and owners. Bad press for an unpopular phrase leads to a new phrase even if the under-lying sentiment is the same. It is important to know what you are talking about, and that is why I always try and lead my discussions with a definition of CSR. On the other hand, better the concept is embedded in an organization than worry about a phrase that may raise hackles especially since decisions in companies are not always taken dis-passionately and objectively. The cigar-smoking CEO based in Dallas or Mumbai and taking rapid decisions is a caricature that may not be far from the truth in many cases!

A closely related concept is the notion of 'corporate sustainability' with its strong overtones of environmental correctness. It's not surprising since the adjective sustain-able arose, in 1987, from the World Commission on Environment and Development (the Brundtland Commission). The definition of sustainable development that is widely quoted is that sustainable development is development that meets the needs of the pre-sent without compromising the ability of future generations to meet their own needs. Often sustainable development is transposed into the word sustainability, since the latter concept was closely concerned with the longer-term issues of environment but has grad-ually come to be concerned with wider issues as well. In particular, many companies,

---

1. This chapter is based upon an interview I did with Dr Nagendra V Chowdary, Consulting Editor, Effective Executive and Dean, IBSCDC, Hyderabad which I have since brought up to date, http://www.ibscdc.org/executive-interviews/Q&A_with_Dr_Michael_Hopkins_8. htm, September 2007.
2. Michael Porter and Mark Kramer, 'Creating Shared Value', *Harvard Business Review*, January–February 2011.

not liking the implications of the word 'social' in CSR, tend to use the notion of corporate sustainability, which, in turn, some have defined almost similarly to my own longer definition as: 'Corporate Sustainability aligns an organizations products and services with the stakeholder's expectations, thereby adding economic, environmental and social value (PricewaterhouseCoopers)'.

There is a noticed return to CSR since COVID-19 started, even though many companies took on board the notion of corporate sustainability and many now produce 'sustainability reports'. Often these reports tend to cover a company's environmental concerns and a few so-called CSR projects (more on the latter in Chapter 18). For instance, the Dow Jones Sustainability rankings put ABB as number one in the Dow Jones on its "sustainability' index and notes that there is mounting evidence that the financial performance of performing sustainable companies is superior to that of companies that are ranked lower.

I thought at one time to move from Corporate Social Responsibility (CSR) to Corporate Sustainability (CSu). There was a strong semantic attraction for that since it is clear that the notion of sustainability has an attractive ring about it to the hard-pressed CEOs trying to keep, and raise, shareholder value as well as keeping an eye on a plethora of social concerns. While responsibility appears, on face value, to do with the 'nice' things a company should do rather than keep in business and work on shareholder value.

However, excluding the word 'social' from CSR leaves us with the phrase 'Corporate Responsibility' and is, to use an ugly but apt expression, simply throwing the baby out with the bath water. I define social to include economic and environment (precedence is set by the fact that most universities have Schools of Social Science that include sociology, economics, political science, environmental sciences, etc.). If the word 'social' is left out of CSR, then it is not so clear what is implied. It could imply attention to corporate governance and agreeing to obey the law. But even that latter sentiment, although praiseworthy, falls down in many countries; for instance, Uzbekistan has rigorous laws about labour standards but, in practice, ignores most of them. Thus, corporate responsibility, without the qualifying word 'social', adds further confusion.

Does CSR Differ in Different Regions or Countries of the World?

The short answer is yes. I think it is because different gurus who rise to prominence tend to dominate their local space to the exclusion of all others. For instance, the shared value idea of Michael Porter originally considered only two stakeholders: customers and shareholders. Nestle took up this idea with vigour, but today (see Annex) have included more stakeholders too. India was heavily influenced by Mauritius, which falsely thought CSR was essentially charity and advocated that 2 per cent of company profits should be allocated to so-called CSR projects. Happily, today, helped a little I think by my own efforts, both countries are slowly moving to more of a multi-stakeholder dialogue (see Chapter 12).

It is not easy to know how CSR is adopted in so many countries across the world when so many have different criteria – CSR Projects in India for instance – and even within countries there are many differences, including India, where its top company, Tata, has adopted a multi-sector CSR view and has greatly widened its perspective to include the 2 per cent aspect of CSR but also its multi-stakeholder view.

What Has Been Your Experience in Having Worked with Many Companies on Their Corporate Social Responsibility Initiatives?

I suppose with my business hat on, I should not really say this since I guess we ought to be hard-nosed profit-seekers, but my main experience has been, in one word, 'enjoyable'. I have met wonderful people in corporations who are serious and concerned about the major issues of the day as well as the role their own companies play as social organizations and as economic ones. In each company we have worked with, we have found an astonishing understanding of the issues, with each one having a varied approach. There is certainly no one model that fits all.

Do You Think Given the Fact that Research on Corporate Social Responsibility Had Been Widening Its Horizons and Continues to Attract Varied Interests in the Subject, Not Enough Has Been Fructified in Actual Practice?

It depends, too, on what part of the globe you are talking about. Corporations, especially in Europe, are ahead of most university research departments. European researchers, and the UK in particular, tend to aim at research journals because of the way research incentives are handled. Business people rarely read academic journals. For instance, economists would read the *Journal of Economic Literature* or doctors would read the *British Medical Journal*. There is no journal that business people immediately go to. In the USA, arguably, the academics are ahead of the corporates in thinking about CSR, but that is gradually changing as the *Harvard Business Review* and the *Journal of Business Ethics* grapple more with social responsibility concerns.

Recently, after the seminar I gave at Nairobi's Rotary Club in August 2020, I was asked whether the South, the euphemism for developing countries, was noticeably different from the North. On reflection, it does seem as if the CSR project movement has taken off more than the CSR strategic view espoused here and in my previous books. India has been trapped in its 2 per cent of profits to CSR project point of view, which is a legal requirement. Other countries in the South have not looked at almost any form of legislation for any aspect of CSR. This will probably change as transparency (essentially anti-corruption initiatives) takes off as citizens become more and more angry at the pilfering of its politicians and their influencers, the rich private sector and overseas financiers, especially from China and the Gulf. China is very different from India and most other countries, with claims coming from luminaries such as Simon Zadek that China has its own sets of CSR standards and aspirations. I think such positive claims are unlikely, as Hong Kong's descent into dictatorship and South Sea Islands become illegally occupied, one word that is sorely needed as parts of the CSR world suffers, and that is democracy!

What Is the Importance of Corporate Social Responsibility Initiatives? Why Should Companies Embrace Them? Can CSR Be a Competitive Advantage for Companies?

This question covers three of the key CSR questions. Briefly, CSR is, in a sense, obvious. There is no need to provide a lot of evidence that treating stakeholders responsibly, which includes actions such as listening to employees, ensuring good consumer relations, avoiding corruption, ensuring transparency in operations, rewarding suppliers on time, having a clear mission statement, avoiding unnecessary pollution, involving local communities, etc., will be good for business and, therefore, improve a company's reputation and profitability. It is amazing, however, how many companies do not follow this simple idea. Just go to Germany and experience often rather poor customer relations! I have never understood how that is good for business. Yet the famous maxim of Warren Buffet rings true today as ever before: 'reputation takes decades to earn and only minutes to destroy', especially now with social media so prominent.

Other than anecdotal evidence, there has been an increasing interest in empirical research linking the business case to CSR.[3] In one of my company's regular http://www.mhcinternational.com/monthly-features/, Adrian Henriques cited a study of top US companies that found a good correlation between an explicit commitment to an ethical approach to business and market value added. Of the 500 largest US companies, those with a code and a strong commitment to ethics had an average market value added three times than that of those without any commitment. The same study also found that those companies in which the ethics executive was a member of the professional Ethics Officer Association had a lower correlation with good performance. The conclusion drawn from this is that the commitment matters far more than the code. Henriques noted that perhaps the most promising correlation was between good social performance in relation to staff and corporate performance. In the UK, Investors in People claimed that the return on capital employed is double the national average and pre-tax profit margin is 50 per cent higher where their staff management approach is followed. The reasons for such a dramatic relationship revolve largely around greater staff motivation, resulting in reduced costs, increased invitations to tender, increased sales, improved customer/client retention, improved productivity, increased customer satisfaction and improved quality of service/product. Henriques' main conclusion was that there is little evidence that good social or environmental performance leads to poor financial performance.

---

3. See also Michael Hopkins and Roger Crowe, 'The Business Case for CSR', *International Journal of Business Performance Management* 5, no. 2/3 (January 2003). DOI: 10.1504/IJBPM.2003.003261.

How Do You Distinguish between Corporate Social Responsibility and Corporate Philanthropy?

When the individuals belonging to a company actively engage themselves in a philanthropic activity, for instance Bill Gates (through his Bill and Melinda Gates foundation), etc., would it constitute a corporate philanthropy or individual philanthropy? In fact, as I argue in Chapter 18, I distinguish between CSR and philanthropy. CSR is a system-wide concept that touches all the stakeholders of a corporation. CSR, as I define it, does not concentrate on only one stakeholder but philanthropy, 'the practice of performing charitable or benevolent actions' does. Most, if not all, philanthropy is devoted to items that governments should be doing (health grants to developing countries, help to the handicapped, drugs for HIV/AIDS, for example). And their failure should not be the preserve of corporations. However, since the government is one of the stakeholders of a corporation, there is nothing to stop corporations offering their management and technical skills to the government to improve or introduce programmes to help vulnerable groups. Corporations exist to make profits. There is nothing wrong with that; only the way profits are made is the concern of CSR practitioners. Philanthropy does little or nothing to help companies make profits, while all CSR activities are linked to improving a company's bottom line.

Is There Any Distinction between Corporate Responsibility and Corporate Social Responsibility?

I am reluctant to drop the term social in my definition, as noted above, simply because the word social conveys what CSR is all about. Dropping the term does lead to blurring as the question rightly implies. I include economic, financial and environmental issues in social, thereby avoiding the problem of only looking at social issues that may simply be a cost, not a business benefit, such as paying above market wages for social not economic reasons. But it is true that some companies prefer to use the term 'Corporate Responsibility' rather than 'Corporate Social Responsibility'. My above postulated cigar chomping CEO in Dallas mistakenly believes that including the word social means introducing socialism through the back door! Therefore, my own feeling is that better to use 'corporate responsibility' as a term than not caring about the issue at all. A deconstruction of the term corporate responsibility that includes all stakeholders will, eventually, lead a company to CSR.

Let's look at some hypothetical instances. An oil refining company pledges its support to an afforestation project. A large retailer decides to slash its fleet size by 35 per cent. A paint manufacturing company undertakes to clean up the local waters. On the other hand, a software company's employees work for a day in a month in a local community hospital. A company adopts and funds a local school. Of these, what can be characterized as CSR initiatives and corporate responsibility initiatives?

Treating all stakeholders in a socially responsible manner means that isolated initiatives focused on one or two stakeholders, although welcome, do not mean that a company can assume it is socially responsible. Further, I would look at all initiatives and assess how they contribute to a company's bottom line this might sometimes be oblique such as contribution to a company's reputation or reducing risk. Happily, one action often leads to another and they are correlated in a statistical sense. Employees who are allowed to work a day a month for a good cause are likely to be treated well by their employer and, therefore, are more productive and long serving.

What's 'social' in their responsibility? Companies benefit immensely from CSR initiatives as the image improves and propels business prospects. The (un!) intended consequences are quite fathomable. Adam Smith observed, 'It is not from the benevolence of the butcher, the brewer, or the baker that we expect our dinner, but from their regard to their own interest. We address ourselves, not to their humanity but to their self-love.' Are corporates, therefore, doing what is the minimum expected of them, rather than doing a 'selfless' service to the society in which they operate?

The key question, as Adam Smith would no doubt approve, is not the pursuit of profits per se, but how profits are made. The pursuit of profits at any cost has led to some spectacular collapses, Enron being a case in point. Today it is more difficult to pursue profits at any cost in many parts of the world. Nevertheless, there are parts of the world that have only just started thinking and worrying about 'process', such as Wal-Mart in the USA, and large areas such as China that will, if our theory is correct that CSR is good for business, be forced to become more and more socially responsible simply to preserve their markets. Spiked toothpaste may be a blind from the USA to reduce Chinese imports, but true or not China will have to become more transparent, including independent auditing, to preserve the market share.

Now, is there a minimum that companies must do to satisfy what is, as you ask, 'expected' of them? A risky strategy I believe, since lack of response in one area of stakeholder engagement could well nullify the advantages earned in another area. Interestingly, many large corporations these days are ahead of what is expected of them; for instance, companies, surprisingly, would welcome legislation in many social areas simply to create a level playing field. "The beggar thy neighbour" policy that I wrote about in my book *The Planetary Bargain*, and summarized and updated in Chapter 6, is a dance to the death since one company undercutting another will eventually lead to poorly paid employees and, eventually, poor consumers. CSR helps to avoid the latter.

Do You Think Every Form of Business Should Undertake Corporate Social Responsibility Initiatives?

Many a times it is argued that for small companies (although their societal impact can be substantial) this can be a luxury that they can seldom afford.

We found through my CRITICS Rate Your Company survey,[4] also available on all mobile phones, that large companies (more than 1,000 employees) and small companies (less than 50 employees) were more socially responsible than medium-sized companies (51–1,000 employees). Our analysis revealed that small companies tend to be

---

4. https://play.google.com/store/apps/details?id=com.incode.jodirishta&hl=en&gl=US, accessed 20 November 2020.

very responsible simply because they are small and often are family concerns. Families, in general, do treat each other well. Large companies are in the public eye and are either forced to behave socially responsibly or understand the business case arguments and are aware of the benefits. Medium-sized companies, we hypothesized (since we did not know), have grown out of the small business phase and are now being professionally managed in order to survive. Or, they were big but are dropping out of sight. In each case, it is 'backs-to-the-wall' as survival is the key concern. No time for fripperies, management fads, going to conferences, keeping up with the Joneses, no, survival is everything.

So, would CSR help or hinder medium-sized companies? (I dealt with small and large companies above.) There is no in-depth empirical analysis that I can draw upon. But CSR is obvious. Treating people well, including customers and suppliers etc., must be good for business. Therefore, arguably, the best CSR-induced medium-sized firms will perform better than those without CSR.

Perhaps one area may defeat my logic on the natural environment. As I write this, in front of me is a farmer (a small businessman) and I can see his old van with its doors propped closed with a length of wood. Inside, from time to time, it is stuffed with one of his dead calves or cows. Eventually these may be disposed of legally at a supervised dump or, at much less cost, simply dumped in the stream at the back where my young children can no longer play! I won't go into the reasons why I am powerless to complain; you would have to understand the power of the agricultural lobby in French local administrations for that. But these sorts of acts, repeated a million times all over the world, show that a problem exists and that CSR is far from their thoughts. So, is CSR a luxury small businesses cannot afford? It is perhaps obvious that small businesses that do not observe CSR are luxuries we cannot afford!

Should Companies from Some Industries Be More 'Socially Conscious' than Other Industries?

There does seem to be a tendency for visible companies, such as oil and petroleum, chemicals, textiles, automobile, shipping, steel, airlines and aerospace, food, pharmaceuticals, etc., to be very active in CSR. Companies whose activities are less visible, such as banks, information technology services, financial houses, property companies, etc., which are mainly in the service sector, do seem to be less socially aware than those mentioned. Google, for instance, collaborates with China to filter content so as to obtain competitive advantage. To date, Google has produced a code of conduct and corporate governance guidelines but no CSR report although since 2017 it has produced an environmental report.

Service companies also affect our way of life; there is no doubt that they should also show the same commitment to CSR as do more obvious agricultural and manufacturing companies. One has to simply ask who funds non-socially responsible companies and you quickly find the biggest investment funds and banks. Would Halliburton have promoted its lobbyist friends to launch the war on Iraq if it had been considered a socially irresponsible company and therefore outed by investment fund managers? Hardly!

How Do You Assess and Distinguish between Corporate Social Responsibility Initiatives of Companies from Developed World and Companies from Emerging Economies?

The definition remains the same, of course, wherever the company is based. Consequently, stakeholder initiatives should be of similar nature. In practice, however, CSR initiatives vary greatly from region to region and country to country. For instance, in the Middle East, a company tends to focus upon corporate philanthropy because of Islam. The notion of other aspects of CSR, including whether corporate philanthropy is the correct approach, is rarely covered.

One issue of huge contention has been the application of ILO core labour standards. Neither the ILO nor the World Trade Organization (WTO) has broached the subject of whether to include labour standards in trade agreements. Objections have been voiced by developing countries that argue, rightly or wrongly, that this is protectionism through the back door by the developed countries. The argument is that emerging economies cannot afford the level of labour legislation experienced in the richer countries simply because they are developing and need to reap benefits from cheap and unskilled labour.

As so often is the case, however, the issue is much more complicated than as so simply stated here. Briefly, therefore, the notion of CSR should be the same but the devil is in the detail. And the application of CSR, as so often is the case, must be applied on a case-by-case basis with the broad principles in mind.

Are Corporations Doing Enough on Corporate Social Responsibility?

Most large corporations have CSR activities, and nearly all now produce social reports of one form or another. Clearly, the level of intensity varies from one company to another. Models of best practice come and go. Royal Dutch Shell was at one point the leader, as was British Petroleum, and there are many rankings these days that purport to say who is the best and who is the worst. Coca-Cola's report is currently highly regarded by many.

In recent years, there has been a slight move away from social concerns as the issue of global warming and company carbon emissions take centre stage. Clearly an important issue, but the intensity of change reflects the current fad as much as the seriousness of the issue. There is no doubt that companies must be swift to cope with current concerns or their reputation will suffer. However, we in the social responsibility movement must continue to make companies aware of the balance of the various issues in the CSR portfolio by continually pointing out the business case options.

I warn some commentators that criticizing companies for not following CSR activities must be carefully balanced with what companies see as their benefits. It is no use driving a company into the ground through over-insisting on ridiculous commitments. A company not making profits will quickly go out of business, which, in general, CSR practitioners would not want to happen!

Has the Relevance and Importance of Corporate Social Responsibility Grown with Increased Globalization?

The short answer is yes. No doubt that globalization has made the world a smaller place with information quickly being passed from one part to another in seconds. Two hundred years ago, one of the most famous victories in British history, that of Nelson at Trafalgar, took weeks to reach London. Today, drones over Iraq are controlled instantaneously from a US military base in Florida.

The same is true for companies. Reports of poor treatment of workers in Vietnamese shoe factories greatly embarrassed Nike, who had received a clean bill of health from former UN Ambassador Young. The debate ran for some time and forced Nike to introduce very careful controls. But Nike's HQ was in a land that has an open press and freedom to publish (despite attempts in recent years to curb these hard-won freedom).

Of those countries that are more closed and host large companies one immediately thinks of China, with, in general, much poorer records than their counterparts, say, India. But, as noted above, China is playing with fire. There is a real danger of a huge consumer reaction to the purchase of Chinese goods should news of poor-quality control, environmental damage and labour abuse start to bite in its main export markets! Other rogue nations will also be in trouble as world attention translates into commerce.

What Is the Role of Regulation in Ensuring High Standards in Corporate Social Responsibility?

A question that often arises is whether regulations, such as mandating companies to devote a certain percentage of their revenue to CSR initiatives, can be made mandatory. The issue of regulation for CSR was, at one time, one of the hottest topics on the CSR agenda. However, the flight of some companies from the USA fearing the heavy costs of the Sarbanes-Oxley legislation has weakened enthusiasm for any new legislation.

Yet another argument cited as a common reason given for why new legislation would set CSR back is the lowest common denominator argument. This suggests that if there were legislation on CSR, then companies would deliver what the law requires, but not more.

The following are the pluses and minuses of CSR regulation:

Pluses
1. It would help companies avoid the excessive exploitation of labour, bribery and corruption.
2. It enables companies to know what is expected of them, thereby promoting a level-playing field.
3. Since many aspects of CSR behaviour are good for businesses (reputation, human resources, branding, easier to locate in new communities, etc.), legislation actually could help to improve profitability, growth and sustainability.
4. Rogue companies would find it more difficult to compete through lower standards.

Minuses
1. Additional bureaucracy, with rising costs of observance
2. Costs of operation could rise above those required for continued profitability and sustainability
3. Critics already argue that the CSR of companies is simply to make a profit, and legislation would increase the vocalization of these concerns
4. Reporting criteria vary so much by company, sector, country and they are in constant evolution.

Happily, more and more companies are already focusing voluntarily on CSR issues, but it is clear in the light of the poor corporate governance seen, which resulted in both the Enron and World Com debacles, that some further form of legislation is necessary. It is clear that zero regulation is out of the question. Similarly, complete regulation of all aspects of CSR could bring industry to a halt, and thus there is a need for something between the two extremes.

But the key question remains, who will be the regulator?

Government? In the USA, the Security and Exchange Commission is to play an enhanced role at least as far as something called 'corporate responsibility' is concerned. In Europe, the EU has already stated its position as being on the side of the voluntary, which will relieve many anti-EU lobbyists (check new rules).

The UN? In emerging economies, we would normally look toward the UN but we know that the UN is not a regulatory body and can only suggest changes to national legislation.

The Corporate Sector? Like it or not, voluntary will be the status quo for the foreseeable future with only a few companies interested in legislation to create a level-playing field. This means that CSR advocates/consultancies, such as our own (MHCi), will more and more become the 'unacknowledged legislators of mankind' (with apologies to Coleridge, who was referring to poets) in helping companies and governments find their way.

What Is the Role of Leadership in Ensuring High Standards in Corporate Social Responsibility?

A question covered in Chapter 15, should a leader lead from the front so as to balance shareholder interests and stakeholder's interests? Over 70 per cent of CEOs surveyed by the World Economic Forum as far back as January 2004 agreed that mainstream investors would have an increased interest in corporate citizenship issues which, in turn, is a closely related, albeit rarely defined, parallel concept to CSR. Experience has shown that without the CEO of a company being closely attuned to implementing CSR, it – and, perhaps, the CEO! –will not go very far.!

A key component of any CEO's contract is, of course, the responsibility that his/her company must perform well on profits. To promote CSR, it would be very useful to include in their contract a clear commitment to social and environmental objectives. According to a friend, a former CEO of Hays PLC, given that most CEOs have, on average, four years in their job, such a suggestion will not be popular. The first year is normally spent learning the ropes, the second and third years are when something can actually be done and the fourth year is spent working out a compensation package for his/her untimely removal! My friend's experience at the time decades ago was that he could go along the environmental route since his company was mainly a shipping and trucking company, but social issues could hardly be touched.

Yet, such a suggestion is not wildly off beam. An important suggestion of the Higgs report on corporate governance in the UK in 2002 was a call for appraisal reforms to make boards more effective. There is a trend to make management of the largest companies more accountable, and the Higgs Report was influential to that end at least in the UK.

What could a CSR clause look like in a CEO contract? The lawyers would have to take over here, but elements of what could be included can be found in the World Economic Forums CEO Statement on Global Corporate Citizenship of 2002. It recommended that CEOs and boards exert leadership in four basic areas:

1. Provide leadership
   Set the strategic direction for corporate citizenship in your company and engage in the wider debate on globalization and the role of business in development.
2. Define what it means for your company
   Define the key issues, stakeholders and spheres of influence which are relevant for corporate citizenship in your company and industry.
3. Make it happen
   Establish and implement appropriate policies and procedures, engage in dialogue and partnership with key stakeholders, encourage innovation and creativity in problem-solving and build the next generation of leaders.
4. Be transparent about it
   Communicate consistently with different stakeholders about the company's principles, policies and practices in a transparent manner, within the bounds of commercial confidentiality.

What Is the Role of Business Schools in Sensitizing Their Students to the Importance of Corporate Social Responsibility?

In the mid-1990s, when I first started working in this area few, if any, business schools around the world had basic ethics courses. This has certainly changed, and it is rare, indeed, to find a business school that does not include some element of CSR in their courses. The number of dissertations and doctorates has increased exponentially, and there now exist MBAs in CSR. I, myself, started a research centre at the Middlesex University Business School, founded and directed a diploma course on CSR at the University of Geneva over 2007–2013 and started a doctoral programme at the Geneva Business School. Happily, aspects of all still remain. Rarely a day goes past without a prospective student asking me to suggest a school to go to.

So, in reply to the question, the role is important and is growing of business schools in teaching and researching aspects of CSR. Influence of their graduates on CSR is now gaining in impact.

The New Digital Economy and How This Will Change and Expand CSR and Sustainability

Technology always changes the world. The fourth Industrial Revolution is now with us as the internet is everywhere. How will this affect CSR? It will affect CSR enormously for five main reasons. First, probably and maybe the most important, will be that social media will ensure that no company or institution can hide behind company walls. Not only disaffected employees can find space but also legitimate concerns from all stakeholders, especially those outside the company in supply chains, customer product complaints from snapchat, to TikTok, to Instagram and now, what seem older, e-mail, LinkedIn, Facebook and Twitter.

Second, amid major global disruptions brought about by the COVID-19 pandemic, there is little doubt that it is a moment for innovative companies to bring forward new ideas and innovations, and already these aspects can be seen in platforms like Uber, Airbnb, Amazon, Wikipedia, LinkedIn, Twitter and Facebook; also, dating apps like Tinder have considerably changed over the years people's attitudes towards specific consumption patterns and the ways they connect.

Third, the investment/financial industry is also changing as ESG (Economic, Social, Governance) issues rise to the fore with sums as high as 34 trillion dollars mentioned worldwide. These coupled with new technologies such as the blockchain industry are, as the other technologies, not without controversy.

Fourth, innovation is likely to increase as people travel less and work either from home, or much nearer to home. Office buildings in the centre of major cities will be used less or used in different forms. There will always be a need for people to get together face-to-face, but this will be much more efficient in the future since time for busy entrepreneurs will always be at a premium.

Fifth, personal responsibility as well as how companies treat their key stakeholders will get a huge boost as issues such as 'Your customer problem is now your problem' dominate. Then, since legal compliance issues are multiplying, there will be an increased scrutiny of Supply Chains, and green washing will be much harder.[5]

What Does the Impact Measurement of CSR Mean?

The measurement of impact of CSR/Sustainability is fairly complicated. Once a CSR programme has started, how does one measure how effective it is? Similar to finding a

---

5. Some of the above ideas were inspired from a presentation by David Simpson in August 2020, and from an interview by Dukascopy TV with Michael Hopkins also in August 2020, see https://www.linkedin.com/posts/dukascopy-tv_the-world-after-the-pandemic-activity -6701447257453031424-9Fyw, accessed 18 August 2020.

reliable vaccine in COVID-19, a control group is necessary to judge effectiveness. But how can one find an exactly similar company where a CSR programme has been implemented compared with the one that has? Nearly not feasible and is a standard problem in economics where one can hardly have a control group country. Thus, impact measurement must measure what happens to a set of key indicators. How to choose the key indicators? In fact, one needs a conceptual framework to decide what the key issues and then indicators to measure progress are. The H-CSR-M model provides such a framework. But are there better ones than mine? Let's have a brief look as I did in more detail in my paper of around 60,000 reads to date on ResearchGate.[6]

The main measurement systems

Six main systems, with indicators applied to companies around the world, have been chosen for comparison. Unless otherwise stated, the source of information in this section comes from the various websites that each index generator maintains.

Business in the Community (BiTC)

The Corporate Responsibility Index is a voluntary, self-assessment survey that provides an annual benchmark of how companies manage, measure and report their corporate responsibility. The index is open to all companies in the FTSE 100, FTSE 250 and the Dow Jones Sustainability Index (DJSI) and to Business in the Community member firms that have a significant economic presence but are not listed in the UK.

FTSE4good

The FTSE (Financial Times Stock Exchange) Group produces the FTSE4Good index series, which gives investors an opportunity to invest in companies meeting globally recognized CSR standards. Even though it requires a large amount of data, and the index has been significantly changed over time to allow for human rights and environmental requirements, the majority of companies managed to meet the new selection criteria.

Dow Jones Sustainability Index (DJSI)

The Dow Jones Sustainability Indexes (DJSI) were established to track the performance of companies that lead the field in terms of corporate sustainability. The Dow Jones Sustainability Indexes consist of a global and a European set of indexes. The global indexes, the Dow Jones Sustainability World Indexes (DJSI World), consist of a composite index and five narrower, specialized indexes, excluding companies that generate revenue from alcohol, tobacco, gambling, armaments and firearms, or all of these

---

6. https://www.researchgate.net/publication/247831664_Measurement_of_corporate_social _responsibility/citations?latestCitations=PB%3A343361783, accessed 17 June 2021.

industries. This set of indexes was first published on 8 September 1999. The European indexes, the Dow Jones STOXX Sustainability Indexes (DJSI STOXX) were first published on 15 October 2001. For each of the Dow Jones Sustainability Indexes, a guidebook is published, outlining the Corporate Sustainability Assessment methodology, index features and data dissemination, periodic review and ongoing review, the calculation model and the management and responsibilities.

Business Ethics 100

The US-based *Business Ethics* magazine's widely quoted ranking of US companies, the 100 Best Corporate Citizens, has been produced since 1999. Service to a variety of stakeholders is the essence of good corporate citizenship. That's what the 100 Best Corporate Citizens listing is about. While traditional measures of success focus on stockholder return, this list defines success more broadly. Using social ratings compiled by KLD Research & Analytics of Boston – plus total return to shareholders – the *Business Ethics* list ranks companies according to service to seven stakeholder groups: stockholders, community, minorities and women, employees, environment, non-US stakeholders and customers.

AccountAbility (AA) Rating®

The Accountability Rating® was launched on 23 June 2004 to coincide with The United Nations Global Compact Leader's Summit in New York, where many of the G-100 companies covered by the index – world's 100 highest-revenue Companies – were in attendance to discuss business' leadership in a global society. The index has been developed by the NGOs, AccountAbility and csrnetwork. It measures the state of corporate accountability by ranking individual companies on their global sustainability performance.

Global Reporting Initiative (GRI)

GRI recognized that developing a globally accepted reporting framework is a long-term endeavour. It noted that, in comparison, financial reporting is well over half a century old and still evolving amidst increasing public attention and scrutiny. The methodology is extensively and clearly presented in their reports that can be found online.

The lack of a clear definition of what the GRI is trying to do continues into the lack of a clear concept. We read that the guidelines do not 'provide instructions for designing an organisation's internal data management and reporting systems; nor, offer methodologies for preparing reports, nor for performing monitoring, nor verification of such reports'.

A topic covered by GRI in some detail, unlike many of the other measurement sets is the question of 'boundaries' or the footprint of a corporation's core activities. To resolve this knotty problem, the GRI framework emphasizes the importance of extensive interaction with stakeholders to determine appropriate reporting boundaries.

Are Economic, Social and Governance Investors Helping CSR?

COVID-19 has transformed the role of government in economies around the world.[7] Borrowing and spending increased, and as stock markets – especially the stocks of the IT companies – boomed in many countries, companies were expected to improve their profits. Indeed, public support for companies started to become conditional on business behaviour, which also serves the public interest right across the world. Conditions included not operating in tax havens, raising environmental standards, limiting executive pay and extending financial support to staff and suppliers.

In June 2020, a group of ESG investors with assets of €11.9 trillion wrote to the European Commission and to heads of government calling on companies that receive 'government bailouts, grants, loans, tax concessions and temporary equity purchases' to be required to 'enact climate change transition plans consistent with the Green Deal and Paris Agreement goals'.

Institutions that signed the Principles for Responsible Investment and the Principles for Responsible Banking, and also who are among the most influential capital investors in the world and, as such, will be on the front line of recapitalizations are expected to meet the need for better public health, more equitable access to labour market opportunities, and speedy action to decarbonize the corporate sector.

Strong public support for responsible investment is only part of the picture. A financial case matters just as much, according to Catherine Howarth, who is chief executive of ShareAction, a responsible investment charity. She noted that the UK's new Stewardship Code, launched in January 2020, was already raising and influencing standards around the world through 'the responsible allocation, management, and oversight of capital to create long-term value for clients and beneficiaries leading to sustainable benefits for the economy, the environment and society'.

To conclude, right across the world, investors are looking to ESG and sustainable investments. All realize that climate change and so many other social disturbances are simply not good for business. Yes, we can quibble about the huge amounts of money being invested in attack aka defence! But that will have to await my next book!

---

7. https://www.ft.com/content/1f93c77d-4eed-490d-861e-1fb613245225, accessed 12 August 2020 FT.

Chapter Six

THE PLANETARY BARGAIN UPDATED

Introduction

My first book on Corporate Social Responsibility (CSR) was written in 1994 titled *A Planetary Bargain: CSR Comes of Age* (aka published as *CSR Matters*) with the aim of promoting social and economic development as we move into the next millennium. In this chapter, I shall outline the main ideas – updating them where appropriate – of that book.

Clearly, CSR and similar and related concepts such as corporate sustainability, corporate citizenship and corporate responsibility, as well as the older concerns with business ethics, business in society and the ethical corporation, now matter and have taken root at an even faster pace than I envisaged at that time. The significantly revised version of the earlier book updated the material and reflected the major changes from 'CSR Comes of Age' - the sub-title of the earlier book - to a broader concern with 'CSR Matters'.

Yet, more than 25 years later, unemployment remains stubbornly high in most of the richest nations of the world, poverty persists in the developing nations and inequality has risen sharply. The rich have seen their wealth increase as wages stagnate. Globalization protests have subdued, especially with the global fight against the corona virus. But the social protection gained for people in Europe over the nearly 80 years since the end of the Second World War is under continual threat as costs rise. And the richest nation in the world, the USA, struggles to retain its social protection provisions that are more meagre than Europe and even 'elected' a maverick president, leading to environmental weakening, health sector reductions and a war on migrants. At the time I asked whether all would end with the world's production going to the lowest common denominator, that is the country with the lowest social costs, the paltriest wages, the poorest working conditions and those with the lowest pensions for the old. The trend seems to be heading this way as inequalities deepen, yet this is in no-one's interest. That concern has been surpassed as inequalities both within and between nations increase (see Chapter 8).

Poor consumers in developing countries would very much like higher living standards, and the sorts of social protection accorded to workers in Germany (say). Transnational corporations need customers for their goods, something not helped by the rising unemployment associated with downsizing or impoverishment in developing countries.

To reverse these negative tendencies, the book's main thesis was that there was a need for a worldwide compact – a planetary bargain, in other words – between the private and public sectors. In this bargain, the public sector would help private organizations to operate with clear ground-rules, and the private sector will pay more attention to longer-term social development issues than ever before. What such a bargain could include, why it is necessary and who should be involved are the themes that ran throughout that book. One clear outcome was the UN Global Compact that I had, indeed, suggested to UNDP in the early 1990s when I was working on the UNDP Human Development Report. Kofi Annan himself personally thanked me when we shared a plane trip together. As an aside, a problem with being the originator of big ideas, and I have had at least four in my life, is that others will always claim to have been there before you with slight variations of those ideas, or you have been too junior for anyone to accept that such a non-descript chap such as Hopkins could be ahead of the game!

The first of these four big ideas was the introduction of the basic needs approach to the ILO and their 1976 World Employment Conference; second, the proposal to create a Global Compact of the private and public sectors in 1992; third, the introduction of the key stakeholder approach to CSR as well as the first to apply a measurement system to examine progress in 1994; fourth, the creation of the slogan and application of turning black gold (oil) into human gold (human capital) in Azerbaijan in 1999, eventually taken up by President Aliyev. Interestingly, the success of each of these ideas is that so many others claim them as their own. In fact, to be a successful consultant is to make the client believe it was his or her idea!

What Is a Planetary Bargain?

A Planetary Bargain (PB) will mean more of what I forecasted and what I originally called, in the early 1990s, socially responsible enterprises (SREs). I rephrased as CSR later, although that was mentioned in the PB book. There I had written that CSR now matters and has taken root at an even faster pace than envisaged when the hardback version of this book was written some four years ago. I devoted sections of the book to explain the main differences and similarities between these concepts. The book also reflected the change from 'CSR Comes of Age', the sub-title of the earlier book, to a broader concern with 'CSR Matters'.

I had argued that, in time, it will not be possible to conduct business without being socially responsible. This is inevitable and I have been more or less on target with that prediction. The book argued that new rules or corporate laws in this area may well be unnecessary, because corporations will see for themselves, and many have seen this already, the need to behave more responsibly in the social area. The book did argue for a 'level playing field' in which a minimum set of rules for corporate behaviour is required. However, it did not argue for new sets of complex rules simply because these would make it even more difficult for corporations to operate and, in turn, would encourage further hopping from one advantageous country to another. If the same rules could be applied universally, many corporations would accept CSR since a level playing field would apply for all. But, despite halting steps in this direction by such bodies as the EU and countries such as France, an agreed set of rules for CSR activities is unlikely and hence a world consciousness of stakeholders such as consumers, employees, local communities, etc. will be better placed to create this level playing field. But I was not so correct there and both the Global Reporting Initiative and the ISO 26000 have grown and flourished over time. There are also many other standards and contributions now covering issues such as human rights, ethics, corporate governance, etc.

I asked whether the private sector could do more than just be good at business. It was the underlying thesis of the PB that being a socially responsible enterprise was not only good for business; it was actually better for business in terms of long-term profits and stability. It was not my intention in the PB to suggest areas where the private sector could make profits through helping social development directly – they are their own masters at this. For instance, the private sector has been helpful in housing projects for low-income groups, providing credit through the banking system, promoting education through private educational institutions and so on. But CSR is not just about corporate philanthropy, as the book argues; it is about a new management and strategic philosophy for companies large, medium and small.

At the time, there had been few attempts at quantification of what was meant by CSR in the literature, and what did exist, mainly through the social screens of ethical investment companies, is largely subjective. When I started research in this area in 1992, I had intended to rank the Fortune 500 companies from 1 to 500 on a HDI index (human development index following the United Nations Development Programme's work). This task proved beyond my resources but launched me, nevertheless, some eight years ago into this field. The book captured my efforts at determining a conceptual framework for these indicators and then examines how I calibrated them for the UK. The previous chapter covers how those ideas have developed until today.

But I could not present indicators without first looking at what others have done in the field of CSR – and there is a lot. So I critically reviewed that work in the first seven chapters. In these, I also develop the elements of an economic theory of socially responsible enterprises, where I showed, mainly through case studies and anecdotal examples, that social responsibility not only has strong philanthropic undertones but also, just as importantly if not more so, has sound economic reasons too. By this I mean that it is increasingly in the economic interest of business, and consequently of societies, to engage in socially responsible activities. If it is not in the fabric of companies today, then these companies, more than likely, will not exist tomorrow. This is why, in the book, I argued the need for a planetary bargain.

The main work at that time in the area of CSR had been in the USA and, more recently, the UK. The book drew most of its examples from these two countries. Many other countries in both the First and the Third Worlds were starting to take the concepts, ideas and practices seriously, and I covered some of these experiences too.

What sort of planetary bargain could help increase corporate profitability while not resorting to the bargain basement was, of course, the book's central theme. Gradually, the United Nations, the World Bank, ILO, OECD, UNCTAD, UNESCO, UNDP, UNICEF, UNRISD, UNEP, the UN's Global Compact and the WTO, as well as the burgeoning number of private networks of enterprises and NGOs such as the Social Venture Network (SVN), EBEN (European Business Ethical Network), Business for Social Responsibility (BSR), Business in the Community, Global Reporting Initiative (GRI), World Economic Forum (WEF), World Business Council on Social Development (WBCSD), AccountAbility, the International Business Leaders Forum (IBLF), the Caux

Principles, etc., all came to grips with the global issue, but then had not seen CSR as a global voluntary planetary bargain.

It was my hope then that the book would contribute to making the issue of CSR a worldwide process, and that beggar-thy-neighbour polices, of countries and enterprises, would be a thing of the past, as the peoples of the world move towards a global agreement with the private sector. The next millennium would have to be the age of CSR, I argued, and after 20 years there is no doubt that much has moved forward. Climate change, which I covered only sparingly,[1] has probably moved forward more than any other topic despite the recent buffoonery of the USA in withdrawing from the Paris accord. As I write, not only is COVID-19 killing many Americans because of poor leadership but also California is once more ablaze as the globe heats up.

Guidance for the Future from the Planetary Bargain

I had written in the PB that the future within which companies operate will be entirely different from what we see today. This future will be created partly by the private sector, and, increasingly, by the visions that socially responsible companies have and will have. The future is not just being created by enterprises, although these are having a bigger influence than ever before. Think tanks, universities, governments, NGOs, communities and inspired individuals, all play their part. Reflections on this future here are, of course, pure speculation based on perceived trends of the moment.

In the PB interviews with 48 company leaders were cited and, briefly, six major forces for change were identified. First, technological developments transforming markets, revolutionizing information and communications and creating new possibilities for what, how and where work is done. It is still relevant today, especially with COVID-19 changing working habits.

Second, the globalization of markets, supply chains, work and capital would, and now has, become a phenomenon that has continued, with China now playing an even bigger role than before.

Third, new employment patterns with the rise in importance of the knowledge worker, the growing numbers of self-employed people and small businesses, the erosion of the traditional concept of the job as full-time, permanent and male, and the consequent changes in the role and outlook of trade unions. In fact, work has become even more precarious and the gig economy of short-term working has advanced substantially.

Fourth, new organizational structures were said to be emerging with the networked organization, the reduction and streamlining of corporate centres, the subcontracting of whole functions and the growing use of independent specialists. A trend that has continued.

---

1. Note my climate change coverage is minimal not because I don't think it extremely serious but because so many other people write about the issue that anything I say here will be repetitious; however, I do have a short section on climate change as a key big issue in Chapter 17.

Fifth, environmental issues are becoming of critical importance for business, not only because of the rising threshold of public concern and expectations, but also because of the need for business to fulfil a significant role in helping to solve global environmental problems. No change since then and hardly any improvement has been observed although companies are now much more aware.

Sixth, the death of deference means pressure on companies from more demanding employees, customers and communities, who expect their individual needs and values to be respected. Stakeholder capitalism has enhanced these demands, and our suggestions that employees also act in a responsible manner to their employers has not advanced as much as hoped.

To these I added a seventh, the decline in government and the need for large-scale enterprises to take on more of the responsibilities formerly seen as the sole preserve of governments. This book attests to that movement, but we haven't arrived there as yet.

In addition to the above, the PB also examined what businesses would look like in a new 'CSR' world. And I speculated, as we moved towards the next century, on what sort of socially responsible business we could expect to see. With change occurring very rapidly, it was not completely possible to separate changes in the social arena from the technological or economic ones. Clearly, technology would increasingly require fewer natural resources for the same products, which, in turn, are more and more efficient. The replacement of copper wiring by glass fibre made out of abundant silicon (which is in sand) is just one example of this. In the future, too, we shall see less and less the need to travel to a place of work. Production will be more or less entirely carried out by machines, and the main jobs will be in the service sectors – communication, care and social delivery. It is facile to say it, but there is no need for unemployment when the world is crying out for teachers, the old require increasing amounts of care and so on. All those forecasts, not so difficult on make on reflection, have come about.

I was wrong when I thought that production would pay for this through a more efficient distribution system of the fruits of production. That, as will be covered in Chapter 8, has seen a worsening of inequalities as the rich get richer and the poor and middle classes stagnate. I predicted that less travel to work would be required – increasingly this will happen because of, and after, COVID-19 but even before – and many services would be carried out in people's own backyards. This, I thought, would lead to increased fulfilment in work and a reduction in the tremendous pressure felt today by those employed and in the long hours of work, even as others cannot get a job and, despite their inherent skills, are resigned to long hours of leisure that is ruined by the lack of income. Unfortunately, the latter picture is still with us in many countries.

I had noted that the planet could not support the consumption and rate of natural resource use for everyone at today's levels in the USA (the USA has the highest level of consumption per capita in the world). The USA will change; signs of this are there already – for instance, the move towards healthier foods; towards greater vegetable consumption, which requires less land than meat; towards smaller cars, more energy-efficient homes and so on. Some will say that the change is far too slow and that catastrophe is just around the corner. There has certainly been what we hope was just a hiccup as many trends reversed with a moron as president, for some the catastrophe is already with us, as a walk in the streets of Calcutta or a mile from the White House in Washington or even the streets of Kiev all illustrate. There will be an equilibrium point at which the world will settle – the poorer countries will become richer, while the richer countries may have to give up those social provisions that destroy incentives, as we see today in France and Germany. But this does not mean impoverishment and less caring: many social services can be delivered more efficiently and cheaply than they are today, and socially responsible business will contribute to the large voluntary efforts that already deliver many social services.

The creation of dozens of billionaires even as there exists mass poverty is not sustainable. The remarkable offer of a billion dollars by Ted Turner to the United Nations several decades ago was an excellent example of what is likely to be the new mood. More on these issues in Chapter 8 on inequality.

Nevertheless, as this new world took shape, large enterprises did start to become more socially responsible than many governments. And 'compassion will be one of the most important characteristic business leaders will need for success a decade from now', according to executives of Fortune 1000 companies surveyed by Cornell's Johnson Graduate School of Management. The socially responsible companies in this new world have started to care for all its stakeholders, the Code of Ethics has become longer, and a planetary bargain where rogue companies are punished by consumers and governments alike has arrived, accelerated by social media, which was unknown before this new world took shape.

The workers, who are also consumers, did see a new world of environmentally socially responsible products, although those left behind by society, for whatever reason, were not increasingly cared for by the haves in so far as the have-nots also had to work to help themselves. But yes, owners and investors are certainly more socially responsible while making profits, and these, as I argued in the 1990s, were closely shadowed by social and ethical investment funds, now known as ESG or SRI investment.

I end this chapter by noting one prophecy that still needs to come true for a future, that will not be one where each company vies to outdo its competitors through beggar-thy-neighbour policies. Right now, as despots sprinkle the globe, there will be competition between companies, but will there be a level-playing field brought about by increased global cooperation? And the conflict between government and governed, where the former spends and the latter pays, will gradually draw out to new social arrangements where the private sector becomes kinder and gentler in their own and society's interest – the 'acceptable' face of capitalism within a new planetary bargain. I still hope and foresee the latter.

What Could Be the Next Evolution of CSR?

There is little doubt that the lack of responsibility in markets has led to today's current financial turmoil and recession in most international markets. The private sector has taken a huge blow, but there is agreement that no one wants too much control by governments – although the exact division of public and privately provided goods is one of the greatest economic dates of today. CSR does provide many of the elements of a solution, but its ideas were largely ignored by many of the big financial players to date, and has led to increased public sector involvement in the governance of corporations. As Thomas Friedman noted in the *New York Times*[2]: 'This financial meltdown involved a broad national breakdown in personal responsibility, government regulation and financial ethics ... That's how we got here - a near total breakdown of responsibility at every link in our financial chain, and now we either bail out the people who brought us here or risk a total systemic crash'.

However, if you adhere to the theories of Adam Smith, you may disagree about a larger role for the public sector. Smith argued more than 200 years ago that the general welfare was better served by people pursuing their enlightened self-interest than by misguided attempts to serve society.

Note that CSR is a strategic approach to managing a company, not simply an add-on.[3] CSR encompasses all stakeholders of a company, not just a few. CSR is concerned with treating the stakeholders of a corporate body ethically and in a responsible manner.[4] Yet, others misleadingly define CSR to be simply philanthropy or, perhaps worse, as sacrificing profits in the social interest. This is wrong: the central point is how profits are made, *not* profits per se. Yet today, companies have lurched more and more against CSR, as exemplified by their seeming move to embrace 'corporate sustainability' or 'corporate citizenship'. This is aided and abetted by the 'think tanks' of change such as the consultancy *SustainAbility* or *The Global Reporting Initiative*. If either embraces the tenets of strategic CSR, then perhaps we should worry less. But it does appear that those who embrace the last two 'phrases' have lurched either towards more environmentalism (sustainability) or more community involvement, either at home or abroad (citizenship). These points are exemplified in GlobeScan and Sustainability's 2009 Survey of Sustainability, which focuses on climate change.[5] They list a number of urgent sustainability which could easily have been drawn up in 1970 after the celebrated report, and book, by Denis Meadows et.al *The Limits to Growth!*

This does not imply that the GlobeScan report has little interest to CSR, since the issue of environmental sustainability is a key area of CSR discussion. My worry is that a focus on future concerns might lessen the focus on current and past concerns, of which widespread poverty (mentioned by GlobeScan, to be fair) has been with us for far too long and global warming could well lead to the next pandemic. Already we have seen widespread damage from burning forests, especially, but not only, every summer in California and in a country that is supposed to be advanced.

---

2. Thomas Friedman, 'All Fall Down', *New York Times*, Op-Ed, 25 November 2008.
3. See http://www.mhcinternational.com/corporate-social-responsibility/publications/csr-strategy. html, accessed 22 November 2009.
4. Michael Hopkins, (2003) *The Planetary Bargain – CSR Matters* (London: Earthscan, 2003). First published as: Michael Hopkins: *The Planetary Bargain: Corporate Social Responsibility Comes of Age* (Macmillan Press, 1999).
5. GlobeScan and Sustainability, '*The Sustainability Survey 2009*', available from GlobeScan, GlobeScan Incorporated, 65 St. Clair Avenue East, Suite 900, Toronto, Canada M4T 2Y3.

What Can We Expect from Corporations?
What Will Be Their Role?

According to my company's own mail bag, CSR is still attracting interest across all markets – from China to Pakistan to Nigeria to Brazil – each with differing rationales. In a poll conducted by *The Economist Intelligence Unit* of 566 US-based respondents, even over a decade ago, 74 per cent said that CSR can help increase profits. In fact, CSR is not expensive, although the respondents did think that financial philanthropy would be reduced over the coming years.

An example illustrates simple, but powerful, applications of CSR. When the three CEOs of Ford, Chrysler and GM came to Washington DC at that time to plead for a $US25 billion bailout of their companies, the Senate committee was scandalized that the three CEOs each flew in their private jets from Chicago to DC. At a time of recession, socially responsible CEOs would, at least, have shared the same jet or, better still, travelled commercially!

Normally, an article written today on this topic would announce that we are in uncertain times and we don't know how the future will unfold. But, in fact, the future is more certain than ever before, especially for CSR. The continuing turmoil in markets shows a role for more stakeholder engagement and legislation in previously unregulated areas. Take **Lehman Brothers** for instance. They stated in their 2007 letter to their shareholders that 'Strong corporate citizenship is a key element of our culture. We actively leverage our intellectual capital, network of global relationships, and financial strength to help address today's critical social issues.' However, as one commentator noted, 'Lehman Brothers did not produce a CSR report, but they produced a philanthropy report. Even if they had gone further, it seems unlikely that the complex nature of how they created wealth would have been a feature.' A pity they didn't look more at their key stakeholders such as their rating agencies through examining their progress in today's form of multi-stakeholder CSR/Sustainability Reports. Lehman Brothers did produce social responsibility reports but they extolled the virtue of their philanthropy but did little else. With a proper concern for CSR, I am convinced that Lehman Brothers would have had a great chance of survival. I had approached them, without success, and suggested they take a hard look at their rating agencies, but my advice was ignored. Even today, the incredibly powerful rating agency S&P (Standard and Poor's) ignores the topic completely – Lehman Brothers collapsed at the end of 2008.

While employment and production from the private sector is likely to contract in the near future, CSR compliance can be expected to increase. CSR will become more important as regulation for the ethical behaviour of companies becomes more and more important.

Chapter Seven

IS IT THE RESPONSIBILITY OF
CORPORATIONS TO CREATE JOBS?

Modern methods of production have given us the possibility of ease and security for all; we have chosen, instead, to have overwork for some and starvation for others. Hitherto we have continued to be as energetic as we were before there were machines; in this we have been foolish, but there is no reason to go on being foolish forever.

Bertrand Russell [1932. See full transcript on http://www .zpub.com/notes/idle.html, accessed Dec 2011]

There is much talk about creating jobs today as unemployment inexorably stays high around the world. Two issues immediately follow from such a statement. First, what do we mean by unemployment, and second, why do we need jobs? Many people would say that I am splitting hairs and people need jobs of almost any kind. Let me discuss these two questions before I move to the main discussion of this chapter, which is on whether we can expect corporations to resolve the issue of jobs.

What Is Unemployment and Why Are Jobs Needed?

The unemployment rate has a numerator, number of people not employed, and a denominator, the labour force. Both are measured by labour force surveys, and the indicator most often cited is the definition provided by the ILO. Briefly, the ones not employed are those who did not work for money or income in kind for at least one hour in the previous week or day prior to the survey. Those in the labour force have to be in the allowed age range and, if not employed, must have made an effort to find work in the previous month. Thus, one can be employed, for instance, even if income is ridiculously low. One cannot be unemployed if one has become discouraged from looking for work. The remarkable changes in the unemployment rate in the past decade in the USA, for instance, had as much to do with the private sector increasing employment as it had to do with labour withdrawing from the labour force because they had become discouraged after not finding employment for some time. Long-term unemployment is a considerable problem and one can only imagine the terrible hardship of the people it impacts upon.

But we must also examine what constitutes a job. Bertrand Russell ably wrote, reproduced in this chapter's epigraph, that we seem to have our priorities mixed up. People obviously need to work when that is the main way of receiving income. Yet, we treat all employment as the same when most struggle to survive on what they receive, while, as the worsening income distribution statistics across the world demonstrates, some are benefitting enormously from current circumstances. Distressingly, as Krugman so often shows in the pages of the *New York Times*, most of these high-income earners do nothing to create employment. Worse, they make bets on outcomes that often make things worse. One only has to remember the collapse in financial institutions and the bailout of too-big-to-fail institutions to know that financial betting has been supported by many governments through deregulation and massive financial transactions to banks.

Increasingly, having a job doesn't bring with it rewards necessary for basic survival. With attacks on reducing deficits through reducing public expenditure, we are increasingly left to the private sector to find the jobs. Cutting public expenditure in recessionary times, especially those that are job related, has struck many as foolish (as I argue later in this chapter). Again, Krugman describes the hope that the private sector will take up the slack because confidence will increase as the public sector declines as hoping for a magic 'confidence fairy'. The hope that the private sector will invest in a recession belies the fact that corporations are hoarding a vast amount of wealth that is not being invested. This was shown when Trump gave corporations in the USA a one- or two-trillion-dollar tax refund. As commentators noted, 'the 2017 tax cuts have largely served to line the pockets of already wealthy investors - further increasing inequality - with little to show for it'.[1] Furthermore, the private sector will tend to invest not necessarily according to national priorities but across oceans, where emerging markets provide higher returns.

The result of increasing unemployment

Nonetheless, one of the main results of increasing unemployment coupled with declining wages has led to a worsening income distribution as the now-famous work of Picketty has illustrated.

Europe has not escaped either. As Cockburn wrote in *CounterPunch*, 'The argument against the eurozone is that hard-faced Euro-bankers—their killer instincts honed at Goldman Sachs, Wall Street's School of the Americas—have the power to act as the bully-boys of international capital and impose austerity regimes from Dublin to Athens, scalping the poor to bail out the rich.' This, in turn, is what the Occupy movement is all about, i.e. their starting point is highly unequal income distribution and their protest is to try and do something about it.

CSR an answer?

Returning to the main point of this chapter, as unemployment levels remain high and will probably stay that way for the next year or so, now exacerbated by COVID-19 lockdowns, until reflation and inflation encourage a different model as I shall point out

---

1. https://www.americanprogress.org/issues/economy/news/2019/09/26/475083/trumps-cor-porate-tax-cut-not-trickling/, accessed 18 June 2021.

later in this chapter, should corporations be doing more to create employment? Is this part of their social responsibility?

The short answer is that probably they should do something. As I noted above, the longer answer is what sort of jobs are we talking about anyway? Creating jobs for their own sake simply to transfer money so that it can be spent takes us into the trap so ably summarized in the Russell quote above. There are many types of employment, yet much less is currently required to supply us all with the goods we need. What we really need is a system that recycles wealth earned into people's hands as fairly, and sustainably, as possible. Unfortunately, we have not found an adequate way to do that. Communism attempted this and failed as market mechanisms were not allowed to work and shortages of just about everything replaced unemployment. It also led to concentration of power in non-transparent, repressive, vicious people and non-functioning committees. The market system works well as long as it has a strong dose of democracy, although it does tend to move to a cyclical inheritance of creating unemployment in recessions often caused by excess public expenditure and then on things with hardly any forward investment multiplier such as tanks, drones, aircraft carriers, nuclear weapons, etc., which we hope are not to be followed by a trumped-up war.

CSR for private corporations also means addressing social benefits and living wages, both of which are subjects of continuing international debate and not something I can either resolve or shall discuss in this chapter. Suffice to say that the one area that is in immediate need of attention is the question of socially responsible restructuring. As employment reduces, firing someone immediately with little or no warning subjects the victim to many more hardships than simply losing a source of revenue. Depression, feelings of failure and hopelessness quickly ensue. We all know it is easier to get another job, assuming they exist, if you are already employed. Socially responsible restructuring and retraining would address that issue and even keep the 'fired' on board as retraining and access to infrastructure, such as an office, are provided. Both require little cost, although complications of job security in our age of essentially service sector jobs and more of working from home needs imaginative solutions. Not often realized is the devastating loss of human capital that can hardly be re-invigorated as jobs return and demands for lost skills increase. A highly skilled laid-off service sector worker is hard pressed to keep up with new technology as one's iPhone replaces another's blackberry. The loss to a nation is hard to calculate but may easily drop future economic growth by several percentage points.

But large corporations themselves, many will be surprised to know, do not create many jobs directly, probably not more than 3 per cent of world employment.

Obviously, the structure of the business population varies between countries, and so does the distribution of employment. For example, in Greece, Italy and Portugal, micro-enterprises account for more than 40 per cent of employment, while they represent around 10 per cent or less of employment in Israel, the USA and Luxembourg. In most countries, small and medium-sized firms (SMEs), i.e. those with less than 250 employees, account for the majority of jobs. The implication is, often, that therefore investment should be made in SMEs since they create jobs more rapidly than larger firms. However, anyone familiar with input-output matrices will know about direct as well as indirect effects. Put simply, a small- or medium-sized enterprise needs larger enterprises and/or the public sector to provide the demand for their goods and services. Regrettably, there is little or no research on that issue.

Yet, corporations are concerned about poor income distribution and high unemployment simply because, for most of them, they need markets for the goods and services they produce. In fact, the US Chamber of Commerce showed the Chamber's concern on JOBS during Obama's time even if the prescriptions and books cited in their website might miss a number of key points since they are noticeably against Keynesian stimulus during recession. As if President Obama didn't know, huge numbers of letters marking out 'JOBS' were plastered on the Chamber offices located just across the road from the White House, where they could be seen clearly.

The US Chamber website acknowledged that Americans have become increasingly concerned about the economy; however, their faith in the free enterprise system remains strong, according to a survey by the US Chamber of Commerce. While government efforts to stimulate the economy are considered useful in the short term, Americans believe that it's the free enterprise system that will grow their economy and create jobs over the long term. It is surprising, therefore, that the US Chamber has been one of the, if not the, biggest lobbyist against just about any action by the Obama government, including its stimulus package (variously agreed to have preserved or created 700,000–3 million jobs, the large range indicating the difficulty of estimation), while paradoxically admitting that 'government efforts are useful in the short-term'. In fact, the right form of stimulus to create jobs in the USA was not entirely used; for instance, about a third was used to cover tax relief. The point, of course, to use a pun, is where to put the pointer between private markets and public intervention. One of the books missed by the Chamber was that of John Maynard Keynes (see below), and no lover of the public purse was he, as he made a fortune working from his home with his stockbroker.

Under the guise of CSR, corporations need to start thinking how much of government support they think the economy should absorb and where they come in to promote jobs. Providing lobbyist funds to the most outspoken and not well-admired politicians is self-defeating. But even corporations are rent-seeking, i.e. will invest in areas that are in their own best interest. Simply encouraging the corporate sector to create jobs such as providing tax relief on investment, for instance, may not necessarily work directly. There is a tendency to set up protectionist barriers to prevent the sorts of picture happening that we see in the graph. However, creating jobs overseas also means creating overseas consumers.

How to Avoid a Recession in Market Economies

The British economist John Maynard Keynes found the answer in the 1930s. Briefly, his story relies on the fact that economic growth is based upon the growth of private and public consumption and investment, and the balance of trade of goods and services (the Keynesian equation see below).

Employment cannot rise unless there is economic growth that is not merely jobless growth due to solely productivity growth. In the absence of private consumption and investment and a poor trade balance, the only source of growth will be the public sector.

Now with today's urge to reduce deficits, the *only* solution has to be the private sector. But when that is not growing, as now, and when interest rates are historically low, it makes sense to borrow to invest and/or provide transfer payments to the unemployed.

But, right across the world, few countries are currently borrowing to invest. The main outcome will simply be rising unemployment and continuing recession. So, sorry, the *only* solution is stimulus unless the private sector thinks that low consumption will suddenly reverse. But it won't without a stimulus.

It is a sad fact of our times that strident action with a hint of violence gains more attention than peaceful words. Protests at Wall Street, and then across the USA because of COVID-19 linked to racism, showed that big business certainly needs to do more as the distribution of income worsens in our major economies, and the drivers of this mess, online banks and financial institutions, emerge unscathed. We have been here before. Remember, it was Keynes who was the inspiration that helped resolve the recession of the 1930s through his recommendation to increase effective demand.

CSR has been the tool that dreamers such as myself have suggested to curb the excesses of exploitation, worsening income distribution and the excesses of capitalism. Thus, for many years the twin ideas of free markets and CSR to curb the excesses of the former have been in vogue and we have seen that the CSR model has actually worked somewhat for many large corporations. Especially now under COVID-19, many banks are moving to ESG and sustainable investment. As ever, those who pretended to act responsibly, and some of those through published social or sustainability reports, have not helped to convince an increasingly sceptical public – Enron, WorldCom, Madoff, Lehman Brothers, TepCo, etc. – to see that a radical change is actually taking place among many corporations: Unilever, Wal-Mart, Nestle, IBM, Ford and the tech companies, among others.

Need for Government Responsibility

Nevertheless, the corporate sector still has a long way to go regarding responsibility. What is more surprising, if not depressing, is that government responsibility has not worked so well even in democratic societies. Don't forget that it was the government that gave financial markets the opportunity to dice and slice mortgages through deregulation, followed soon after by the collapse of asset prices and a recession that we have all experienced, and probably will be repeated as I write with governments around the world now borrowing and spending more than ever before.

It is interesting to see the Republican Party Presidential debates every four years in the USA. Each candidate, in pursuit of their dream of being the head of government, preaches for smaller, or even *no*, government. Rare is it to see applicants for posts in other fields denigrate the institution they want to work for!

The result of this confused thinking led to the rise of the Tea Party that wanted to vastly lower taxes and dismantle government (except defence, of course). Similarly, the reaction of Occupy Wall Street protestors believed that their efforts would lead to improvements in the distribution of income, reduce poverty and create employment. Both have appealing platforms but both have misguided solutions. When interest rates are very low, government borrowing can be used to promote economic demand to lead to increased economic growth, incomes and employment. This *can* all be done with a more responsible and even a smaller government. None of us want a 'BIG BROTHER' government that taps our internet and phones, tortures prisoners, fights ridiculous wars and provides us with an incomprehensible tax code while reducing legislation for financial institutions. That was the path we saw in the USA when the new mafia was there and what we saw in Russia under Putin. But the fear is that repetition could occur with someone as extreme but better coordinated.

Moreover, we need responsible governments for a whole host of reasons as well as one that thinks about what it can do to promote CSR within companies.

Should There be More or Less Taxes to Stimulate Growth and Employment?

To answer this question, we must not ignore Keynes's basic equation since the soothsayers in our societies today just seem to misunderstand one of the basic and most essential stories ever written. The story is based around this simple equation:

$$Y = C + I + E - M$$

What the equation means, at its most basic, is that output is equal to consumption plus investment plus exports minus imports. Thus, to grow output (Y), or supply, we need to increase one or more of C or I or E (or demand) and reduce M. Now, C is private plus government consumption. If private consumption is stagnant, as is the case across the industrialized world, one or more of public consumption, I (public or private investment) or E (exports) must rise. Favourite for many countries has been import (M) substitution, which in turn may convince governments to restrict imports that can be produced locally. This is always a popular choice in democratic countries since importers generally can't vote, but it leads, at least in the short term, to price increases of the traded goods.

Yet, in many countries conservative forces want to reduce the public part of both investment and consumption in the hope that the private part picks up. They also want to reduce taxes so that private consumption picks up, and corporations have more resources to invest. So, are corporations irresponsible for not investing or are governments irresponsible for not introducing more stimuli? Well, something has to move somewhere or we get stagnation and a recession.

Keynes' solution was a counter-cyclical policy whereby the public sector stimulates the economy and all the other components of the equation move up. I won't discuss imports here nor technology, but note that employment rises when Y, or output, rises under the assumption that imports don't take up the slack and/or technological gains don't depress employment as productivity rises.

Still with me? Tack onto the above interest rates (now historically low) and inflation (also low); you can see that raising interest rates to curb inflation (as the European bank has done) will simply reduce I and hence Y unless C or E are rising fast. This is happening in Europe, and output is declining while unemployment rises.

Now, how would CSR work in that equation? Keynes was certainly in favour of government responsibility.[2]. Indeed, if we link CSR to his equation, we can see, using today's terminology, that 'Y' needs to be 'sustainable' and fairly distributed, 'C' needs to be conducted responsibly and energy saving, 'I' must be socially responsible investment, 'E' and 'T' must be non-exploitative and harm-free. All these 'new' concerns do, in fact, give rise to new forms of economic growth (of the sustainable kind) and different forms of employment.

But if even one of the aforementioned conditions is voided, we are in for trouble. For instance, what happens when the rich get richer, as in many industrialized economies, and their taxes reduce even as taxes on the poor and middle classes increase? Well, we have seen what happens in both Greece and the UK in recent years. Ignorance of the Keynesian equation simply leads to recession in many cases.

Now, how would CSR work in that equation? Keynes was certainly in favour of government responsibility. Indeed, if we link CSR to his equation, we can see, using today's terminology, that economic growth needs to be 'sustainable' and fairly distributed, that consumption needs to be conducted responsibly and in a way that saves energy, that investment needs to be socially responsible, and that trade must not be exploitative and use harmful products. As it happens, all these 'new' concerns do, in fact, give rise to new forms of economic growth (of the sustainable kind) and different forms of employment.

Despite the wonderful essay of Bertrand Russell on lauding idleness, he does also note that 'what a man earns he usually spends, and in spending he gives employment. As long as a man spends his income, he puts just as much bread into people's mouths in spending as he takes out of other people's mouths in earning.'

Despite the reluctance by many politicians to reread Keynes in today's recurring recessions even with the hindsight of 75 years since his great work, counter-cyclical stimulus is required. But we also need both corporate and public responsibility to create the sort of sustainable development we would all like to see across the whole planet. Certainly, large deficits have complicated matters and governments must keep a close watch on bond markets in the coming decades. Yet, the political bias in both the USA and Europe is to favour short-term stimulus by lowering taxes but not raising spending with an eye on long-term deficits through cutting public spending and raising taxes. This dual balancing act is, in fact, exactly what Keynes recommended. When times are hard, increase stimulus, including public consumption and investment, but quickly move to balance deficit budgets when growth returns. The danger in our economies today is that the former is happening too little, while the latter, which depends on the former, simply may not occur in time, leaving debt to rise to hazardous levels, thereby,

2. Note that to be unemployed one must be both in the labour force and looking for work, yet not have found work for pay or in kind for at least one hour in the reference period beforehand [ILO international definition].

as Samuelson points out in his famous text book *Undermining Keynesian Economics as Taught in Standard Texts*, leading to perpetual unemployment and recession.

Robotics, Trade, Jobs and Whose Social Responsibility?

The question of technology replacing jobs has a long history. Perhaps the most famous were the notorious Luddites of early-nineteenth-century Britain. The origin of the name Luddite is uncertain, according to Wikipedia, with the movement possibly named after Ned Ludd, an apprentice who allegedly smashed two stocking frames in 1779 and whose name had become associated with machine destroyers to protect jobs. The Luddites were heavily criticized as being in the way of progress although others described them as not against technical change but in favour of fairness - see Guy Standing 'Apology to Ned Ludd' in chapter 1 of his recent book, *The Corruption of Capitalism*. Yet Luddites appear often in contemporary society – most notably Donald Trump during his 2016 US presidential bid. The consequence of Trump Luddism, echoed by Bernie Sanders on the left of the bid, has also led to a huge attack on trade and implicitly technological progress itself.

So, some facts. There is no doubt that technology destroys obsolete jobs. Nor that importing cheaper goods and services from technologically more backward countries also destroys jobs. Happily, the new technological progress leads to higher levels of productivity and new jobs in more technologically advanced industries. Further, trade is mutually beneficial in that it allows countries with low levels of skills to reach higher levels of employment through exporting to richer countries, while richer countries may export technologically advanced goods to poorer countries. Germany is a good example of the latter and achieves unemployment rates less than 5 per cent through exporting high-technology machines.

Yet, there is a downside in that the new jobs may not be as plentiful as before and, more importantly, the old jobs either become obsolete or are in less demand because they are essentially low tech.

There is some evidence (Silicon Valley in the USA, for instance) that high-tech jobs bring higher wages than the obsolete jobs they replaced. Both Germany and the USA have experienced lower rates of unemployment in the past few years, of less than 5 per cent, suggesting that the swap process in jobs accompanied with higher rates of growth of GDP has worked. But, again, the downside is that the labour force in the USA has reduced - workers with obsolete qualifications simply withdrawing from the labour force (discouraged workers) – thus, the unemployment rate, which is, of course, numbers unemployed divided by the labour force, should actually increase! Thus, curiously, the number in unemployment doesn't change, but the unemployment rate actually goes up. Curiously too, when jobs start to increase and unemployed numbers fall, discouraged workers come back into the labour force and are likely to be unemployed, thereby again increasing the unemployment rate.

Another indicator of the health of an economy is the homelessness rate. In the USA, homeless numbers have actually reduced even as unemployment has remained stubbornly (in the early part of the Obama administration) high despite benefits having been drastically reduced by an uncaring Republican-dominated Congress. The preceding pararagraphs, if you are still with me, demonstrate that the interpretation of employment/unemployment statistics is not easy!

Two further problems are that the discouraged workers live on vastly reduced savings and that obsolete workers have to retrain and relocate. This is where a socially responsible government steps in and should provide benefits to discouraged workers living on or under the poverty line and compensates workers to retrain. Germany has done this, but the USA, with its Republican Congress and Senate, simply refused to introduce benefits. Trade does lead to jobs being lost by the low skilled, or even the wrong skilled. Yet the new higher-skilled jobs in the new trade should be better paid and should also be taxed to allow the displaced workers to benefit. If this is not done, then there are disgruntled former workers. But blaming the result on trade, again as the Republicans have done in the USA while not providing unemployment benefits, is nonsensical. Quickly followed by a war on trade is likely to lead to an even larger loss in jobs, as well as higher import prices as retaliatory trade barriers are also thrown up, thereby reducing exports as their price increases.

The worsening income distribution around the world suggests that the benefits of technical progress are accruing to the very rich and not the majority of the working population. But why should this new wealth not be distributed fairly? Curiously, our governments have become less socially responsible and have moved towards less taxes for the rich and fewer benefits for the poor and/or unemployed.

My main conclusion is that technological progress through increasing use of technology (such as robotics) should be welcomed since new technologies reduce the drudgery of life. Yet, both our public and private sectors should be mindful that those who suffer from being replaced by technological progress should be compensated. That income distribution around the world is worsening suggests that the technological progress and increased trade that are occurring have not led to an increase in the social responsibility of governments. So readers, await more politicians of the ilk of Bernie Sanders and Jeremy Corbyn. Much as I like aspects of their programmes, my hope is that the latter types do not damage technological progress or the private sector or trade. So far, the phrase 'private sector' rarely falls from their lips except in derogatory terms. The truth is, as ever, more complicated than that. The social responsibilities of both our private and our public sectors deserve a much higher consideration than up to now.

Chapter Eight

INEQUALITY AND POVERTY INCREASE AS CALLS FOR BASIC INCOME RISE AS A RESULT

Introduction

Inequality is increasing across the world, and many companies are becoming phenomenally rich, especially in the USA, according to Paul Krugman.[1] He notes that such inequality hurts many more people than it helps and wonders why there has not been a bigger political backlash with demands for higher taxes on the rich, more spending on the working class and higher wages. In fact, he shows that policy has mostly gone the other way. 'Tax rates on corporations and high incomes have gone down, unions have been crushed, the minimum wage, adjusted for inflation, is lower than it was in the 1960s'.

Inequality around the world has also been famously documented by Thomas Piketty's[2] 2013 classic book *Capital in the Twenty-First Century*, based upon 15 years of empirical research. That book has since been updated in 2019 to *Capital and Ideology: Scholarship without Solutions*, in which, according to some the French economists, data-driven analysis of inequality offers a flawed prospectus for change. Piketty's new book is full of indignation at our world and calls for nations to enact massive redistribution programmes to reduce inequality.

Piketty wants steeply progressive taxes on income, wealth, carbon emissions and bequests. Yet, like myself, he is not enamoured by communism — he does not want the state to hold all property. Small-sized and medium-sized businesses have an important role to play, he argues. He prefers 'temporary ownership', due to which successful businesspeople will not accumulate wealth but will see it taxed, giving others the chance to succeed. The government will use the revenues to create a more egalitarian educational system, give a sizeable capital endowment to every young adult so that they can study more or open a business, and ensure everyone has a minimum basic income of 60 per cent of average after tax income. That I discuss later in this chapter.

---

1. https://www.nytimes.com/2020/07/01/opinion/inequality-america-paul-krugman.html ?action=click&module=Opinion&pgtype=Homepage, accessed 23 September 2020.
2. *Capital in the Twenty-First Century*, by Thomas Piketty, translated by Arthur Goldhammer (Harvard University Press RRP£29.95/Belknap Press RRP$39.95), 696 pp.

Examples of stupendous wealth and yet minimal taxation on the wealth are legion. We know about Trump's reluctance to declare his income, followed by countless lawsuits alleging corruption. The cases are difficult to prove because of numerous wily lawyers.

Picketty noted in his earlier book that today's rich are largely the idle rich — people like the late Liliane Bettencourt, the L'Oréal heiress, who collected returns on enormous amounts of financial wealth but allegedly paid tax on only a small part of her fortune. What could be the harm in taxing people like her?

Yet, much of the increase in top incomes in the USA came after the 1980s, after the Reagan tax cuts. As Eric Zwick and his co-authors showed in a paper published by the National Bureau for Economic Research,[3] business people moved towards corporate structures such as partnerships, where what was earlier shown as wage income was now misleadingly shown as profits or income to capital. Correcting for this, they find that most top earners in the USA today are the self-made 'working rich', such as lawyers, doctors and car dealers, deriving their income from their skills rather than their physical or financial capital.

Yet, Piketty pointed out that during the post-war years between 1950 and 1980, both Europe and the USA enjoyed strong growth even with high progressive taxes. Yet, as now, there was plenty of disillusionment with high taxes and big government within Britain and the USA, long before the Soviet Union started crumbling. Progressive taxation rose in the early twentieth century, then fell back from the 1980s. Piketty's single-minded focus on taxation and redistribution obscures his key argument on inequality. Tax policy cannot be the only cause of, nor solution to, inequality.

Tax evasion is a major tool of the rich and famous, as a glance at the *New York Times* on the tax affairs of the president shows. Nicolas Kristof[4] writes about what is really happening in the USA. For instance, a homeless African-American woman named Tanya McDowell was imprisoned for misleading officials to get her young son into a better school district. She was sentenced to five years in prison in 2012, in part for drug offences and in part for 'larceny' because she had claimed her babysitter's address so her son could attend a better school in Connecticut. Kristof concludes: 'We imprisoned the homeless tax cheat for trying to get her son a decent education, and we elevated the self-entitled rich guy with an army of lawyers and accountants so that he could monetize the White House as well.'

So yes, as Rhymer Rigby in the *Financial Times* noted,[5] 'the super-rich have a history of doing well out of a global crisis and as usual the wealthy find themselves ready to ride the rebound'. Rigby notes that the twenty-first-century epidemics have tended to raise inequality and favour the better educated. The IMF adds that the solution is some

---

3. Matthew Smith, Danny Yagan, Owen M. Zidar and Eric Zwick, 'Capitalists in the Twenty-First Century', NBER Working Paper No. 25442, Issued in January 2019, Revised in June 2019, see https://www.nber.org/papers/w25442.pdf

4. https://www.nytimes.com/2020/10/10/opinion/sunday/trump-taxes.html?action=click &module=Opinion&pgtype=Homepage, accessed 10 October 2020.

5. https://www.ft.com/content/9c9d1ec2-8898-11ea-a109-483c62d17528, accessed 11 October 2020.

sort of 'New Deal', which could involve measures such as expanding social assistance systems, boosting public work programmes and progressive tax measures. Unless this happens, those who have a 'good pandemic' will be those who have a good year nearly every year. More on this when I discuss basic income next.

Warren Buffett's view — that in the longer term, most investors will be fine — hints at the bigger picture. If we look at recent global crises before the pandemic, the 'merely' rich as well as the ultra-rich have done pretty well. According to the Pew Research Center and the Survey of Consumer Finances, both in the USA, the wealth of the US family at the median point — the middle of the income ladder — was lower in 2016 than in 1998. Those lower down the ladder did even worse. By contrast, upper-income families 'were the only income tier able to build on their wealth from 2001 to 2016', adding 33 per cent.

So, do crises ever hurt the wealthy? The crash of 1929 caused some of the rich to suffer horribly. Robert Searle, president of the Rochester Gas and Electric Corp, gassed himself after losing $1.2 million, while James J Riordan, president of the County Trust Company, shot himself in the head.

Poverty

The pandemic has pushed hundreds of millions of people towards starvation and poverty. According to Ishaan Tharoor of the *Washington Post* and *World View*,[6]

> Financiers and traders on Wall Street may be starting to feel optimistic, but for most people the gloom is only deepening. In the United States, thousands of people continue to die of covid-19 each week, while some 30 million people remain unemployed. Industrial output and consumer spending are still well below pre-pandemic levels, with experts pointing to evidence of spiraling inequality as winter approaches. In Europe, a second surge of infections has triggered warnings and shutdowns, compounding the continent's economic jitters.

Yet, the worst pain is centred in the developing world. Even though poverty had started to reduce over the past two decades, mainly because of the economic success of China, poorer nations are floundering amid massive public debt and shortfalls in state revenue. All the while, the roughly 2 billion people who eke out a living in the world's informal economies face varying degrees of deprivation. The World Bank noted that the COVID pandemic would undermine international efforts to bring down the global extreme poverty rate to 3 per cent by 2030 and projected that existing poverty levels would grow in years, 2020 to 2021, for the first time since the 1990s. The war in Europe started by Russia in 2022 is also likely to impact both European and world poverty levels as inflation rears its ugly head. While some 160 million people in Asia alone may be forced below the poverty line, according to the Asian Development Bank. In Latin America, that figure is around 45 million people, according to a recent UN study.

David Beasley, the executive director of the UN's World Food Program and winner of the 2020 Nobel Peace Prize, warned during a September 18 briefing that a 'wave

---

6. https://www.washingtonpost.com/world/2020/09/25/pandemic-pushes-hundreds-millions-people-toward-starvation-poverty/, accessed 11 October 2020.

of hunger and famine still threatens to sweep across the globe'. He said his organization needed close to $5 billion to prevent 30 million people from dying of starvation.
According to the agency, some 135 million people around the world faced acute food
insecurity before the pandemic, and that number is expected to double this year.

UNICEF, the UN Children's Fund, calculated that 872 million students in
51 countries are unable to head back to their classrooms. More than half that number
live in circumstances where remote learning is impossible — a scale that suggests a
generational crisis in education.

As hospitals and clinics around the world remain swamped because of COVID-19,
UNICEF feared new declines in infant and maternal health. 'When children are denied
access to health services because the system is overrun, and when women are afraid
to give birth at the hospital for fear of infection, they, too, may become casualties of
COVID-19', Henrietta Fore, UNICEF's executive director, said in a statement. 'Without
urgent investments to re-start disrupted health systems and services, millions of children
under five, especially newborns, could die'.

Campaigners who have led the charge to reach the UN's poverty-eradicating 'sustainable development goals' warn of an epochal reversal. 'We have celebrated decades
of historic progress in fighting poverty and disease,' wrote Bill and Melinda Gates in
their foundation's annual 'Goalkeepers' report. 'But we have to confront the current
reality with candor: This progress has now stopped.'

Even with the $18 trillion of stimulus pumped into the global economy, mostly by
wealthy governments, the International Monetary Fund projects a cumulative loss of
some $12 trillion by the end of 2021. A separate study from the International Labour
Organization found that the pandemic has already wiped out $3.5 trillion in income
from millions of workers around the world. By the ILO's calculations, projected global
working-hour losses in 2020 will be the equivalent of some 245 million lost jobs.

But it's unclear how much more wealthy governments are willing to give in the face
of their own budget crunches. 'Developing countries have been exposed to manifold
shocks in a context of anaemic global growth,' Stephanie Blankenburg, the head of debt
and development finance at the UN Conference on Trade and Development, told the
Financial Times. 'The international response has been extraordinarily hesitant — way
too little, way too late.'

Thus, the focus may have to fall on private donors. 'Worldwide, there are over 2,000
billionaires with a net worth of $8 trillion. In my home country, the USA, there are
12 individuals alone worth $1 trillion,' said Beasley of WFP. 'In fact, reports state that
three of them made billions upon billions during COVID-19. I am not opposed to
people making money, but humanity is facing the greatest crisis any of us have seen
in our lifetimes.' In fact private companies have stepped up across the world and funnelled billions into development efforts of all shapes and sizes. At the same time, a few
have made billions, as cited above. Can private companies do more? As will be seen in
Chapter 18, I argue strongly for transfers from the private sector to be as sustainable
as possible through something I call sustainable philanthropy. In summary, I argue
there that interventions should be sustainable as far as is possible in the sense that the
initial investment should also lead to a strategy to move NGOs into especially social

enterprises. They should also follow at least a 3-M approach, where the aid is not only transferred to the poor recipients (micro level) but also takes into account government policy (macro level) and then the management of the same (meso level).

What Can Companies Do to Stem Inequality?

Is rising inequality coupled with increased wealth something that companies should see as one of the big issues of the day? Certainly, the SDG Goal 10 on reducing inequalities urges such action and advocates by 2030 to progressively achieve and sustain income growth of the bottom 40 per cent of the population at a rate higher than the national average. But ultimatums, aspirations or lectures are simply not going to work. Yes, companies can increase worker pay through socially responsible actions. But the tendency of companies is always to reduce wages. Companies react negatively to Keynesian pump priming even though that increases effective demand.

Thus, why would companies not be strong advocates of pump priming in a recession? This is not clear, since companies still tend to avoid any discussion on a public policy that might increase their expenditure through taxes or other benefit losses. I think we may have to simply accept that reducing inequalities in the distribution of income is simply not going to happen for most companies. Perhaps, the nearest they would accept is investment in skills and education.

Elements of a Worldwide Poverty Alleviation Strategy

So, what could be the elements of a worldwide poverty alleviation strategy? As far back as the mid-1990s, Godfrey (1995) has imaginatively placed Sen's theory coupled with Chamber's sustainable livelihood ideas in a table that juxtaposes the causes of poverty with a number of policy interventions required to alleviate them. I have used and modified that table (see Table 8.1) as the basis to develop the elements of the proposed poverty alleviation strategy. Again, as in the previous section, it is doubtful whether companies will heed any of the suggestions in the table. Possibly, those who have signed up for the SDGs, in which they are asked to report, may refer to SDG, where Goal 1 emphasizes: End poverty in all its forms everywhere.

In Table 8.1, the left-hand column lists some of the main causes of poverty that comprise both the endowment or ownership of a bundle of assets and a mapping of exchange entitlements. The middle column (drawing upon ideas of sustainable livelihoods) identifies the policy intervention implied in each case. For instance, the ownership bundle of the poor can be augmented by policies which affect their acquisition not only of land but also of human capital and of assets purchased on credit. The right-hand most column illustrates how each intervention fits into the 3-M framework described above - remember that macro is overall policy, meso is the institution/delivery mechanism and micro is the direct contact with people. Hence, one can see for some policies both meso and micro aspects or both macro and meso aspects. In a sense, all interventions have all of 3-M, but those categorized in Table 8.1 are the *main* types of activities in each case.

Table 8.1 Causes of poverty and typical policy response

Causes of poverty: Standard of living of the poor depends on	Intervention in favour of the poor	3-M Policy
(a) The *endowment* or ownership bundle of the poor (e.g. land, labour power, other assets) or the *supply* side of the equation	• Reallocate assets (particularly land) to them and ensure their access to sustainable common property resources • Ensure their access to clean water, health care, sanitation and other socially provided goods and services • Ensure their access to high-quality schooling and adult literacy classes • Ensure that their acquisition of assets is not constrained by lack of credit	Meso (developing institutions) and micro (direct contact)
(b) The *exchange entitlement* mapping (or *demand* in the economy) is affected by:		
(i) Whether employment can be found, for how long and at what rate	• Follow policies on government budget, exchange rates, interest rates, wages, deregulation of the economy etc., which favour employment, creating growth • Set up system of safety nets for seasonal and cyclical bad times, e.g. food-for-work or public works schemes	Macro Meso and micro
(ii) What can be earned by selling non-labour assets, compared with the cost of what is to be bought	• Ensure fair markets for non-labour assets (particularly land, housing, livestock) • Ensure their access to efficient and equitable distribution system within a stable macro-economy • Consider subsidies to the goods they consume, e.g. food stamps	Macro Meso Meso and micro
(iii) What can be produced with own labour power and other obtainable resources or resource services	• Follow policies on government budget, exchange rates, interest rates, wages, deregulation of the economy, etc., which favour employment, creating growth • Remove restrictions on their livelihood activities and stop harassment • Reorient research towards their crops and livelihoods • Ensure their access to knowledge for sustainable livelihoods • Ensure that their access to resources/inputs is not constrained by lack of credit	Macro Meso Macro and meso Meso Meso

(Continued)

Table 8.1 (Continued)

Causes of poverty: Standard of living of the poor depends on	Intervention in favour of the poor	3-M Policy
(iv) The cost of purchasing resources or resource services and the value of the goods that he/she can sell	• Remove barriers to their entry into production of high-value commodities • Ensure their access to an efficient system for transport/marketing, and necessary skills • Consider subsidies to their inputs and outputs, e.g. tax credits	Meso Meso Meso and micro
(v) Entitlements to social security benefits, and liability to pay taxes	• Ensure that the benefit system, if any, covers them effectively. Include a basic income for the poorest • Exclude them from coverage of direct taxes, fees, etc.	Meso
(vi) Intra-household	• Change legal and property rights • Increase education of females • Raise consciousness of males	Macro and meso Meso and micro Macro, meso, micro
(c) Poor management	• Improve system of governance • Capacity-building	Meso

Source: Michael Hopkins. A short review of contemporary thinking about anti-poverty strategies for sub-Saharan Africa. Prepared for UNDP Economist's meeting, Lome, Togo, Jan 21-23, 1997, available on Researchgate.net

Basic Income and Corporate Social Responsibility: Is There a link?

The idea of an unconditional universal basic income has three historical roots. First, the idea of a minimum income first appeared at the beginning of the sixteenth century. Second, the idea of an unconditional one-off grant first appeared at the end of the eighteenth century. And, third, the two were combined for the first time to form the idea of an unconditional (now universal) basic income near the middle of the nineteenth century.

In the vein of Bertrand Russell, some have suggested the need for a basic income to be paid to all individuals in society. This income would replace the myriad of public subsidies currently allocated, thus providing income when there are no jobs, and be enough to meet basic needs.[7] Clearly, production systems can provide direct access to the goods we need without full employment. A basic income would therefore, theoretically, be very attractive. But beyond the calculation of whether it could be afforded comes the process of passing the necessary legislation through our democratic institutions.

---

7. Guy Standing, *Basic Income: And How Can We Make It Happen?* (London: Pelican, 2017).

Claims of basic income proponents[8]

Help us rethink how and why we work

Contribute to better working conditions

Downsize bureaucracy

Make benefit fraud obsolete

Help reducing inequalities

Provide a more secure and substantial safety net for all people

Contribute to less working hours and better distribution of jobs

Reward unpaid contributions

Strengthen our democracy

Provide a fair redistribution of technological advancement

End extreme financial poverty

These are indeed laudable and welcome objectives. Few in the CSR world would object to any of them. Perhaps 'include all stakeholders' would satisfy all corporate and private sector institutions. Thus, there is a link between the two concepts of CSR and BI, and the main benefit for them would be to raise effective demand for their products and services.

Most, if not all, of the above 11 points would appeal to corporations under CSR. Perhaps three key issues of BI implicate CSR more than the others.

First, should all corporations commit to better working conditions, such as pay a living wage[9] to all its stakeholders or simply continue to respect minimum wage legislation and only a few of their stakeholders, such as their employees?

Second, should corporations reconsider their tax contribution to promote a BI in the countries where they operate? Proponents of BI see corporations as a fat cow to be taxed more to ensure a BI.

Third, the increasing inequalities in the distribution of income in the world are leading to unrest and uncertainty among billions of people. Only a few companies will benefit from that (simply because there are always winners and losers) but the losers will far outweigh the winners. Increases in income of the poorer part of the population through BI will lead to increased consumption, and therefore economic growth – again beneficial to private companies through increases in Keynesian demand. Yes, such growth could lead to increased inflation, and yes there could be further damage through economic growth from unsustainability. CSR, when seen as corporate sustainability, focuses upon sustainable growth.

---

8. http://www.basicincome.org.uk/reasons-support-basic-income?recruiter_id=4616 Note the list is in the order presented in the referenced website and their priority not necessarily mine, accessed 4 January 2018.

9. https://www.theguardian.com/society/2017/nov/05/working-poor-skip-meals-living-wage -foundation-poll

Basic income support

With time, universal basic income (UBI) has gradually been transitioning from the radical left into the mainstream. For instance, in the UK, its Green Party Policy is picking up steam among SNP and Labour MPs and has been advocated by commentators, especially in the *Guardian* newspaper.

Supporters of the idea got a boost with the news that the Finnish government, in 2016, piloted the idea with 2,000 of its citizens with positive results. Under the scheme, the first of its kind in Europe, participants received €560 (£473) every month for two years without any requirements to fill in forms or actively seek work. If anyone who receives the payment finds work, their UBI continues. Many participants reported 'decreased stress, greater incentives to find work and more time to pursue business ideas'. In March 2009, Ontario's Provincial Government in Canada started trialling a similar scheme. In the UK, it has been championed by the RSA think tank, and the city of Glasgow is considering a pilot. Across the continent, experiments are running not only in wealthy Finland but also Italy and the Netherlands, and it was a key plank in the platform of Benoît Hamon, the defeated socialist candidate for French president. There are also many small-scale experiments going on to channel BI to poor people and check out such ideas that BI recipients will find jobs easier, will be healthier, will seek education, etc. The old but persistent idea that welfare simply encourages people to be lazy and 'scroungers' is also being tested[10] even though such a notion has been widely debunked.

The deceptively simple idea of offering every citizen a regular payment without means testing or requiring them to work for it has backers as disparate as Mark Zuckerberg, Stephen Hawking, Caroline Lucas and Richard Branson. Ed Miliband, former UK Labour Party aspirant leader, chose the concept to launch his ideas podcast.

BI pros and cons

BI, as a *Guardian* article by Ellie Mae[11] shows, is not without its detractors, and she warns: 'Love the idea of a universal basic income? Be careful what you wish for' and the above 11 points suggest all sound great. But does BI have a sting in its tail?

Let's start with the positives. It could produce a partial solution to robotics taking over jobs if that happens – my own view is that robotics are beneficial to humankind but they do make many jobs obsolete and, as such, the technological revolution should be encouraged while training and subsidies should be used to help displaced workers.[12]

---

10. Overview of Current Basic Income-Related Experiments (October 2017): see http://basicincome.org/news/2017/10/overview-of-current-basic-income-related-experiments-october-2017/, accessed 13 January 2017.
11. Ellie Mae O'Hagan, 'Love the Idea of a Universal Basic Income? Be Careful What You Wish For', *The Guardian*, UK, 23 June 2017, https://www.theguardian.com/commentisfree/2017/jun/23/universal-basic-income-ubi-welfare-state
12. https://www.linkedin.com/pulse/robotics-trade-jobs-whose-responsibility-dr-michael-hopkins/, April 2016, accessed 15 January 2018.

Of course, BI is a temporary help to such displaced workers as they seek more training and/or higher-paying jobs.

It could be more efficient than existing benefit systems because zero bureaucracy makes it cheaper to apply. It could finally implement Bertrand Russell's famous analysis of 'In Praise of Idleness' and the end of work as drudgery and the beginning of work as a service to all.[13] Today, there is understanding of CSR among most companies, and the key issues are how to make profits while being socially responsible and to satisfy the stakeholders that are prominent. These now include its shareholders but also, at least, its management and corporate governance, its employees, suppliers, the government, media, communities and its customers.

But the main problems is who is going to pay for BI, and what is it going to cost?

Costs of BI

BI proponents have rarely worked out the costs of a decent UBI. Supposing everyone of UK's 65.1 million people were given GBP6.70 an hour, the UK minimum wage, for every working hour in a year. The equivalent of 40 hours per week for 52 weeks would be GBP907 billion, or around 33 per cent of UK's current GDP. The tax revenue to GDP in the UK in 2016 (OECD figures) was just about the same at 32.5 per cent. Thus, advocates of a UBI would have to allocate *all* tax revenue to a UBI that was reasonably modest and equivalent to a minimum wage for all. In fact, there is *no* general agreement on what level to set a BI. Years ago, I posited that a basic income should cover a family's basic needs, but that income was often above minimum wages. Note too that basic needs include the services offered free by the government, such as primary education, safety and some aspects of health. Further, should a BI exceed or equal a minimum wage or a basic needs income? However, if the BI is the same as the minimum wage, clearly unskilled workers in dirty or dangerous or boring jobs will be tempted to stop working. So, then the BI should be less than, or even supplementary to, the minimum wage?

So any takers, anyone?

Thus, my own view is to provide a basic income for the poor but not everyone. This means making BI conditional and not universal for everyone, rich or poor. Although I oppose most conditional benefits, because the conditions are so complex to police, I think some are necessary. In Kenya, where just about everybody has a mobile phone and uses them to receive and make payments, transferring benefits is relatively straight-forward using a technique we have called geo-fencing. During COVID-19, the idea was to provide cash transfers to vulnerable families in the urban slums, thereby increasing mutual support between beneficiaries, reduced tensions and improved relationships

---

13. http://www.independent.co.uk/news/business/news/finland-universal-basic-income-lower
    -stress-better-motivation-work-wages-salary-a7800741.html# Finland experiment

within the community. Even better news is that each Ksh1,000 of cash assistance can generate more than double that, most of which will be spent locally. Then, with cash, people were able to buy what they most needed, whether food, rent or other essentials.

A huge difficulty is that corruption has led to most cash distribution schemes failing. There are too many steps to take, with slow and bureaucratic government mechanisms. So, our suggestion was that a basic income should be sent only to areas where poor people live, distributed via MPESA (the Kenyan mobile money system transfer that just about everyone uses) to those with mobile phones. Of course, some will have more than one phone and others none – estimated at a mere 3 per cent in the slums. But the sharing culture there would reduce the hardship of the few without.

Our technical contacts at mobile phone companies could identify most poor people in the vicinity of a transmission mast through a technique known as 'geo-fencing'. Yes, some people who don't need the cash would be included. But if distributed after curfew it would exclude passers-by. Worse, some who desperately need the cash might also get excluded. However, geo-fencing ensures that it is the people in need who do obtain the cash, while corruption can just about be eliminated.[14]

My friend, Guy Standing,[15] noted,

in your calculation of net cost and your rejection of Basic Income for the rich, you have missed out the effect of my proposal to replace tax allowances with the Basic Income and to have a flat rate of income tax. Tax allowances are not counted as Government spending but rich people get the full benefit of the basic and intermediate tax allowances. In the UK the first £11,000 is tax free and the next £32,000 is taxed at 20%. These allowances when used in full (by rich people) cost HMRC (UK's tax authority) more than the basic income we are discussing. There is obviously much scope for tweaking, and I have not considered the 45% tax rate.

Basic income for the wealthier always seemed to me a bridge too far. Standing is adamant about not paying conditional benefits, but I think there must be a way to benefit the poorest and those affected with unemployment or underemployment from the coming robotic expansion.

Then, on costs 'Social protection spending amounted to £231 billion in 2015/16, about 35% of all public spending. This doesn't just include benefits and tax credits; personal social services like child protection are included in this figure, as well as pensions paid to former public sector employees'. https://fullfact.org/economy/welfare-budget/. So, it does look as if a basic income that replaced all social protection could be affordable if the benefit was as low as the current state pension.

---

14. Drawn from Michael Hopkins, Mike Eldon, Bob Munro and Christian Vater, 'Roll Out Basic Income for the Poor in Slums', *Business Daily*, Kenya, 21 April 2020. See https://www .businessdailyafrica.com/bd/opinion-analysis/columnists/roll-out-basic-income-for-the -poor-in-slums-2287496, accessed 12 October 2020.
15. The 'father' of basic income, see his book Standing, *Basic Income: And How We Can Make It Happen*.

But social protection[16] includes health (18.9 per cent), education (13.2 per cent), welfare (24.5 per cent), state pensions (12.1 per cent), etc., which I guess basic income aficionados would not wish to defund? Thus, I think basic income is a great rallying device, but its economics are doubtful.

The UBI tax implications could mean no free health service, no defence, no new roads, no education to identify just a few and, of course, no government.

The worry about robotics and artificial intelligence replacing most, if not all, jobs is a serious but, nonetheless, contentious issue. Some even reject current notions of CSR and sustainability and argue that if everyone received a basic income, then we would not need to worry so much about the responsibility of business, nor, presumably, other corporate bodies such as NGOs and public institutions.

I leave the last but one word to Gemma Telow of the *Financial Times*,[17] who noted that

> being imprecise allows Standing to defend the idea on all sides. On the one hand, he argues basic income - by being unconditional - is preferable to welfare systems which require low-income people to face high marginal tax rates when they move into work. Yet he defends against the common critique of UBI - that paying the same income to everyone would either be prohibitively expensive or worsen inequality and poverty - by saying that a basic income 'does not imply ... the replacement of all other welfare benefits'. In the real world, you cannot have it both ways.

She continues:

> At the outset, Standing urges readers to 'approach this book with as open a mind as possible'. He says he has given 'the devil the best tunes ... so readers can weigh the arguments for themselves. But evidence is not impartially marshalled and he seems blind to glaring inconsistencies in his logic. In the same breath as saying a basic income could be funded by 'scrapping the plan to replace the Trident nuclear missile system' he dismisses a *Guardian* editorial that asked 'Would this be money better spent on the NHS?' as 'prejudicial, deliberately and wrongly implying that basic income would deprive these vital public services of resources'. Everything has an opportunity cost.

Concluding Remarks

In conclusion, it is clear that poor people are poor because they simply don't have any, or enough, money. If you, or I, dear reader, were parachuted into a very poor region, most, if not all of us, would survive simply because we have money or the means to access money through friends or even via our credit card companies or our bank. Consequently, a basic income for all poor people would help enormously. Thus, the CSR of companies and non-private institutions to provide basic incomes would help

---

16. https://fullfact.org/economy/what-you-need-know-about-treasurys-tax-statement/
17. https://www.ft.com/content/ccc8ff92-7083-11e7-93ff-99f383b09ff9, July 31 2017 by Gemma Tetlow.

their reputation enormously while providing the poor with the means not only to survive and live longer but also to buy those companies' products. Income distribution would improve and help to prevent social unrest. But, and this is the key, basic income should not be provided to people above the poverty line and those whose basic needs have been satisfied. Consequently, and this is at the heart of proponents of basic income, there must be some form of conditionality. Middle class and rich people simply don't need more money to meet their basic needs. The very rich hardly know what to spend their money on. In Africa, where I spend half my time, only the very poor don't have walls around their houses. While in Europe, where I spend the other half of my time, only the very, very rich have walls around their homes. But should income distribution continue to worsen, the walls will get bigger. A basic income for the rich would only help them to add another brick or two in the wall. A basic income for the poor would not only help the poor to survive and live longer but also help the walls of the rich to come down.

So Universal BI is laudable but unsustainable. However, given the widening gap between the rich and the poor in the UK, and globally, in favour of the rich and the escalating political, economic and social risks that involves corporate support for a targeted and conditional BI should be a part of their CSR commitment to also treat fellow citizens responsibly and ethically, and especially the poorest.

As CSR gets more and more popular, and encompasses all institutions not simply private ones, the link with basic income is clear since CSR simply cannot ignore the debate on basic income. My view, as spelled out here, is that CSR should embrace a basic income for all poor but not to all, and certainly not to the very rich. The other battle to be fought, and CSR proponents have been weak on this, is the link to income distribution. It is in no one's interest for a few to be barricaded to protect their wealth while the outside continues to fall behind. And talking about battles, with the war in Ukraine in full tilt as I write, is it not time to talk about a basic war expenditure which would avoid the extremes of today and focus on the minimum for basic protection against one's enemies?

Chapter Nine

CSR AND THE SDGS: THE ROLE
OF THE PRIVATE SECTOR[1]

In the global market, the private sector not only has a great responsibility to act on sustainability issues, but also a great opportunity to build new sustainable markets. [15 Swedish CEOs]

In addition to eliminating poverty, the new framework will need to address the drivers of change, such as economic growth, job creation, reduced inequality and innovation... the private sector can get involved, including aligning CSR strategies with the SDGs, encouraging skills-based volunteering for SDG progress among employees, including global causes in your workplace giving campaigns, and raising awareness of the SDGs and efforts to achieve them among staff and the public.[2]

Introduction

The Sustainable Development Goals (SDGs) present the United Nation's view of the future of development until 2030. Their predecessor, the Millennium Development Goals (MDGs), finished in 2015 and were deemed successful, but this was largely because of the success of China in achieving a huge reduction in poverty.[3] Did the private sector have anything to do with that success, and will it be even more involved in the future? Yes, we think so, as the quote above and this chapter suggests.

---

1. Thanks to Prof. John Lawrence, Columbia University, New York and former senior UNDP Director for comments and suggestions based upon an earlier draft.
2. See US Chamber of Commerce Foundation, https://www.uschamberfoundation.org/blog/post/corporate-engagement-will-be-critical-sdgs-success/43828
3. According to UNDP, between 1990 and 2005, more than 470 million people in China were lifted out of extreme poverty, see 'China, the MDGs, and the Post-2015 Development Agenda'. UNDP 2015.

What Happened?

It was in the year 2000 that the United Nations brought together more than 180 member nations at the Millennium Development Summit in a global effort to initiate progress towards eight MDGs.[4] These all had specific, measurable targets associated with each goal, across a broad spectrum of poverty eradication, human development and environmental sustainability concerns.[5]

To update the MDGs and more, the SDGs function as a guide that UN member states will use to frame their policies from January 2016 through 2030. This means that almost all members of the UN – well 193 countries out of a global 196 – have signed up unanimously to make these goals a priority for the next 15 years. And, unlike the MDGs (which were developed by a relatively small group and perceived as relatively non-participatory by many stakeholders), the UN conducted the largest consultation programme of its kind to ensure that all countries and groups would be a part of creating the SDGs, including 11 issue-based and 83 national consultations, as well as door-to-door surveys.[6]

Some success was achieved in the MDGs, as noted above, but the way the goals were selected were both 'limited and top-down, lacking the kinds of consultative engagements that are expected in today's information age. Further, the goals themselves were seen as focused mostly on less developed countries, in the context of anticipated aid donations from the more industrialized world. So, despite some gains inequalities persist and progress was uneven'.[7]

What Are the SDGs?

The UN felt it had considerable success[8] in eliciting the world's attention to the MDGS, hence the new 17 SDGs,[9] which, nevertheless, differ importantly from MDGs although they build on them both conceptually and institutionally. Identifying the SDGs took several years, and their scope is more extensive. They aim to bring in multiple interests and actors from public and private sectors as well as civil society. Most significantly, the

---

4. See http://www.un.org/millenniumgoals/
5. http://www.icsu.org/publications/reports-and-reviews/review-of-targets-for-the-sustainable-development-goals-the-science-perspective-2015/SDG-Report.pdf
6. This foregoing paragraph is largely based upon http://charity.org/press/news/corporate-engagement-will-be-critical-sdgs-success
7. Ban Ki-Moon, UN Secretary General in Foreword to the Millennium Development Goals Report 2015.
8. The UN says 'The Millennium Development Goals (MDGs), are the most successful global anti-poverty push in history. Governments, international organizations, and civil society groups around the world have helped to cut in half the world's extreme poverty rate. More girls are in school. Fewer children are dying. The world continues to fight killer diseases, such as malaria, tuberculosis and AIDS.' see http://www.un.org/millenniumgoals/mdgmomentum.shtml
9. See http://www.un.org/sustainabledevelopment/sustainable-development-goals/

SDGs have already attracted significant private sector interest, and the UNCTAD has suggested a plan to attract private investment,[10] not only in goal/target identification, but also in the early stages of moving towards their achievement as we shall see below.

Private Sector Involvement

Corporate involvement in the MDGs had been sporadic and restricted, partly because of the primary focus on poorer countries. In some sectors (e.g. health, information technologies, environmental control), the private sector was on stage almost by default for its role in supply lines for drugs and other crucial commodities and utilities. The SDGs, however, are universal, not only crossing all sectors, but also signed onto by all countries as nationally relevant to their individual agendas with many more opportunities for private sector involvement (see Table 9.1).

Global public consultations were held on how to partner with the private sector in the post-2015 agenda.[11] Refreshingly, it was immediately apparent that commercial interests at many levels would have to be directly concerned in both goal selection and specific measures of achievement across time. Broad agreement was evident as to the crucial contribution of business and industry as 'drivers' of socio-economic progress. The corporate role was seen as encouraging public sector policy to drive sustainable commerce and trade, working towards building trust through greater transparency and accountability, and promoting a constructive localized environment for small and medium enterprises. Surprisingly, when a senior member of the UNGC (UN Global Compact) asked me about funding, I said why not contact the companies that helped you put them together. The result? Still on their to do list I think.

In my book on CSR and development, I insisted on including the private sector in development issues.[12] Thus, the remainder of this chapter outlines some of these issues and underscores the critical role of private enterprise in SDG achievement.

Interestingly, the private sector's role in achieving the MDGs had hardly come up in UN discussions at that time.[13] Yet, when the UN began reviewing MDG progress in 2012, the results in areas such as hunger and sanitation were sobering, according to Olav Kjørven, then a special advisor to the UN Development Programme.[14] His team

10. http://unctad.org/en/PublicationChapters/wir2014ch4_en.pdf
11. Engaging with the Private Sector in the Post-2015 Agenda. Consolidated Report on 2014 Consultations. UNIDO and the UN Global Compact. 2014.
12. Michael Hopkins, *CSR and International Development* (London: Earthscan, 2007).
13. In fact, I failed in my attempt to have a Human Development Report (HDR) devoted to development and CSR and the private sector when I worked as an adviser to the HDR in the 1990s. My presentation was topped at that time by a much better one on Human Rights that won that day!
14. See more at http://www.scidev.net/global/sdgs/analysis-blog/focus-on-private-sector-competition-can-deliver-sdgs.html#sthash.5xSbDZZI.dpuf

Table 9.1 Examples of private sector involvement per SDG

SDG issue	Meaning	Private sector involvement
1. Poverty	End poverty in all its forms everywhere	Pay living wage, reach out to families and communities
2. Food	End hunger, achieve food security and improved nutrition and promote sustainable agriculture	New methods of sustainable crops and products
3. Health	Ensure healthy lives and promote well-being for all at all ages	Word with public health sectors to develop cheaper and more appropriate products
4. Education	Ensure inclusive and equitable quality education and promote lifelong learning opportunities for all	Work with public sector to ensure supply of appropriate skills and education
5. Women	Achieve gender equality and empower all women and girls	Gender equality in companies
6. Water	Ensure availability and sustainable management of water and sanitation for all	Nestlé has shown the way with big push on clean and available water
7. Energy	Ensure access to affordable, reliable, sustainable and clean energy for all	Government to provide incentives and adequate tax and pricing structure to mobilize alternative energy private sector
8. Economy	Promote sustained, inclusive and sustainable economic growth, full and productive employment and decent work for all	Private sector led
9. Infrastructure	Build resilient infrastructure, promote inclusive and sustainable industrialization and foster innovation	Sustainable construction to lead to many new companies
10. Inequality	Reduce inequality within and among countries	Accept fairer tax regimes
11. Habitation	Make cities and human settlements inclusive, safe, resilient and sustainable	New technologies for construction will lead to more new companies and innovation
12. Consumption	Ensure sustainable consumption and production patterns	Major efforts required by retailers and supply chains
13. Climate	Take urgent action to combat climate change and its impacts	Needs massive private sector innovation
14. Marine	Ecosystems Conserve and sustainably use the oceans, seas and marine resources for sustainable development	Shipping and fishing industries to innovate and then expand rapidly

(Continued)

Table 9.1 (Continued)

SDG issue	Meaning	Private sector involvement
15. Ecosystems	Protect, restore and promote sustainable use of terrestrial ecosystems, sustainably manage forests, combat desertification and halt and reverse land degradation and halt biodiversity loss	Millions of new products and companies required with government incentives
16. Institutions	Promote peaceful and inclusive societies for sustainable development, provide access to justice for all and build effective, accountable and inclusive institutions at all levels	Companies to respect local laws, weed out corruption and benefit through enhanced reputation
17. Sustainability	Strengthen the means of implementation and revitalize the global partnership for sustainable development	Huge opportunities for public-private partnerships in sustainability agendas

decided that many targets - for example, to do with employment, the environment and the delivery of key services - could not be achieved without the private sector.[15]

The MDG goals launched in 2000 amid aggressive but unsuccessful campaigning against the Washington Consensus pro-market economic policies had excluded the private sector from planning. 'Nobody was thinking about the private sector because the private sector had won the debate', Kjørven explained. Then, after the financial crisis, people realized that to make progress on energy, food, liveable cities and job provision, the private sector would have to be brought into this process.[16]

With this in mind, SDG planning proceeded along three tracks: consultations with policy experts, national consultations of citizens' priorities and private sector consultation, managed by the UN Global Compact. The process highlighted at least two key ways tech companies could make a difference. First, the priorities survey helped put access to technology on the agenda. Goal 9 on infrastructure development includes a target to 'provide universal and affordable access to the internet in least developed countries by 2020'. In an era when global job growth is likely to come from high-tech industries, and where all businesses increasingly require the use of technology, the digital divide between rich and poor countries is a major obstacle to development.[17] That goal was prescient as I write these words on the Kenyan coast as well as discuss worldwide via Zoom, helped by superb internet coverage.

---

15. See more at http://www.scidev.net/global/sdgs/analysis-blog/focus-on-private-sector-competition-can-deliver-sdgs.html#sthash.5xSbDZZI.dpuf
16. Ibid.
17. http://www.scidev.net/global/sdgs/analysis-blog/focus-on-private-sector-competition-can-deliver-sdgs.html

Similarly, Goal 17 on international partnerships emphasized technology as a key area where rich countries could transfer expertise to poor ones. This is an opportunity for technology companies that can distribute phones and tablets, install telecommunications infrastructure at low cost and help other industries use technology to thrive in the Global South.[18]

'Further, data companies have helped develop tools to monitor SDG progress. These include telecoms firms BT and Verizon, which support a UN initiative on the Sustainable Development Solutions Network, an online platform where development practitioners, governments and businesses can share practices and progress related to the SDGs'.[19]

UNIDO[20] found, in analysing its consultative feedback on SDGs from businesses worldwide, that

> respondents saw corporate sustainability regimes as one way of improving regulatory frameworks, for example, via better understanding by all parties as to importance of data quality and reporting procedures. It was suggested that closer cooperation between public and private sectors might lead to incentive structures such as reduction of penalties for more corporately responsible firms, or rewards for compliant behavior including preferential awards of procurement tenders.

Moreover, successful development, UNIDO argued,[21] leads to enhanced markets and more consumer demand. Thus, health, education and employment goals are seen by businesses as fostering national investments in human resources on both supply and demand sides. 'CSR in the context of South-South collaboration must also move beyond traditional notions of philanthropy to embrace principles of sustainability and harness the transformational power of a shared value approach focused on people'.

As noted in two recent Human Development Reports of the UN Development Programme (2014, 2015), a resilient and healthy economic climate is conducive to greater private investment in the virtuous circle of sustainable human progress (see Table 9.1). As evidence shows repeatedly, although large firms are often the loudest voice of the private sector, small and medium-sized enterprises (SMES) are inevitably the backbone of commerce everywhere. Their capacity and access to assets (physical infrastructure, finance, internet connectivity) are highly constrained by several factors onto which the SDGs have brought strong light. The SDGs open up a new space

---

18. See more at http://www.scidev.net/global/sdgs/analysis-blog/focus-on-private-sector-competition-can-deliver-sdgs.html
19. http://www.scidev.net/global/sdgs/analysis-blog/focus-on-private-sector-competition-can-deliver-sdgs.html#sthash.5xSbDZZI.dpuf
20. Engaging with the Private Sector in the Post-2015 Agenda. Consolidated Report on 2014 Consultations. UNIDO and the UN Global Compact. 2014.
21. Ibid.

for SME partnerships with large firms, through subcontracting, locking in to already established supply chains, or transportation arrangements. More particularly, CSR in both large and SMEs will enhance such aspects as trust, living wage, fair trade, less pollution, more human rights, community development as well as other key stakeholders and issues.

SDGs, Systems Thinking and CSR

One issue of concern for me is that the SDGs tend to be more of a list, mainly of the issues that the UN deals with. Nothing wrong with that but if one took a systems approach where all aspects that affect the ultimate goal of development were to be included. One might first order the SDGs into objectives or targets and then the processes to achieve those targets – such as I have done in Figure 9.1.

Then we see key targets become three: anti-poverty; health and well-being; and reducing inequality. One might go further and suggest that the ultimate objective is increasing 'well-being'! Especially, as I have already noted, life expectancy at birth is the ultimate indicator of development.

Returning to systems thinking and adding in CSR to Figure 9.1 leads to Figure 9.2.

As can be seen, a first approach at moving towards a systems approach would include other key processes such as responsible people, democracy, responsible business, responsible institutions and even responsible leadership. These issues are all discussed in various chapters in this book.

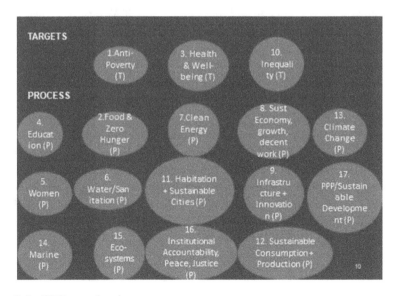

Figure 9.1 SDGs reordered.

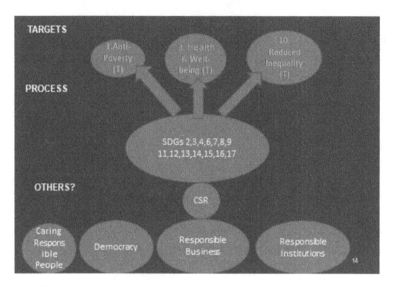

Figure 9.2 SDGs systems approach.

Practical Approaches to SDGs[22]

How have companies approached SDG implementation in practice? Here I look at three companies: SAB, Interface and Marks & Spencer. SAB, a major brewing company, struggled with measuring the likely impact of its SDG work. They were faced with 159 targets and decided to translate them into four key areas of action, asking (1) Is there a relationship between SDGs and their business case? (2) How would it impact on the company's licence to operate and their reputation? (3) What would their potential be to enhance innovation and growth? and (4) What would this mean for the company's priorities socially, both internally and for society as a whole? Their biggest priority, clearly because they are a brewer, was the operational impact on issues with water, both use and disposal of waste. On further reflection, they discovered that societal priorities were actually critical to answer the kind of business they were. Hopefully, this book will provide further food for thought!

Their further concerns, as they funnelled down into their company operations, were more specific and again fourfold, namely: (1) SAB could not simply cherry-pick the SDG that emphasized exciting stuff on their commercial agenda but had to look further into their responsibilities; (2) a strong need to partner with companies and stakeholders who would have more insight than SAB; (3) a clear understanding of SAB's business model and the key risks and opportunities and not simply relate to Goals 3, 7 and 8 but

22. This section relies heavily on a webinar conducted by Ethical Corporation on 16th August 2018, where key participants included Anna Swaithers, former Head of Sustainability at SAB; Munish Datta, Head of Plan A at Marks & Spencer and John Khoo, Interface. Thanks to both Munish and John for permission to use the above remarks and their comments on them.

to go past them even if a clear commercial opportunity didn't present itself; (4) the measurement of the impact of SDGs are key but SAB still had some way to go in reporting, but more than a report was required and steps to link impact measurement to actual results were needed.

Interface, according to the company's website, is 'a world-leading modular flooring company with a fully integrated collection of carpet tiles and resilient flooring'. One problem their spokesman mentioned was the need to avoid so-called SDG Washing, i.e. paying only lip service to the SDGs and carrying on as usual. Clearly, a need to prioritize which SDG to focus upon without, as SAB, 'cherry-picking'. Interface still had to prioritize and chose to focus upon SDG12 to create responsible products; SDG13 on Global Warming and to continue to make all their products carbon-neutral. They noted that the indicators generated by the SDGs tended to be very much government-aligned and so needed to rework them to reflect their business environment. This was especially true of SDG17 on partnerships and led them to work with two degrees on their manufacturing 2030 programme. They also chose SDG14 on networks which led them to work with the Zoological Society and thereby focus on plastics and their disposal. Clearly Interface felt that such a partnership was required for that major issue.

The business case was key, and interface had therefore examined how best they could grow their business while reflecting upon the SDGs. They noted that a collaboration between GRI and the Global Compact led by PwC had led to a useful collaboration of ideas, especially the issues of how best to work and promote SMEs.

Marks & Spencer (M&S), a retail company with 80,000 employees, were pleased to work with the SDGs as it was one of the first comprehensive approaches to development. A 2017 report of the BSDC suggested that the adoption of the SDGs by companies could lead to an additional amount of business, totalling at least US$12 trillion a year by 2030 and generating up to 380 million jobs, mostly in developing countries.[23] That sum could be hampered by the cost of inaction, such as interrupting the move towards a low-carbon economy. M&S had been involved in development issues since at least 2007, if not before, and dealt with 'big issues' right across their value chain, such as using renewable energy sources as much as possible, not using landfills for waste disposal and collecting obsolete clothes for distribution to poorer people. In the M&S Plan A report for 2018,[24] they have mapped their 100 commitments in the development area to the SDGs and, unsurprisingly, don't cover all SDGs. Clearly, their investors are pleased to get a good return, such as their focus against modern slavery has helped their supply chain. They admitted that one of their biggest challenges was connecting what they are doing on SDGs to their public and are using a PR company to do that.

---

23. https://www.wbcsd.org/Overview/News-Insights/General/News/Achieving-the
    -Sustainable-Development-Goals-can-unlock-trillions-in-new-market-value, accessed 20
    August 2018.
24. https://corporate.marksandspencer.com/plan-a/report2018, accessed 20 August 2018.

What More Could Corporations Do to Promote Development?

Development assistance is key in many countries. This would best be done with existing development agencies such as the UNDP, who have vast experience in development. Clearly, MNEs should not replace the UN, nor government's own efforts. Simply, the power and wealth of MNEs need to be harnessed in positive development efforts. Should these efforts be in addition to the taxes that MNEs pay anyway? There is no easy answer. But many taxes that MNEs pay in developing countries are misused. A democratic government will tend to use tax revenue in ways that benefit its electorate so as to ensure re-election next time around. Yet most governments in developing countries are not democratic. So, should MNEs be involved in those countries and, if so, what should they exactly do?

First, MNEs should evaluate their position based on existing relations with the government. Clearly, if a host government simply says how we use your taxes is none of your business, then the MNE can decide whether to stay or leave. Second, where possible, the MNE can, at least, assist the government in ensuring that tax revenue is used effectively to promote development. MNEs have vast experience in tax issues and could well lend some of this experience to develop capacity (better governance) within governments. Third, when MNEs carry out their own development projects, these should draw upon the development experience available in NGOs and local UN offices such as the UNDP. Fourth, MNEs are not the government and obviously cannot, nor should not, carry out the major programmes of the government such as education, health, security or employment systems. But MNEs can be involved as an agent of positive change through lending their expertise to improving efficiency in government programme delivery. Fifth, if more than one MNE is involved in a developing country, they should work together to ensure increased efficiency of development programmes in the host country.

But how much will all this cost? How much of its time and money should a MNE invest in any of the above-mentioned activities? There is no easy answer to this question. It is worth bearing in mind, however, that a MNE is involved in many of the above-mentioned processes as much as by default than a clearly thought-out strategy. A MNE has to be continually involved with the host government negotiating all sorts of deals from land acquisition to taxation to import and export. Often these discussions will influence government policies and changes will be made. So, what I am suggesting here, at least as a first step, is to place the myriad of discussions with the government in an overall development framework. The more transparency, the better, since the MNE will then be seen to be working in the country's best interest rather than colluding in smoke-filled darkened rooms. Thus, the MNE strategy in any particular country could be framed with a clear idea as to the benefits and costs of its intervention in terms of its own bottom line and, also, in terms of its benefit to development. Some of these are highlighted in the Table 9.2.

Table 9.2 Corporate development to promote SDGs

Actions	Benefits to MNE	Disadvantages to MNE	Benefits to SDG development
1. Anti-corruption culture embedded throughout organization	a. Reputation enhanced b. Costs of delivery of services and products reduced	More difficult to win contracts	Increased efficiency as poorly managed projects are eliminated and good projects properly monitored
2. New investment in LDC	Take advantage of cheap labour Closer to raw materials	Increased costs of ex-patriate managers and local training Increased costs in management Need to deal with host government and local institutions	1. Increased employment and incomes 2. Enhanced external trade position
3. Improving community relations	Reputation enhanced	1. Increased costs 2. Increased criticism if badly designed	Well-designed projects can create sustainable development
4. Philanthropic actions	Reputation enhanced	Increased costs Will need to continue pay-offs if project design is non-sustainable	One-off actions are rarely sustainable
5. Development assistance	International reputation enhanced	1. Accused of becoming a new United Nations 2. Entering unfamiliar territory	1. Obtain expertise from practical managers 2. More resources available than from international public sources 3. Less strings tied to development assistance
5. Capacity Development	Reputation enhanced	Few, if existing skills are used but there is management cost	Sustainable training can never be lost, essential for development

Suggested SDG Actions Linked to CSR

The UN together with the GRI and WBCSD have provided an action programme to help companies cope with how to deal with SDGs, known as SDG Compass, from which I have drawn up the following guidance notes. One key issue is that such a manual is helpful for large companies that have the time, staff and budget to comply but exceedingly difficult for small-sized and medium-sized companies. Happily, the suggested steps in this book to identify key issues for each of their key stakeholders is exactly what the SDG Compass recommends,[25] and I can comfortably state that:

1. CSR is the driving force to meet SDGs and more
2. CSR is treating key stakeholders responsibly
3. CSR must now address BIG ISSUES via its annual CHARTER on BIG ISSUES

The Compass lists the three key instruments of UN principles that apply universally to all companies, namely: the ILO Tripartite Declaration of Principles Concerning Multinational Enterprises and Social Policy, the UN Global Compact Principles and the UN Guiding Principles on Business and Human Rights. But none actually refer to the SDGs, simply because the UN standards were completed years beforehand – for instance, the ILO standards were first drawn up in 1976 at the World Employment Conference, where, in fact, your author was present while introducing the basic needs approach to development. Compass also adds the ISO 26000 Guidance on Social Responsibility as well as the more regional guidelines such as the OECD Guidelines for Multinational Enterprises. An inventory of existing principles, standards and guidelines as well as other business tools is available at www.sdgcompass.org

Compass does complicate the issue by suggesting companies consider their entire value chain – from the supply base and inbound logistics, across production and operations, to the distribution, use and end-of-life of products – as the starting point for assessing impact and defining priorities. Details and examples are given on the Compass website.

Happily, their and my processes are perfectly compatible as they agree that 'engaging stakeholders' both internally and externally is key to the SDG process and that 'paying close attention to their issues, interests, concerns, and expectations will help identify and build a full understanding of your company's impact on the SDGs'.

Clearly, reporting and communicating is important, and Compass provides details on their website. Frankly, if companies would produce a 'Big Issue' annual report, they could cover most SDG issues and even more. Indeed, as Compass agrees with my own statements and lessons learned that over the last decade, the 'practice of corporate sustainability disclosure has increased dramatically in line with stakeholder demand for information'.

Furthermore, a company's list of material issues is likely to include the strategic priorities identified in the Compass website. And the site states that priority areas do not have to be highly significant to be deemed a priority for reporting, especially if companies can make use of independent external assurance as a way to enhance the credibility and quality of their reports.

---

25. https://sdgcompass.org/, accessed 8 October 2020.

Concluding Remarks

So, as argued in previous chapters, as well as the SDG remarks here, CSR can pave the way for development. CSR has paved the way for corporations to examine their wider role in society in ways that have not been as widespread as is becoming the case today.

Clearly, governments will be the overall arbiter of development through the public purse. But their failure in many developing countries has provided an empty space that must be filled by another entity, and the main alternative is the private sector and its champions, the large corporations. As UNCTAD's Secretary-General Mukhisa Kituyi said[26] while opening the meeting on 30 October 2019 at the Palais des Nations in Geneva, Switzerland, 'More and more financial decision makers are demanding information on the business risks and opportunities associated with climate change.' He noted also that '130 banks (one third of the global banking sector) signed up to align their businesses with the Paris Agreement's objectives and the SDGs while asset managers representing nearly half of the world's invested capital – some $34 trillion – demanded urgent climate action and a phase-out of fossil fuel subsidies and thermal coal power worldwide'.

---

26. https://unctad.org/en/pages/newsdetails.aspx?OriginalVersionID=2223

Chapter Ten

IMMIGRATION PLUS BUSINESS
IN CONFLICT AREAS

Social Responsibility Solution to Refugee Crisis

Watching the unfortunate refugees across the world trying desperately to salvage their lives gives a new meaning to the lack of social responsibility across the world. Anyone reading this chapter in their relatively secured homes could easily suffer the same fate. Yes, even you dear reader can suddenly become a refugee and thereby feel the desperation. So I am sure most, if not all, readers are highly concerned with the situation we see in our daily news.[1]

What we don't see is that refugees generally tend to be well-educated, peace-loving and very capable of using their skills – they must be very capable given the absolute horrors they experience to arrive on often hostile shores in search of a better life or simply to survive the local massacres and violence.

Germany's announcement in 2019 of welcoming one million refugees was just what the doctor ordered, albeit without controversy for Angela Merkel at the time. These refugees were mainly Syrians and were well educated and mainly young men. There will be no doubt a few hoodlums among them, but probably much less than the indigenous population. For instance, it is striking that, according to the think tank Global Research in 2011, US citizens were nine times more likely to have been killed by a police officer than a terrorist!

The social responsibility of Merkel in fact had a strong business case – there is no point in carrying out CSR activities if it is not positive for the business or institution and what we call the 'business case'. A quick calculation shows this: one million active young men and their families will spend easily a minimum of 5,000 euros a year, i.e. about 5 billion euros which as a proportion of Germany's GDP of around 3.5 trillion euros is 1.4 per cent. In 2019, economic growth in Germany was a modest 0.6 per cent, so Germany could easily treble its 2019 economic growth rate merely by absorbing such refugees!

So social responsibility for the refugee issue is crucial for the future of their as well as our countries. Let me count the ways:

---

1. Check out this 7-minute video by the author published on 23 October 2015, https://www .youtube.com/watch?v=vbtQvtYKMFY

1. War is totally destructive. The famous conundrum of the Prisoner's Dilemma in Game Theory showed us that compromise allows everyone to gain. So why must we be hostage to socially irresponsible arms dealers, military unthinking and socially irresponsible leaders, including the so-called religious ones?

2. In refugee camps, CSR is essential to prepare people for their journey home, where, believe it or not, most would return given appropriate conditions.

3. Hostile reception by the social irresponsibility of the far right in rich countries across the world can only be reduced by showing the population how destructive such views are. Also, as I showed above for Germany, such views are against prosperity and will also lead to unnecessary violence between small groups of people wrongly convinced that refugee inflows will lead to economic decline, and prejudice the unfortunate immigrant themselves. One must also be aware that, as Europe ages, immigration is actually essential for Europe's economic and social prosperity. If only the UK Brexiteers could have understood such an obvious point.

4. Within countries themselves is the oft-forgotten problem of the Internally Displaced People (IDPs). They need strong doses of CSR to cope with their own pressing problems among which are an intense programme to increase their skills.

Finally, I am an immigrant having left my country, the UK, long ago. Let me thank the wonderful people I have met in all the countries that have allowed me to settle over the past decades – USA, France, Switzerland, Colombia, Malaysia and Kenya!

Doing Business in Regions of Conflict: Can CSR Help[2]?

Business continues even in regions of conflict. But what does corporate social responsibility really mean under conflict conditions? How can business not make the situation worse and how far can private enterprise go in actively building peace?

In fact, there have been notable exclusions and many failures. One of the biggest in recent years has been the almost total lack of social responsibility of our financial organizations and rating agencies – for instance in their misguided application of social responsibility Lehman Brothers was only interested in philanthropy as was Enron, believe it or not, and we know both subsequently collapsed! While the rating agencies such as Standard & Poor's and Fitch lamentably have nothing on their websites and seem to do whatever they wish without regarding the implications of their decisions – for instance, downgrading US debt during the discussion over the US budget ceiling simply raised borrowing costs and lowered confidence. When what was needed in the USA to reinvigorate its economy was (and is) greater confidence and greater spending to help unemployment. With interest rates low, creating debt is practically free. Standard and Poor's simply raised the cost of debt while ignoring its impact on unemployment which remained stagnant.

---

2. An earlier version of this section was given as a speech at an event in London hosted by the Norwegian Embassy on 9 May 2012 organized by International Alert and moderated by BBC presenter Zainab Badawi.

Another major failure and strongly related to the topic of conflict, as President Eisenhower warned us in 1961, is the military–industrial complex (MIC). In his last speech, as President, he said 'In the councils of government, we must guard against the acquisition of unwarranted influence, whether sought or unsought, by the *military industrial complex*. The potential for the disastrous rise of misplaced power exists and will persist'. He warned that defence spending levels and even the wars the USA would fight were disconnected from actual security needs. They were driven instead by the profit and power interests of the MIC who benefited from militarization and war.

In fact, since the fall of the Berlin Wall, the hoped-for peace dividend materialized only slightly as US defence expenditure fell from 6 per cent of GDP in 1990 to 3.5 per cent at the end of the Clinton administration but climbed rapidly to 6 per cent again by the end of the Bush era in 2008 – it stood at around US$700–800 billion at the end of the Trump Administration, dwarfing the amount of about $190 billion spent on education from public funds in 2019.

In conflict situations of which there are far too many – Somalia, Syria, Congo, Yemen, Pakistan, Afghanistan, Iraq … the list seems to go on and on – the private sector has three options:

1. Deliberately create conflict to benefit themselves.
2. Lobby to benefit from conflict.
3. Actively reduce conflict to benefit themselves.

Let's look in more detail at the three options.

Companies create conflict to benefit themselves

One of the most brazen of all interventions by the private sector occurred 60 years ago, when BP was called the Anglo-Iranian Oil Company (AIOC). AIOC was complicit in helping and convincing the UK Government, with the help of the USA, to overthrow the democratic Iranian Government of Mohammad Mosaddegh.

In his book *All the Shah's Men: An American Coup and the Roots of Middle East Terror*, Stephen Kinzer, the former *New York Times* bureau chief, told the story of the Anglo-Iranian Oil Company's role in the 1953 CIA coup against Iran's popular progressive prime minister, Mohammad Mosaddegh. Kinzer stated:

> At the beginning of the twentieth century, as a result of a corrupt deal with the old dying monarchy, one British company, owned mainly by the British government, had taken control of the entire Iranian oil industry. So, this one company had the exclusive rights to extract, refine, ship, and sell Iranian oil. And they paid Iran a very tiny amount. But essentially, the entire Iranian oil resource was owned by a company based in England and owned mainly by the British government.

BP was formed shortly after the coup.

On 20 January 1953, Dwight D. Eisenhower took office as the 34th President of the USA, and the first Republican to be elected after 20 years of Democrat control. Along with the partisan shift, the White House retracted and reversed its policy towards Iran and its recent nationalization of the AIOC. Eisenhower's push for a coup d'état, instigated by the CIA and MI-6, stood in stark contrast with Truman's opposition to such policy. BP's role in Iran's descent into tyranny is no trivial historical coincidence. To this day, it is not difficult to find an Iranian living in America who refuses to buy gas from BP.

The coup, led by the CIA's Kermit Roosevelt, TR's grandson, was successful. The Shah, installed as leader, turned tyrannical, leading directly to the Iranian revolution of 1979. Protesters carried placards of Mossadegh through the streets in the course of the overthrow and, once triumphant, many members of Mossadegh's government were restored to positions of power. Within several years, however, the pluralist nature of the revolution receded, and Ayatollah Khomeini tossed out the liberal element.

The coup shattered Iran's nascent democracy and taught Middle Eastern leaders that the West cared more for access to resources and stability than human rights and democracy. 'We are not liberals like Allende and Mossadeghh, whom the CIA can snuff out,' said Ayatollah Ali Khamenei, who was a top aide to Khomeini during the revolution and is now supreme leader in Iran.

Chiquita too, no doubt contributed to conflict. In March 2007, the Cincinnati banana company stunned investors, employees and the local business community by admitting it made regular payments to Colombian paramilitary groups for 15 years, ending in 2004. It said it had no choice – the lives of its employees were at risk.

Companies lobby to benefit from conflict

Do companies such as Xe (formerly Blackwater) Lockheed, General Dynamics or BAE encourage conflict to profit? They certainly lobby the US Congress strongly to increase defence expenditure which, in the USA today for instance, is more than double it was at the end of the Cold War. As noted above, there is not much doubt that Eisenhower's MIC is still very powerful today.

Evidence, as compiled by the Minnesota Arms Spending Alternatives Project, found:

- In 2011, the defence Industry spent $131 million lobbying Congress and devoted nearly $23 million to congressional campaigns.
- Lockheed Martin led the way – spending $15 million on lobbying. This was a great investment as Lockheed received more than $40 billion in defence contracts.
- The top 10 recipients of US government contracts are all defence industries.
- The US Congress in 2012 devoted 59 cents of every dollar it appropriated (Congress controls the discretionary budget) to war or national security.
- There are front groups for defence contractors such as 'The Coalition for the Common Defense' working tirelessly on behalf of industry to prevent cuts in military spending.

Companies need to reduce conflict to operate normally

According to a private source, Shell estimated that around 80 per cent of its costs are above ground. Certainly, in Nigeria, Shell's reputation has run aground due to perceived insouciance in local communities. In Somalia, Shell has several blocks where oil is thought to exist, but they have not done any exploration as yet because of security issues. Many suspect that the increase in interest in Somalia is due to perceived availability of oil riches. *The Guardian* has reported that a former Somali prime minister, Abdiweli Mohamed Ali, after meeting Hillary Clinton and David Cameron at the London Somalia Conference held in February 2012, said that in the future a share of natural resources would be offered in return for help with reconstruction. "There's room for everybody when this country gets back on its feet and is ready for investment", he said.

But the majors are keeping their powder dry. When I asked a Shell contact if they would help to preserve the democratic government in Somaliland and thereby gain preferential access to various possible areas of oil exploration, there was a deafening silence.

Companies' Reputation Improve If They Help to Reduce Conflict

Is there evidence for this reduction of conflict? Certainly, many companies now emphasize helping local communities and offer assistance in all sorts of development projects. They gain customers by working with local communities, for instance, Coca Cola signs are everywhere in Africa and they gain from advertising as well as their local community work. They also gain a good reputation for helping local communities. Yet, as Warren Buffett once said, reputation takes 20 years to obtain and five minutes to lose – e.g. Apple using poorly paid labour to produce iPhones in China.

So which one of the above three options in conflict situations will dominate?

We can be cynical and say that our companies if left to themselves will become, as Terence Ratigan states in the title of his latest book, 'Greedy Bastards'. There is plenty of evidence for that. But I am more positive, and the increasing move towards social responsibility, encouraged by NGOs such as International Alert, social media and activist movements such as Occupy will make companies much more careful in the future.

In Somalia (according to a World Bank study[3]), the economic sectors which have benefited most from the absence of state regulation – financial services, telecommunications and the commerce in consumer goods across national boundaries – have also profited the warlords and spoilers, and have not done much to develop Somalia's critical infrastructure (roads, power grid, water supplies). The latter can only attract private investment when a stable national government (or regional authority) with reliable security forces at its disposal is in place to ensure their maintenance and protection from extortionists or rent seekers.

---

3. https://www.worldbank.org/en/news/press-release/2020/02/27/somalia-to-reestablish -financial-relations-with-the-world-bank-group-after-thirty-years, accessed 24 November 2020.

International Private Sector Conflict Avoidance Efforts

Greater awareness of the risk of 'doing harm' has increased interest in the concept of conflict impact assessment as a subcategory of social impact assessment. The UN Global Compact took up this theme in one of its first dialogues between the UN and representatives of the private sector. In 2002, the Compact published its 'Business Guide to Conflict Impact Assessment and Risk Management in Zones of Conflict'. Meanwhile, researchers and NGOs have been taking this idea forward by developing new conflict impact assessment tools. For example, International Alert published in 2005 both a Macro-level and Project-level Conflict Risk and Impact Assessment tool as part of its Conflict-Sensitive Business Practice Toolbox for Extractive Industries.[4]

But how do presumably intelligent people like Farage in the UK, LePen in France (father and daughter) or Trump in USA live with themselves? They expound a populist message that immigration must be stopped immediately since they argue (mistakenly) that their own country values are being destroyed. Racist values are not being destroyed and this distresses me greatly as so many who read this will, I am sure, agree. It annoys me deeply that articulate people preach a racist story solely so that they may become elected and presumably implement more closed borders.

The war on immigrants and refugees is probably one of the most disgusting habits we have in the world today. For instance, Madame Le Pen in France, do you think that the quality of French wine has not kept up with the rest of the wine producers around the world? Le Pen answer: Stop immigration! Mr Obama? There are many born-to-immigrant kids in the USA who are undocumented, what to do? Chapeau Mr Obama who announces 'I have signed an executive order to give them legal papers'. But the Republican Party: Stop immigration.

Farage makes no bones about the fact that he believes immigration is the reason behind all of societies' problems. For instance, speaking to BBC's Sunday Politics Wales, Farage stated:[5] 'It took me six hours to get here – it should have taken three-and-a-half to four. That is nothing to do with professionalism, what it does have to do with is a population that is going through the roof chiefly because of open-door immigration and the fact that the M4 is not as navigable as it used to be.'

Farage, Le Pen, and others of their ilk blame everything on immigrants. What really annoys me is that these people are articulate and intelligent but they use their skills to get elected on total rubbish that they don't even believe deep down!

Happily and as a Swiss resident, there is something to be proud of as elsewhere European racism rises. On 30 November 2014, in a nationwide referendum, voters in Switzerland decisively rejected a proposal to cut net immigration to no more than 0.2 per cent of the population. The country's 26 cantons rejected the proposal, with about 74 per cent of people voting no.[6] Around 25 per cent of Swiss residents are foreign born.

---

4. https://www.international-alert.org/sites/default/files/publications/conflict_sensitive_business_practice_all.pdf, March 2005.
5. https://www.bbc.com/news/uk-wales-politics-30370570, accessed November 2020.
6. https://www.bbc.com/news/world-europe-30267042, accessed November 2020.

I am proud to say that I am a Swiss immigrant – presumably Le Pen, Farage and others of their ilk wouldn't welcome me!

So where next? I think we all agree that our economies must have a private sector. We know that we cannot regulate everything. Thus, social responsibility of our industries is key for the future. For instance, when former UN secretary general Kofi Annan launched the UN-backed PRI (Principles for Responsible Investment) on 27 April 2006, during the iconic opening bell ceremony at the New York Stock Exchange (NYSE), he was joined by executives from 11 institutions representing $4 trillion in assets. These founding PRI signatories understood that global threats being addressed by the UN – such as climate change, resource depletion, ecosystem destruction and water scarcity – also have the potential to threaten their own investment returns. For these globally significant investors, the challenge is to make investments that do not, over time, undermine the value of their entire portfolio.

Concluding Remarks

International Alert has been very active in Corporate Responsibility and Peace-Building and in a paper commissioned by the Conflict Prevention and Reconstruction (CPR) Unit of International Alert provided an interesting conclusion which reflects at least some of what has been discussed in the preceding paragraphs. They stated[7]: 'Like development projects, international companies may contribute to either peace or war, but on their own will serve neither as the sole source of conflict nor the sole remedy. The most important questions are how to minimize the risk of causing harm, and how to maximize the social benefits of their activities'.

So, as noted in this book, the corporate social responsibility of companies will increase as will their energy in working with Governments to reduce big issues such as conflict. How? Five suggestions:

1. Work with the UN as a partner to reduce conflict by funding peaceful activities such as education. (As far ago as 2002, the UN Compact published its Business Guide to Conflict Impact Assessment and Risk Management in Zones of Conflict.)
2. Use their knowledge to work with governments to develop appropriate skills of the youth.
3. Weapons manufacturers to work on fail-safe mechanisms to make their weapons harmless once their dirty deed is done.
4. Military, security and attack (defence?) industries to publish social reports that encompass all stakeholders.
5. Companies to work with government to increase transparency of their security measures (e.g. drones).

---

7. https://www.international-alert.org/sites/default/files/publications/conflict_sensitive_business_practice_all.pdf, March 2005.

Chapter Eleven

NATIONAL SOCIAL RESPONSIBILITY INDEX (NSRI)

Introduction

Can a country as a whole be judged on its National Social Responsibility (NSR)? In this chapter, I both define and measure a simple index which I then apply to most of the countries in the world for which I have data – around 180 countries – and compare over time since 2009, the date when I first created the index.[1] Depressingly, many, if not most, countries lack social responsibility. The key stakeholders of any nation-state are their citizens and their trading partners. Conceptually, the index uses freedom, well-being and transparency. Consequently, I define their NSR as follows: *a state that treats its citizens fairly, looks after their well-being and is respectful to foreigners – immigrants as well as their trading partners.*

In the rankings I produced, Norway was at the top for the last year for which data were available, 2019, while Sweden topped in the year 2007.

Conceptual Basis

The NSRI, as well as corporations, illustrates that we can also talk about the social responsibility of nation-states. Following the tradition of the Human Development Index of the UNDP which measures development, the index presented here purports to measure their social responsibilities.

A reviewer pointed out to me that such an index by Skoloudis and Gjoberg[2] already exists that follow a similar methodology to myself. My approach is very simple as seen below. Indeed, the same reviewer pointed out to me an even more recent and ambitious project: a UNDP network of 91 Accelerator Labs supporting 115 countries. The UNDP Accelerator Labs are a new service offering works with people, governments and the private sector to reimagine development for the twenty-first century. Unusually for the UN, and UNDP in particular where I had been one of their senior evaluators, their

---

1. http://www.mhcinternational.com/images/stories/national_social_responsibility_index .pdf, accessed 4 July 2009.
2. Antonis Skouloudis, 'Revisiting the National Corporate Social Responsibility Index', University of the Aegean November 2014, Online at https://mpra.ub.uni-muenchen.de /64864/, MPRA Paper No. 64864, posted 9 June 2015 14:38 UTC, accessed 24 November 2021.

Accelerator approach looks at the private sector and relies in many cases on private sector partnerships for its innovation programmes, setting useful precedents for public–private cooperation in public service.

Corporate social responsibility (CSR) is about corporations treating their stakeholders in a socially responsible manner. Similarly, NSR is about nation-states treating their stakeholders in a socially responsible manner. The key stakeholders of any nation-state are their citizens and their trading partners. Consequently, the NSRI is composed of whether citizens are treated fairly, whether the state looks after their well-being and, economically, whether the curse of corruption is widespread.

To measure these three aspects, I have used measures of the freedom of the country, life expectancy at birth and the transparency of a country's operations. The former uses the Economist Intelligence Unit's Democracy Index[3] which, in turn, is based upon five categories: electoral process and pluralism; civil liberties; the functioning of government; political participation; and political culture. And life expectancy at birth which is the best measure of the level of living, on average, of a nation's well-being is drawn from the 2007 and 2019 UNDP Human Development Report.[4] The third indicator used is the nation's transparency and uses Transparency International's Corruption Perception Index.[5]

To a certain extent, one might believe that one is closely related to the other. However, there is nothing, in particular, that would say that freedom would lead to high living standards or that transparency (lack of corruption) means that a society is fair – in fact the intercorrelations between each of the variables is around 0.65 – suggesting that none of the individual variables selected depend very much on any of the others – of course +1 means high correlation, while -1 would mean high but totally reverse or negative correlation. For instance, 0.57 between life expectancy and the democracy index shows that only 57 per cent of a long life can be explained, in simple words, by democracy.

To obtain the final index, following the UNDP's HDI, each variable was scaled between 0 and 1 using the minimum and maximum values in each index and then added up and divided by 3, i.e. the weighting given in the final composite index to each individual index was equivalent.

I have also examined whether those countries who perform well on the NSRI have also done well on COVID-19 prevention. The COVID Safety Index comes from DKG (Deep Knowledge Group).[6] Their analysis utilizes 130 quantitative and qualitative parameters, grouped into 30 indicators and 6 top-level categories (quarantine efficiency, government efficiency of risk management, monitoring and detection, health readiness, regional resilience and emergency preparedness), applied to 200 regions and utilizing 11,400 data points in total to create a composite index capable of comprehensively ana-

3. http://www.economist.com/media/pdf/Democracy_Index_2007_v3.pdf, accessed 1 August 2008.
4. http://hdrstats.undp.org/indicators/2.html, accessed 1 August 2008.
5. http://www.transparency.org/policy_research/surveys_indices/cpi/2007, accessed 1 August 2008.
6. www.dkv.global/covid-safety-assesment-200-regions

lysing the health, societal and economic status of each region in terms of their absolute and relative stability, safety and risk.

Results

As might be expected, of the 180 countries for which data were available,[7] the richer countries dominate the leading positions, with Norway in the year 2019 and Sweden in the year 2007 being at No. 1, closely followed by Iceland and Denmark. The bastions of democracy came further down the list than one might expect with the UK at the 14th position in both years – its civil liberties have been hard hit in recent years because of its over-the-top intrusive behaviour as a response to terrorism as has the USA with a position at No. 21, falling to 24 in 2019 – probably when all new data are in for 2020, the USA will suffer further falls. The rising economic powerhouses, the BRIC group of countries (Brazil, Russia, India and China), came 53rd, 119th, 73rd, and 108th, respectively, in 2007. Although Brazil, Russia and China fell sharply by 2019 to 69th, 139th and 127th, respectively, India rose slightly to 68th despite their PM Modi being increasingly authoritarian.

As might have been expected, the list was propped up by the Central African Republic (178th), Zimbabwe (179th) and Somalia (180th) and those ranks barely moved by 2019. Big upward changes occurred for Tunisia, Botswana, Rwanda and South Africa.

Regarding COVID-19, Switzerland came top in its treatments, although the USA, the UK and France were all hit hard by COVID-19 and ranked 58th, 68th and 60th in COVID-19, respectively. This shows that higher COVID-19 is related to lower National Social Responsibility, in general.

France's democracy was especially hurt by the anarchistic 'gilets jaunes' and its population was one of the worst around the world, ironically it probably stems from its population's freedom to ignore government rules, especially on social distancing and facemask wearing. And it clearly shows the French anarchistic behaviour in the face of state interference even when the state is showing strong national responsibility.

Meanwhile, the UK had suffered from a long period of poor investment in its National Health Service and Nursing Homes as NSR fell sharply over the past two decades. Similarly, the USA has also made an awful job of managing health care for poor people coupled with a leadership responsibility that has fallen under its wayward president who tries to weaken National Health Care since it is called Obamacare and then lies when asked what alternative he suggests. Millions suffer and the poor, and even some of the uninsured middle classes, generally have huge medical bills to contend with. Happily, President Biden is working hard to both increase and solidify gains on the health front.

---

7. For those few countries in this list for which data were not available, the author used his 'judgement' to calculate the missing value. This happened in one or more indices for only five of the countries selected.

Finally, as I write these notes from Kenya, it can be seen from Table 11.1 that Kenya is not doing too well. Kenya rose from 146th in the NSR ranking in 2007 to 120 by 2019 as its 2007 political troubles reduced. Yet as a relatively poor country, it was not able to commandeer adequate testing equipment nor hospital beds and so its COVID-19 ranking was even lower than China, at 147th at the time of writing. Showing the double whammy of poor countries that despite many efforts to control COVID-19 (as in Kenya) cope with the lack of resources leading to undercounting of positive cases due to lack of testing (around 3,000 a day in a country of 49 million) coupled with a lack of personal responsibility, especially by men, to wear masks properly. Although figures are not generally available – my own casual empiricism count only one in three wear masks properly and even worse in public parks according to this author's figures collected during a morning jog of 30 minutes or so in a middle-class area of Nairobi. While in the countryside, including urban centres, few if any wore masks during 2020 and I wonder if a shock is to come, as I write. I certainly hope I am wrong.

As companies increase their take-up of socially responsible behaviour, we see signs of less national responsibility and increasing lack of personal responsibility. Strong responsible leadership is urgently required, albeit sadly lacking in far too many countries to date. 'One interesting sign on the horizon is that countries led by women do seem to be particularly successful in fighting the coronavirus', noted Anne W. Rimoin,[8] an epidemiologist at UCLA. 'New Zealand, Denmark, Finland, Germany, Iceland, Norway have done so well perhaps due to the leadership and management styles attributed to their female leaders'.

Concluding Remarks

Generally, high NSR leads to better health care and lower COVID-19 infections rates. The Scandinavian countries do well too except Sweden that, like the UK and USA, has seen sharp drops in expenditure on its National Health Service and in care for older people. Its socialist experiment worked but led to an increasing turn to far right politics that has shaken the country today. One major exception has been China from where the COVID-19 virus originated but showed its high ranking of 7th in dealing with COVID-19, which meant that a strong centralized Communist government did better to control COVID-19 than most other countries. China's economy is also recovering rapidly as I write. Does this mean that central planning under communism will be an alternative even though China ranked a low 127th in 2019 which was even worse on NSR than its ranking of 108th in 2007? In the rankings I produced, Norway was at the top for the last year for which data were available, 2019, while Sweden topped in the year 2007 (see Table 11.2).

---

8. Cited by Nicholas Kristof in *New York Times* on 14 July 2020, https://www.nytimes.com/2020/06/13/opinion/sunday/women-leaders-coronavirus.html?action=click&module=Opinion&pgtype=Homepage

ANNEX: NSRI DATA ALONG WITH COVID-19 BY COUNTRY AND RANKINGS

Table 11.1   Country NSRI and COVID Rank

Country	2019	2007	COVID Rank
Norway	1	8	14
New Zealand	2	2	9
Sweden	3	1	5
Finland	4	4	24
Denmark	5	3	15
Switzerland	6	7	1
Iceland	7	2	22
The Netherlands	8	5	19
Canada	9	10	12
Australia	10	9	8
Germany	12	13	2
UK	14	14	68
Japan	16	16	5
France	23	18	60
USA	24	21	58
Hong Kong	26	22	13
Italy	35	30	53
Mauritius	39	40	109
Botswana	41	90	122
Greece	43	36	34
Hungary	54	39	18
Tunisia	55	98	18
Colombia	58	57	150
UAE	64	64	11

(Continued)

Table 11.1 (Continued)

Country	2019	2007	COVID Rank
South Africa	66	81	69
India	68	73	56
Brazil	69	53	91
Ecuador	90	94	74
Mexico	92	51	50
Turkey	99	66	37
Rwanda	104	162	199
Tanzania	107	135	194
Kenya	120	146	147
China	127	108	7
Russia	139	119	61
Venezuela	161	99	184
Somalia	176	180	187
South Sudan	180	158	200
Zimbabwe	159	179	151

Table 11.2 National Responsibility Index Rankings for Complete List of Countries from 2007 to 2019

Change 2019 cf 2007	Country		Country
	2007	2019	
-5	2	7	Iceland
-2	3	5	Denmark
0	4	4	Finland
-3	5	8	The Netherlands
4	6	2	New Zealand
1	7	6	Switzerland
7	8	1	Norway
-1	9	10	Australia
1	10	9	Canada
0	11	11	Luxembourg
-3	12	15	Austria
1	13	12	Germany
0	14	14	UK
2	15	13	Ireland
0	16	16	Japan
-3	17	20	Singapore
-5	18	23	France
-2	19	21	Spain
3	20	17	Belgium
-3	21	24	USA
-4	22	26	Hong Kong
1	23	22	Chile
-1	24	25	Portugal
-6	25	31	Slovenia
-6	26	32	Malta
9	27	18	Uruguay
-1	28	29	Israel
-7	29	36	Barbados
-5	30	35	Italy
-2	31	33	Cyprus
-18	32	50	Costa Rica
14	33	19	Estonia
6	34	28	South Korea
1	35	34	Czech Republic
-7	36	43	Greece

(Continued)

Table 11.2 (Continued)

Change 2019 cf 2007	Country		Country
	2007	2019	
10	37	27	Taiwan
?	38		Dominica
-15	39	54	Hungary
1	40	39	Mauritius
-5	41	46	Slovakia
-6	42	48	Saint Lucia
6	43	37	Lithuania
2	44	42	Latvia
7	45	38	Cape Verde
2	46	44	Poland
-4	47	51	Croatia
3	48	45	Malaysia
-4	49	53	Bulgaria
3	50	47	St Vincent/ Grenadines
-41	51	92	Mexico
-18	52	70	Serbia
-16	53	69	Brazil
-5	54	59	Romania
-1	55	56	Jamaica
56	56		Samoa
-1	57	58	Colombia
-9	58	67	Montenegro
-31	59	90	El Salvador
9	60	51	Argentina
-26	61	87	FYR Macedonia
0	62	62	Trinidad and Tobago
-11	63	74	Qatar
0	64	64	UAE
4	65	61	Panama
-33	66	99	Turkey
-8	67	75	Sri Lanka
0	68	68	Albania
-27	69	96	Bosnia
-9	70	79	Grenada
-50	71	121	Bahrain
12	72	60	Suriname

(*Continued*)

Table 11.2 (Continued)

Change 2019 cf 2007	Country		Country
	2007	2019	
5	73	68	India
3	74	71	Peru
?	75		Macao
-25	76	101	Cuba
-14	77	91	Dominican Republic
48	78	30	Seychelles
-14	79	93	Jordan
?	80		Belize
15	81	66	South Africa
-23	82	105	Kuwait
-30	83	113	Lebanon
-2	84	86	The Philippines
-13	85	98	Ukraine
9	86	77	Thailand
-10	87	97	Moldova
-6	88	94	Oman
-21	89	110	Guatemala
49	90	41	Botswana
-4	91	95	Paraguay
3	92	89	Mongolia
-45	93	138	Nicaragua
4	94	90	Ecuador
38	95	57	Georgia
-10	96	106	Honduras
19	97	78	Indonesia
43	98	55	Tunisia
-62	99	161	Venezuela
-12	100	112	Bolivia
-16	101	117	Maldives
18	102	84	Guyana
15	103	88	Morocco
23	104	81	Armenia
22	105	83	Senegal
41	106	65	Namibia
?	107		Kiribati

(Continued)

Table 11.2 (Continued)

Change 2019 cf 2007	Country		Country
	2007	2019	
-19	108	127	China
?	109		Tonga
34	110	76	Vanuatu
-15	111	126	Egypt
63	112	49	Bhutan
28	113	85	Ghana
41	114	73	Timor-Leste
-8	115	123	Madagascar
7	116	109	Algeria
14	117	103	Bangladesh
38	118	80	Solomon Islands
-20	119	139	Russia
-5	120	125	Viet Nam
7	121	114	Saudi Arabia
14	122	108	Benin
12	123	111	Papua New Guinea
-46	124	170	Syria
-19	125	144	Iran
-30	126	156	Comoros
12	127	115	Kyrgyzstan
-2	128	130	Pakistan
7	129	122	Belarus
-4	130	134	Mali
-33	131	164	Libya
-1	132	133	Kazakhstan
-9	133	142	Azerbaijan
71	134	63	Sao Tome
28	135	107	Tanzania
34	136	102	Nepal
-20	137	157	Laos
-2	138	140	Mauritania
10	139	129	Gambia
-9	140	149	Cambodia
41	141	100	Lesotho
-18	142	160	Tajikistan
-31	143	174	Yemen

(Continued)

Table 11.2 (Continued)

Change 2019 cf 2007	Country		Country
	2007	2019	
13	144	131	Uganda
-1	145	146	Haiti
26	146	120	Kenya
11	147	136	Gabon
16	148	132	Ethiopia
6	149	143	Niger
-8	150	158	Uzbekistan
23	151	128	Burkina Faso
36	152	116	Malawi
-18	153	171	Burundi
-8	154	162	Eritrea
4	155	151	Mozambique
-13	156	169	Turkmenistan
9	157	148	Djibouti
-10	158	168	Sudan
-16	159	175	Congo
41	160	119	Zambia
9	161	152	Togo
58	162	104	Rwanda
0	163	163	Cameroon
40	164	124	Liberia
24	165	141	Myanmar
11	166	155	Nigeria
13	167	154	Guinea
31	168	137	Cote d'Ivoire
22	169	147	Swaziland
5	170	165	Equatorial Guinea
4	171	167	Congo, Republic
37	172	135	Sierra Leone
28	173	145	Iraq
-5	174	179	Chad
3	175	172	Guinea-Bissau
10	176	166	Afghanistan
27	177	150	Angola
0	178	178	Central African Rep
20	179	159	Zimbabwe
4	180	176	Somalia

Chapter Twelve

INTERNATIONAL DEVELOPMENT AND CSR UPDATED

Introduction

I started my book[1] on international development and Corporate Social Responsibility (CSR) with a quote from Mark Moody Stuart, a former CEO of Shell. He insisted at that time that people thought negatively of companies. And as you read here not much has changed today, especially as we read every day about companies that have misspent or stolen land, assets and money over long periods, and then people turn to the company and say, 'You made money, but there is little in the country to show for it.' Stuart argued that 'to protest that we paid our taxes is of no avail. It may not be our responsibility, but it becomes our problem. If we want the sort of functioning society in which we can do business, we need to work with others to create the capacities and conditions which sound governance requires'.

But change has been, and is, certainly in the air and my statement to introduce my book a decade ago sounds a little out of date as I wrote then that if the business of business is business, then why should corporations be involved in development? I continued and further stated that governments and their international arms, the agencies grouped under the umbrella of the United Nations, had failed in their attempts to rid the planet of underdevelopment and poverty. The astounding success of China has, in fact, reduced the levels of poverty globally, although the COVID-19 pandemic is again revealing cracks in the global scene. True that large corporations with their power and economic strength have taken a dominant position in society. They will, as my book then argued, need to take much more responsibility for development than ever before and there I spelled out why development seen through the lens of CSR is a useful tool to promote economic development. In this chapter, I summarize what I see today.

But let me digress a little on the United Nations. It is composed of around 200 nations that meet regularly in its HQ in New York as well as in its agencies around the world, especially in Geneva and Nairobi. The UN has a total budget around the same order as the New York Health Department! A lot is expected, and yes, it is a talking shop but isn't that very useful when the talk is about resolving conflict and guiding development assistance? But the best is the unknown; how many wars and conflicts has the UN and its agencies prevented when government delegates chat with each other informally and

---

1. Michael Hopkins, *CSR and International Development: Is Business the Solution?* (London: Earthscan, 2006).

ignore the formal necessities but listen to the informal coffee discussions where (e.g. the delegate bar in UN HQ) you will catch India talking to China, Afghanistan to Colombia and Venezuela to peaceful Norway, etc.

CSR and Development

However, change is in the air as the need to address questions of low living standards, exploitation, poverty, unemployment and how to promote social development in general, has been to date almost entirely the preserve of governments, and they have failed. Clearly, they will continue to have a, if not the, major role to play, even if arguably unsuccessfully and likely to continue to suffer under the sort of attack by the Reaganite 'starve the beast (of Government)' Tea Party wing of the US Republican Party that continues to this day.

At the technical level, the UN has been active, if not too successful: starting from the post-war New International Economic Order in the 1960s, then the basic needs development approach of the ILO (introduced by myself in the mid-1970s) and subsequently taken up by the World Bank under Mahbub Ul Haq and then transformed into Human Development at UNDP, also by Mahbub Ul Haq working in conjunction with Nobel Laureate Amartya Sen. I attempted to convince the UNDP to write more about the private sector and have an issue of the UN Human Development Report (HDR) on CSR. I was given a fair hearing in the mid-1990s in New York by the HDR team in a meeting next to the UN HQ, but was surpassed in that meeting by a brilliant speech on human rights by another specialist. A glance at the 1995 HDR on Human Rights will show how one person gained and I (and I think they) lost! Hence the UN, and UNDP in particular, has rarely ventured into the private sector until recently. As noted above on the short discussion on the UN Accelerator Labs, significant attention has been drawn to the private sector. I note in passing it was at that time I decided to focus much more on CSR to look at the private sector and their contribution to socio-economic development. After 25 years, this is my fourth book on that subject. I still await a HDR on CSR, although sustainability, mainly the environmental version, has become prominent.

Prompted by Jeffery Sachs of Columbia University, it was decided by the UN to issue specific targets to reach within a given time and, in 2000, at the United Nations Millennium Summit, 189 countries produced the Millennium Declaration and endorsed the Millennium Development Goals (MDGs), agreeing to aid citizens in the poorest countries to improve their lives by the year 2015, by focusing on various global issues, including poverty, AIDS and the utilization of globalization. This was followed by the Sustainable Development Goals (SDGs) as discussed in a previous chapter. However, many governments had not acted on their promises, and the gap between rich and poor continues to widen.

Thus, increasingly in the future, the promotion of social development issues must also be one of partnership between government and private and non-governmental actors and, in particular, the corporate sector. This importance is shown by their size. When companies' turnover is compared (incorrectly as it happens since GDP is sales minus costs) with the GDP of countries, then companies appear to be bigger than countries in terms of income and wealth.

Increasingly, CSR is a powerful tool. Its shape has been defined and redefined, but the main thrust is still the socially responsible treatment of stakeholders. I argued in my development book that corporations were (and still are) more important than the UN in spending on development and the quality is rising. It is a strange phenomenon that as a strategic concept such as CSR gains in weight and prominence, the number of sceptics also rises as I have noted previously in this book.

Yet there is not much doubt that this new millennium has embraced the private sector while, at the same time, bringing increased concerns about its power and lack of democratic control. There are other concerns as well in this new century, terrorism and climate change being the most prominent. Yet these two latter concerns have their roots in exploitation, ignorance and greed. Can CSR also help progress in these great societal challenges? I believe it can but, not as I argue in the chapter on CSR and Philanthropy, that philanthropy (charity) is of course welcomed but it must be sustainable.

Clearly, the business of business is business, so why should corporations be involved in international development? I purposely use the term 'international' development to distinguish between development which can occur anywhere such as developing a high speed rail network in rich countries and international development that touches on poorer countries.

So saying, as international development has to take place and given that the private sector, particularly large corporations with their power and economic strength, has now been given their head, should the private sector take much more responsibility for international development than ever before? In this book, I have shown that the 'big issues' of the day can be addressed by corporations, but in my development book I concentrated on the private sector and international development.

The Meaning of Development

The phrase 'sustainable development' has been used by many in the past few years to emphasize environmental concerns. However, the term 'development' has been under scrutiny for at least half a century, if not more. And the word 'Development' itself is a much aligned term. Until the late 1960s, development was considered by most economists to be the maximization of economic growth. It was only in 1969 that Dudley Seers[2] finally broke the growth fetishism of development theory. Development, he argued, was a social phenomenon that involved more than increasing per capita output. Development meant, in Seers' opinion, eliminating poverty, unemployment and inequality as well. Seers work at the University of Sussex was quickly followed by concerns with structural issues such as dualism, population growth, inequality, urbanization, agricultural transformation, education, health, unemployment, basic needs,

---

2. http://cepa.newschool.edu/het/schools/develop.htm

governance, corruption, etc. and these all began to be reviewed on their own merits, and not merely as appendages to an underlying growth thesis.[3]

Despite Seers vigorous efforts, including the setting up of the influential Institute of Development Studies at the University of Sussex in the 1960s, Governments and their international arms, the international agencies grouped under the umbrella of the United Nations (which also includes the Bretton Wood's Institutions the World Bank, International Monetary Fund and the newest the World Trade Organization) have failed in their attempts to rid the planet of underdevelopment and poverty. After half a century and $1 trillion (1,000 billion) in development aid, more than 2 billion people still live on less than $2 a day. Indeed, some of the poorest economies are going backwards.[4]

Corporations and Development

Can, therefore, corporations step in and take the development of nations further? Certainly, the take up by many private sector companies of the SDGs has surprised this author and there are certainly benefits for them to do so:

1. Reputation is improved since it is built around intangibles such as trust, reliability, quality, consistency, credibility, relationships and transparency, and tangibles such as investment in people, diversity and the environment.
2. Access to finance is greatly improved as socially responsible investment (SRI) becomes more and more important. The creation of new financial indexes is also supporting these trends, for example FTSE4Good and the Dow Jones Sustainability Index (DJSI) are publicly ranking the major international companies according to their environmental and social performance.
3. CSR, of which development is a major issue,[5] is an important factor for employee motivation and attracting, motivating and retaining top-quality employees.
4. Innovation, creativity, intellectual capital and learning are helped by a positive CSR strategy. Given that 80 per cent of the value of many new economy companies is now their intellectual capital, its preservation through the positive treatment of internal stakeholders is becoming more and more necessary.
5. Better risk management can be achieved by in-depth analysis of relations with external stakeholders. Factors such as new technologies and changing societal, regulatory and market expectations drive companies to take a broader perspective when analyzing the range of risks they may encounter.
6. CSR positively helps in the building of relationships with host governments, communities and other stakeholders and can be of vital importance should the company

---

3. See, for instance, the discussion in Michael Hopkins and Rolph Van Der Hoeven, *Basic Needs in Development Planning* (Aldershot: Gower, 1983). Michael Hopkins was also fortunate to have Dudley Seers as his mentor, critical reviewer and best of all, his friend – cuddly Dudley died in 1985, his name lives on but is still sorely missed.
4. Simon Caulkin, *The Observer*, Sunday 13 March 2005.
5. Hopkins, *CSR and International Development*.

encounter future difficulties with regard to its investment decisions. CSR gives a company a 'competitive' advantage over companies with poorer images.

7. Greater CSR is linked to the heightened public debate on the benefits and short-comings of globalization and the perceived role of business in this process. Those companies perceived to be socially responsible are, more and more, those companies of consumer choice.

8. The energy, technology and management skills learned and honed in large companies are increasingly being made available for the management of poverty alleviation through such instruments as the UN's Global Compact, Business in the Community, private and public partnerships, etc.

9. There is a growing consensus of a Planetary Bargain whereby beggar-thy-neighbour policies of companies through using the cheapest labour, the most polluting industries etc. are neither in the interests of the companies concerned nor their consumers.

Of course, there are costs and limitations of the CSR approach and the idealisms behind the approach can also hinder its spread as hard-nosed businessmen try and squeeze every ounce out of cost-cutting and profit maximization. But, as the classic study Built to Last[6] has shown, CSR companies perform better for shareholders in financial and market terms, carry less debt and are long stayers.

The Size and Power of Corporations

Before addressing the issue of corporations and development, it is worth putting the power of corporations into context. Straddling the world, these large companies command immense power and reach – Apple announced in 2020 that it had a market capitalization of $2 trillion. Apple's worth has eclipsed that of other big tech firms such as Microsoft $1.6 trillion and Google parent Alphabet $1 trillion. They've left other corporate giants in the dust. Walmart is valued at $381 billion, JPMorgan Chase $300 billion and ExxonMobil $179 billion. Most major Multi-National Enterprises (MNEs) are domiciled in the First World and are owned and controlled largely by citizens of these countries, although 10 of the world's top 15 companies have their base in the USA. There are Third World MNEs too, although numbers are generally small with only around 30 figuring in the Fortune 500 list of largest companies. Yet some are huge and the world's first company to hit a $2 trillion value was Saudi Aramco, which briefly crossed the threshold in December 2019 on its second day of trading.

These figures mean nothing on their own, of course, but note that the World Bank lent around US$15–20 billion a year in the early 2000s, while the annual budget of oft-cited UN agencies such as the ILO was only $0.25 billion. Either figure is microscopic compared with the power and wealth of the largest corporations.

---

6. James Collins and Jerry Porras, *Built to Last: Successful Habits of Visionary Companies* (Century, London, UK, 1994).

A large portion of world trade – figures vary but some estimates put this at 40–50 per cent – is conducted either within the walls of MNEs or at their behest. Their role in development has only recently been acknowledged since only until relatively recently corporations were thought to have as their main focus the maximization of corporate profits. To date, corporations have been generous in philanthropic giving – witness the large amounts dedicated and raised for the victims of the Asian tsunami. Around US$400 million was donated by corporations in the USA in only a few weeks in early 2005. In the UK, according to the London *Evening Standard*, about US$15 million was contributed by corporations – such as US$3 million from the giant Swiss bank, UBS, which set up a UBS Tsunami Relief Fund to bring together individual contributions from staff and clients worldwide. In fact, the 500 largest global corporations in 2004 took a record $7.5 trillion in revenue and earned $445.6 billion in profit. If MNEs followed governments and contributed even a modest amount on the lines of the 0.3 per cent of net income, this would have allocated $13.37 billion for development.

So size alone shows that MNEs can be a powerful engine for development if, of course, this can be shown to be in their interest and they have the wherewithal to go about development.

However, there is no doubt that nation-states will continue to be the power of last resort. Simply because they have the power to tax and allocate huge resources, they can veto MNEs more than the other way around (in industrialized countries at least) and they can pass laws that MNEs, at best, can only hope to influence but not create and implement.

So size alone shows that MNEs can be a powerful engine for development if, of course, this can be shown to be in their interest and they have the wherewithal to go about development. Well, the attraction of CSR is that it is a systems approach which states that the problem is defined and the systems boundary delineated so that all important influences on resolving the problem are taken into consideration to the issue of business in society. Many of the criticisms, as will be seen, stem from problems with concepts and definitions. Now business, in general, is more concerned to stay in business and be profitable than to be concerned with such seemingly academic discussions. This is unusual, since business is usually a stickler for detail – a company can hardly prepare accounts, sell pharmaceuticals, computer software, copper tubing or whatever without knowing exactly the definition of the product they are selling.

Yet, somehow, management concepts are manipulated at ease to fit in with one preconceived notion or other that will please the chairman or the companies' shareholders. This translates into a confusing set of definitions for the same concept. For instance, some such as myself define CSR as a systems approach taking into account both internal and external stakeholders, while others define it as purely voluntary. This confusion leads to a proliferation of terminology in the business in society area – corporate sustainability, corporate citizenship, corporate responsibility, business responsibility, business social responsibility, business reputation, the ethical corporation and so on. However, without a common language, we don't really know that our dialogue with companies is being heard and interpreted in a consistent way. These flaws lead some companies to consider CSR as purely corporate philanthropy, while others dismiss the notion entirely. But there are some such as Shell, BP-Amoco, Co-operative Bank, etc. that see CSR as a new corporate strategic framework.

As you know by now, the definition I give of CSR, of course, does not link directly into why corporations should be involved in development. Although it does note that the key stakeholders outside of a company – the government, the environment, the community, its customers and suppliers – must be involved as much as its own employees or shareholders. So why should corporations be involved in development?

New Way Is CSR

Given the rise in prominence of CSR, my book asked whether there is now more mileage for corporations to be more involved in development than hitherto? There is more interest from corporations than even a decade or so ago in being involved in SDG development. Although much of this interest to date has been in philanthropy (charitable giving) rather than development per se. Clearly, development is a wider concept than purely philanthropy. Development projects are much more complicated than philanthropic or charitable donations that hand over cash directly for a school or hospital however welcome these seem to be. Development means working with local partners as well as the public institutions to create sustainable projects. Much of development, and probably the most effective albeit unsung, is purely creating capacity since the best development projects are those which help people to help themselves.

Clearly, corporations are not experts in 'development' and tend to make many of the mistakes that were made in the post–Second World War crusade against underdevelopment by aid agencies. Stories are legion of companies providing direct grants to projects that are unsustainable or simply allow host governments to feather the nests of the most corrupt among them. For instance, Coca Cola funded a hospital in Mozambique, which was beautiful, modern, equipped with latest equipment, etc. When Coca Cola executives returned to the site a few months later, the hospital was being used as housing for the many homeless people and much of the equipment had been 'sold'.

Moreover, given the power and size of corporations, and the private sector, in general, coupled with the failure of public institutions, corporations must be involved in development. Clearly, to move the case forward, large corporations must also see that there is a business case to be involved in development. The business case for MNEs to be involved in CSR has been made. But involved in development too?

But Why Corporations and Development?

The key issue for corporations is why should they be interested in development as defined above? A sub-issue is if development is so important for companies, why go the CSR route? Above I listed nine benefits. Certainly an impetus has been given to such involvement by the embrace of the SDGs.

Thus one may well ask what are the main actions that corporations could take to enhance corporate social development following the SDGs?

There are both actions within the MNE itself touching its internal stakeholders and actions outside of the MNE reaching towards its external stakeholders. Most, if not all, of the MNE's actions affect development in some way. Some more than others, of course. For instance, good governance of a company written and applied in a code of conduct for boards of directors will impact on development more marginally than direct community-level interventions. Although, clearly, a company policy at board level to assist development would be no bad thing.

An MNE looking at its involvement in development could approach the issue in one or more of three main ways. It could:

Simply say that it is focusing on profit maximization for its shareholders and claim that development is none of its business.
Work on a partial approach such as with the UN Global Compact and support that process.
Engage fully with its stakeholders and explore options for furthering development efforts while ensuring that the actions it takes are fully in line with preserving shareholder value.

The argument in this book is that the third approach is in the long-term interest of MNEs and, of course, is crucial for development to move faster than it has to date.

So, what could the key areas of MNE involvement in development be? This is looked at next.

Development Actions inside the Company

The adoption of a fully-fledged approach to CSR within a company has a number of benefits. The demonstration effect of good internal CSR policies should not be forgotten even though these are indirect and hard to measure. CSR policies inside a company can be a lightning rod for other companies both in the location where the MNE is based and its overseas locations. CSR also makes good business sense in multifarious ways. For instance, consumers develop a higher degree of identification with companies having good policies and practices.

Companies which maintain environmental and health standards; propagate transparent business practices; protect human rights at the workplace; and work against corruption are widely respected and appear as more attractive to shareholders, reduce the possibility of industrial action and maintain a working environment that leads to higher worker productivity.

A strong anti-corruption culture needs to be built within the organization through active support from the senior management. Today, anti-corruption is widely discussed both inside companies and in their dealings with the outside world. Companies, too, see the overwhelming advantages of good governance in the countries where they work overseas and, in particular, the advantages of working with a government that is implementing anti-corruption policies. Much corruption occurs between external sources of finance and the host government. Thus, it takes two to tango on the anti-corruption front. The line between corruption and accepting small gifts or hospitality is sometimes blurred. On the larger stage, many companies are almost forced to pay bribes of kickbacks to win contracts. And this is not only the case in developing countries; industrialized countries have also not been blameless as we know with the Enron scandal, the Credit Lyonnais scandal affecting top government officials in France, Volkswagen in Germany and so on. Even a single dubious payment can come back and haunt a company down the line. Just like payments to blackmailers once started the web of deceit and intrigue can be hard to break. Thus, each company should have a set of guidelines and business principles which must be followed by all staff. This code of conduct needs to be followed at all national and international offices which the company may have. Local business practices and culture must not influence or change the organization guidelines. The system of internal communication and training has to be strengthened to keep all staff aware of the policies and principles.

Create a vision statement on how the MNE can (and does) assist in development. This does not mean simply listing a number of philanthropic activities that the company intends to carry out. Development requires careful thought on how, once an injection of funds has been made, development initiatives can be sustainable, i.e. continue without the requirement for additional funds. Too often, company development initiatives have been dominated by generic global initiatives that are not tailored to suit specific circumstances.

Development Actions Outside the Company

Private Sector Participation for Poverty Alleviation: There is not an awful lot a company can do to reduce national poverty itself. However, working with National Governments to work out how best the private sector can stimulate economic growth for poor people is in the interest of both the government and the company. In addition, public–private partnerships for tackling man-made or natural disasters can also speed up reconstruction activities.

Improving people's skills in a myriad of ways is undoubtedly the best way to create development. Education, training, skill development and capacity development are all aspects of the same issue – improving human skills. MNEs with their wealth of experience in in-house training have an enormous amount to contribute. At minimum, MNEs could be involved in national training policy to ensure the private sector needs are incorporated in government training plans. It may be surprising to some, but many government training schemes in developing countries have little contact with private sector needs. MNEs can also set up, perhaps in partnership with others, courses and organizations to create sorely needed skills.

Small- and medium-sized enterprises (SMEs) are where most new employment occurs in developing countries. MNEs have a role to play either directly, through assisting SMEs to improve their management, marketing, technological and financial skills, or indirectly through ensuring that SMEs as suppliers are not subject to complex contractual paperwork and, once hired, are paid rapidly.

Helping people to help themselves is a key mantra to encourage development. Assisting budding entrepreneurs, or even existing ones through mentoring can help launch new businesses, improve existing ones or even assist government departments to improve their efficiency.

Essential, of course, is to invest in emerging market and developing countries and work towards allowing their exports to be freely imported into the rich countries – a huge and controversial issue that will play out for many decades to come. Will not these new imports hurt local markets in industrialized countries where the MNEs are located and many of their staff? Again, an issue that is being discussed vigorously in the development literature right now. The author's view is that the rich countries will innovate quicker than the LDCs simply because of their higher level of skills and continue to move into brain-intensive knowledge industries. As the LDCs start to move into these markets too, the economic growth that is being created will allow room for many and there is no particular reason for unemployment to rise drastically, but that is another story.

To many, CSR is simply working with the local community. Clearly, improving local conditions is in the interest of MNEs to enhance reputation and preserve harmony. Assistance to local communities can also help to improve purchasing power that leads to an expansion in the market size. But these actions are not as easy as they seem on the surface. Three questions not easily answered are as follows: Where does the role of the MNE start and stop vis-à-vis the local community? What are the key issues to be involved in? Should MNEs be involved in human rights and, if so as many think, what are the limits?

Philanthropy has always been a big part of MNEs' actions in LDCs. But few philanthropic actions are sustainable – not to be confused with environmental sustainability – in the sense of once the project has finished, will the project and its related activities continue? I look in detail at this issue in Chapter 18.

Development assistance is key in many countries. This would best be done with existing development agencies such as the UNDP who have vast experience in development. Clearly, MNEs should not replace the UN nor government's own efforts. Simply, the power and wealth of MNEs need to be harnessed in positive development efforts. Should these efforts be in addition to the taxes that MNEs pay anyway? There is no easy answer. But many taxes that MNEs pay in developing countries are misused. A democratic government will tend to use tax revenue in ways that benefit its electorate so as to ensure re-election next time around. Yet most governments in developing countries are not democratic. So should MNEs be involved in those countries and, if so, what should they do exactly? Firstly, MNEs should evaluate their position based on existing relations with the government. Clearly, if a host government simply says how we use your taxes is none of your business, then the MNEs can decide whether to stay or leave. Secondly, where possible, the MNEs can, at least, assist the government in ensuring that tax revenue is used effectively to promote development. MNEs have vast experience in tax issues and could well lend some of this experience to develop capacity (better governance) within government (note the discussion on taxation in Chapter 8). Thirdly, when MNEs carry out their own development projects, these should draw upon the development experience available in NGOs and local UN offices such as the UNDP. Fourthly, MNEs are not the government and obviously cannot, or should not, carry out the major programmes of the government such as education, health, security or employment systems. But MNEs can be involved as an agent of positive change through lending their expertise to improving efficiency in government programme delivery. Fifthly, if more than one MNE is involved in a developing country, they should work together to ensure increased efficiency of development programmes in the host country.

But how much will all this cost? How much of its time and money should a MNE invest in any of the above-mentioned activities? There is no easy answer to this question. It is worth bearing in mind, however, that a MNE is involved in many of the above-mentioned processes as much as by default than a clearly thought-out strategy. A MNE has to be continually involved with the host government negotiating all sorts of deals from land acquisition to taxation to import and export. Often these discussions will influence government policy and changes will be made. So what I am suggesting here, at least as a first step, is to place the myriad of discussions with government in an overall development framework. The more the transparency, the better, since the MNE will then be seen to be working in the country's best interest rather than colluding in smoke-filled darkened rooms. Thus, the MNE strategy in any particular country could be framed with a clear idea as to the benefits and costs of its intervention in terms of its own bottom line and also in terms of its benefit to development.

In a nutshell, what could a 10-point programme for MNEs involved in developing countries (and about all MNEs involved either directly or indirectly) be?

CSR 10-Point Strategy for Companies

Inside the company

1. Develop a CSR strategy that includes an overall vision for the company's place in development. Decide what benefits and costs emanate from involvement in international initiatives such as the UN Global Compact, SA8000, ISO9000, Fair Trade, ISO26000, GRI, IIRC, etc.
2. Investigate whether the company is paying a 'living wage' within the company and that it is paying its main suppliers properly and on time. If not, why not, and then ask what steps should be taken to move towards this.
3. Work with trade unions to ensure proper environmental and safety regimes within the company.
4. Monitor and evaluate the company's anti-corruption policy on a regular basis.

Outside the company

5. Work with the government in host country to see how the government's anti-policy can be enhanced. Work with local UN and NGO to increase efficiency of development initiatives, including ensuring its tax contributions are used wisely.

6. Be proactive in lending in-house training skills to a wider public.
7. Assist the creation and improvement of SMEs through the setting up of an advisory office and/or joining with other private sector or NGO partners.
8. Be involved in mentoring budding entrepreneurs.
9. Invest so as to support wider development objectives of host country.
10. Ensure community or philanthropic company initiatives are sustainable in the development sense.

Example from Emerging Market Economies

India and CSR

India has made some initial steps in including CSR in its government framework. It is, at the time of writing, not clear exactly how it will influence companies, but it is important to include as it shows that CSR has moved out of the mainly academic and business area as in the past, but now into government responsibility. India is not alone and other countries, such as Mauritius and Denmark, have worked on legal frameworks. India insists that its framework is essentially voluntary, while Mauritius has insisted on 1 per cent of company profits to be allocated to 'CSR projects'. Companies have, of course, reacted in Mauritius negatively against such a law. In India, a legislative provision on CSR was embedded in a new company law and passed by Parliament passed in August 2013.

The Indian law requires companies with a net worth of over Rs. 500 crore (US$80 million), turnover of over Rs 1,000 crore (US$160 million) or net profit of more than Rs. 5 crore ($0.8 million) to spend at least 2 per cent of the average net profit in the immediate three preceding years on CSR activity. However, it isn't mandatory, and apparently boards of the companies will only have to report how much they spent on CSR and explain why they couldn't meet the commitment. The government will not, it seems, even ask them to amplify on that explanation.

Another main provision, and seemingly to come closer to the CSR model of this book, is that companies will have to set up a CSR committee at the board level that must be headed by an independent director on the board. The committee will frame a CSR policy for the company or group and recommend expenditure on various projects. It will also monitor the CSR policy of the company from time to time.

The company will have to provide information on their CSR policy and the attendant spending on the website and in the directors' report, putting all the relevant information in the public domain that can be accessed by the company's shareholder, the media and social activists.

The idea is not to regulate too much which is why the entire principle of CSR has been encapsulated in just one section – Section 135 of the Companies Act 2013 – with five subsections. It is expected that there won't be more than 12–14 rules that are currently under formulation.

The Act encourages companies to spend at least 2 per cent of their average net profit in the previous three years on CSR activities. The ministry's draft rules, that have been put up for public comment, define net profit as the profit before tax as per the books of accounts, excluding profits arising from branches outside India. The Act lists out a set of activities eligible under CSR. Companies may implement these activities taking into account the local conditions after seeking board approval. The indicative activities which can be undertaken by a company under CSR have been specified under Schedule VII of the Act.

Azerbaijan

Azerbaijan is again, unfortunately, in the news as war breaks out again in Nagorno-Karabash and is a country I know well having worked there on and off since 1991. Oil has been the backbone of the Azerbaijan economy since the beginning of the nineteenth century and since the mid-1990s it has become even more important, thanks to huge discoveries of oil and gas in the adjoining Caspian Sea. My main contribution to Azerbaijan development was insisting on turning black gold into human gold which led to an important project that I led with UNDP, and the phrase also caught on becoming UNDP's byline and even used frequently by the current President Aliyev.

BP approach to CSR in Azerbaijan was very helpful in the construction of the Baku to Ceyhan pipeline. Not without controversy, but BP's approach to working with a key stakeholder – the communities adjacent to the pipeline's route – was helpful. It claimed to have spent US$100 million on Corporate Social Investment (CSI – CSR projects were once known as Corporate Social Investment) projects for communities in Azerbaijan, Georgia and Turkey.

As Lord Browne, the former CEO of BP, once stated: I believe that our long-term future depends on our environmental and social performance. Excellence in operational performance generates financial returns, but enduring growth depends on something more – on being a responsible citizen in the world and earning the continuing support of customers, shareholders, local communities and other stakeholders.

To date, Azerbaijan companies, as many others in emerging markets, have focused upon CSI. This is welcome, but it is only a part of an overall CSR strategy. The world's successful and long-lived companies, as the famous book *Built to Last* showed, are those with a clear vision and those that encompass all stakeholders – management, owners, employees, shareholders as well as the external stakeholders customers, suppliers, the environment, and government. These are the reasons that companies such as Coca Cola, IBM, General Electric, Tata and Sony, for instance, have been so successful over a long period of time.

China

China has become very much interested in CSR according to CSR-Europe (a Brussels-based CSR think-tank). Citing Gefei Yin, director and vice-president of China, WTO Tribune and the Development Center for Chinese CSR: 'Despite the impact of the economic crisis, more and more Chinese enterprises are taking steps to integrate corporate social responsibility (CSR) into their business practices', he says. Further, according to a report by the GoldenBee Development Center for Chinese CSR, in 2008 there were in total 169 CSR reports published by Chinese enterprises. While, in 2009, up to mid-2009, the listed companies in Shanghai Stock Exchange and Shenzhen Stock Exchange had already issued more than 330 reports.

Gefei Yin stated that there had been three major achievements in China. Firstly, many enterprises were starting to move forward from a limited view of CSR that focused mainly on looking at responsibility to stakeholders. Using the concept of 'responsible competitiveness', popularized by Simon Zadek, means that enterprises help solve some social problems by using their professional advantages and finally increase their competitiveness.

Secondly, some leading enterprises already integrate CSR into their strategy. For example, Bao Steel has a CSR system, and publishes a Guideline to Implement CSR on which it bases its action. With a comprehensive CSR roadmap, it presents its CSR concept systematically so as to integrate CSR into its daily operations – which responsibilities should be implemented and how to implement them are all clarified and updated accordingly. Although Yin states that 'CSR information disclosure is prominent through the establishment of CSR departments', it is probable that more sensitive issues such as rights, comprehensively treated in most Western companies, are swept under the carpet.

Thirdly, the issue of supply chain management is being addressed given its importance for future exports to discerning foreign consumers. One technique being actively used is CSR-Europe's own web portal that helps Chinese suppliers in improving the capacity of their CSR performance. The portal promotes all the well-known supply chain issues such as health and safety, social dialogue, human rights, corruption, forced labour, child labour, collective bargaining, compensation, freedom of association, discrimination, environment and climate issues, working hours, health and safety. Yet no data exist to see how, or whether, these issues have actually been addressed.

Given the importance of China for international trade and as the holder of around US\$2 trillion of US debt, dealing with errant corporations in China is likely to be handled with kid gloves by Western governments. A hopeful avenue is the reaction of consumers and how long they will tolerate abuses in the supply chain of goods coming from China. Clearly, China would like to avoid such reactions by careful manipulation of instruments such as the CSR portal. On the other hand, the CSR-Europe portal could promote international buyers' capacity to find good Chinese suppliers. At the same time, when they cooperate together, they can boost the build-up of a responsible supply chain. Through a better understanding of the CSR implementation of Chinese suppliers, international buyers can continuously optimize the concept and tools of CSR management in their supply chain.

Iraq

The war on terror, at first sight, seems to be conducted outside the remit of large corporations. And the UN is hardly involved either. Iraq is the major issue of our times and the UN manifestly failed to have much influence. The USA and UK decision to go to war in Iraq started by using the UN and its machinery, but when this failed the invasion and its consequences went ahead anyway. Whatever the merits of the case – and my own view is that the superpowers should have persisted with the UN before the invasion and should also have prepared much better for the aftermath when they actually did go to war – corporations did turn out to be more powerful than the UN. Bob Herbert of the *New York Times* tells us why:

> Dwight Eisenhower, the Republican president who had been the supreme Allied commander in Europe in World War II, and who famously warned us at the end of his second term about the profound danger inherent in the rise of the military-industrial complex. Eisenhower delivered his farewell address to a national television and radio audience in January 1961. 'This conjunction of an immense military establishment and a large arms industry is new in the American experience', he said. He recognized that this development was essential to the defense of the nation. But he warned that 'we must not fail to comprehend its grave implications.

In one of the great deceptive manoeuvres in US history, the military–industrial complex (with George W. Bush and Dick Cheney as chairman and CE.., respectively) took its eye off the real enemy in Afghanistan and launched the pointless but far more remunerative war in Iraq.

The military–industrial complex has become so pervasive that it is now, all but invisible. Its missions and priorities are poorly understood by most Americans, and frequently counter to their interests'.

The chilling words of Herbert provide the background to how some large corporations have become more powerful than democratic institutions, including the UN. In the case of Iraq, this power has obviously not helped development. But it does imply that the more we can hold corporations responsible for their actions, the less likely that large corporations like Halliburton, Boeing, Bechtel or the Carlyle Group can benefit, and influence hugely, our political processes. Halliburton, which had US Vice President Dick Cheney as-one time CEO, built the Guantanamo prison compound for terrorism suspects and donated $709,000 to political campaigns between 1999 and 2002. Bechtel, considered the largest contractor in the world, donated $1.3 million to political campaigns between 1999 and 2002 and is the earlier employer of former defense secretary Caspar Weinberger, former secretary of state George Schultz and former CIA director William Casey. The Carlyle Group had former UK prime minister John Major as Chairman of its European Group until 2004, and he continues to serve as a consultant on energy matters. Perhaps, following the lucrative footsteps of John Major, we shall see how Tony Blair linked to these companies in the future?

Chalmers Johnson had also noted that Eisenhower was overly praised for his concerns. Despite Eisenhower's heroic statement, he was the butcher of Guatemala and the person who authorized the overthrow of Mohammed Mossadegh in Iran in 1953 for the sake of the British Petroleum Company. He also presided over the fantastic growth of the military–industrial complex, of the lunatic oversupply of nuclear weapons and of the empowering of the Air Force. It seems to be only at the end that he realized what a monster he had created.

The UN, of course, also suffered badly in Iraq. Its special representative for Iraq, Sergio Vieira de Mello, was killed when the poorly protected UN HQ in Baghdad was severely bombed in July 2003. The UN continues to be involved, to this day, but its presence is largely based in safer Jordan as its diplomats and civil servants have, for whatever warped reason, become 'legitimate' targets of war.

Could CSR have prevented the Iraq War? Yes. The relations between Halliburton, Boeing, Bechtel, Carlyle and many other corporations in a CSR world would have been intensively examined. Stakeholders would have been held publicly accountable and socially irresponsible actions such as supporting war efforts for personal gain would have been stamped out. Naive? Perhaps. But right now, large corporations are more powerful than the UN, and more powerful than many nation-states.

Concluding Remarks

So, can CSR pave the way for development? The short answer is yes. CSR has paved the way for corporations to examine their wider role in society in ways that have never been done before. CSR is a systems concept that touches every part of a company and has both positive and negative effects. The wide role of CSR coupled with the power and technological capacity of corporations and also with the failure of most development efforts to date provides additional impetus for corporations, and the private sector itself, to be more involved in development than ever before.

Clearly, Governments will be the overall arbiter of development through the public purse. But their failure in many developing countries has provided an empty space that must be filled by another entity, and the only one around is the private sector and its champions, the large corporations. It is relatively easy to argue the obverse that corporations should stick to making profits and leave development for governments. But this is a dance to the death, since the market left to purely profit maximization has been unable to fulfil social roles such as reducing unemployment, creating primary and secondary education for all, tacking the major diseases of the Third World and so on. Only time will tell whether corporations will take on this new challenge, although, as we saw with India, legislation may well creep up upon them if they don't start to act. To a certain extent MNEs will engage in development simply to ward off problems such as rising energy prices, resentment at offshoring, consumer boycotts and the like. But whether they will take on the wider challenge of development and how they will do this if they decide to go forward are still subjects of intense discussion.

The truth is, the real energy in CSR is coming from the business side, not the social side.

Companies are starting to realize that ethics, stakeholder relationships and external conditions affect their competitive position. They realize that the more they build up their internal ethical culture, the more productive and dedicated their employee teams become. The more they actively manage their stakeholder relationships, the more they leverage their business ecosystem. The more they actively engage with their external environment, the more effective their internal resources become.

Over the next few years, I would submit that concepts like 'social capital', 'stakeholder relationship management' and 'sustainable development' are going to become much more mainstream and widespread, and that there will be a transformation in the management of the field.

Take 'social capital' for example. Companies are going to start developing tools to measure their organizational productivity, industry productivity and business productivity. Concepts like 'social friction', 'transaction costs', 'trust building', 'trust substitutes', 'trust brokering' and the like will become more commonplace as companies transition from hierarchical systems to network systems with hubs and nodes. The implications of the information and communication technology (ICT) revolution are going to remake the way people see themselves, their organizations and their ecosystems.

At first blush, stakeholder relationship management (SRM) might seem like a subset of this concept, but SRM is going to be a widely plumbed field in its own right. As we move from three networks to 500 TV channels, 250,000 non-profits to 1.5 million (in the USA alone, not to mention worldwide), and hundreds of millions of voices and perspectives on social media and the other components of the internet, SRM is going to rapidly evolve.

But if social capital management and stakeholder relationship management would seem to place CSR in more of a brand/reputation/marketing/communications/legal continuum, the assistance, recovery and development challenges that we are seeing seem to be pulling CSR in a more strategic planning and operational direction.

CSR practitioners are increasingly having to learn site selection criteria, community design, urban planning, GIS mapping, project cost/benefit analysis, time value of money, critical path theory, systems integration and a host of other disciplines to help them determine the context and the value of their social investments.

What used to be simply an exercise in charity is increasingly becoming a discipline for determining where businesses operate, how they operate and why they do what they do as opposed to other alternatives. As these disciplines take hold, expect the field of corporate citizenship to transition rapidly.

In Chapter 18 on philanthropy, I shall look at a few specific development case studies and suggest a quick methodology on how to evaluate their effectiveness. The case studies have been drawn from this author's actual experience with a large multinational corporation.

Chapter Thirteen

DO THE MEDIA INCITE TERRORIST AND MILITARIZATION OUTRAGES: WOULD MORE SOCIAL RESPONSIBILITY HELP?

Introduction

The terrorism of today had its roots in the exploitation of societies in the past. I am not an apologist for terrorism. There is no way any sane person can tolerate the destruction of people's lives through indiscriminate acts. As Thomas Friedman wrote in the *New York Times* nearly a decade ago: 'a suicide attacker disguised as a health worker blew himself up near a crowd of about 150 people who had gathered for a ribbon-cutting ceremony to open an emergency ward at the main government hospital in the city of Khost. A few days later, at a Baghdad college, a female suicide bomber blew herself up amid students who were ready to sit for exams, killing 40 people'. Could CSR have helped prevent any of this? This is demanding a lot but, turning back the clock a little, there are two important occurrences that illustrate what happens when CSR is not practised.

London Bridge Borough Market Terror

Cordoned off in a group near the London terrorist murders, I interviewed a posse of personalities of the main TV channels, namely CNBC, CNN, ARD, ITV, Sky, BBC, Al Jazeera, RAI and France 24. I had travelled there by coincidence the morning after from Cardiff where I had witnessed the UEFA European Final as part of my contribution to the CSR RESPECT activities of UEFA.

To each I asked 'Do you think that your live broadcasts actually contribute to terrorist acts because you give the terrorists what they want which is publicity?' They were there to report live on the terrorist act the night before on 3 June 2017, where 11 people died, including the 3 perpetrators, at London Bridge and Borough Market. The response of the journalists was unanimously, 'we report to give the public what they want – so they may be informed'.

But, I asked, don't you think you are given the terrorists what they want – i.e. oxygen for their outrages?

We must report, they all insisted. Otherwise, we are not doing our job. They then threw their hands in the air and said they didn't want to be censored. Further, social media and the internet send out the stories quicker than they must provide live pictures of the event location even though there is basically nothing to see.

My suggestion was that they should only report once the outrage is over and all the facts are in, and not for all channels to blanket the airwaves for days on end, thereby giving the terrorists what they want – publicity and oxygen for their despicable acts.

There was some sympathy for my view but none, with the exception of CNBC, suggested action.

My further suggestion is that the news channels should come together, under their CSR, to voluntarily *not* report on terrorist outrages until a reasonable time has passed.

There were *no* takers. The media *must* do more, they were there for at least three weeks more after my own reporting on now long-passed events. Who gains? Unfortunately, the slain terrorists who knew they would occupy the front pages for days. And soon, no doubt and certainly not to my liking, will come copycat murders.

Alternative Terrorist Philosophies

The Koran is much more similar to the Christian Bible than most people realize. Specifically, the Koran *very* clearly states that suicide, under *any* conditions, is banned and a terrible sin. An example is in Sura 3, Imran's Family (3.139), 'It is not for any soul to die, save by God's permission written down for an appointed time'.

The curse of Islamic terrorism *does* have a cure. There are two main reasons that terrorists act without fear – paradise and publicity. Coupled with those may be added some form of hope for prosperity for them and their families who are, in general, impoverished.

Paradise

It is inconceivable to believe that murdering innocent civilians of whatever faith and then killing oneself gives one the right to enter paradise. No religion was ever created to provide shelter and respite for murderers, thugs and villains. In fact, *hell* is most certainly the endpoint for all those past and, unfortunately, future persons who commit outrages. I simply do not understand how, if you kill someone at total random, this qualifies you for paradise. We in civilized society (and that exists in 99% of *all* countries in the world) must make such unfortunates aware that, if they believe in biblical texts, then the logical conclusion of their self-inflicted death is perpetuity in *hell*.

I urge governments, religious leaders and, indeed, most people in the world who wish to lead a civilized and socially responsible life to make the above message as clear as is possible in their writings, speeches, sermons, social media texts and in their family circles.

Publicity

I am a supporter of the freedom of the press, but also human rights. I do not propose legislation but I propose, as noted above, the major news outlets get together (press, TV, social media) and come up with a socially responsible code of practice. We cannot continue with the notion of the public's right to know. Know what? How many people have been uselessly killed? No. I see a world where the attention is passed not to the above but to my proposition.

Arguably, many murderers carry out their acts mainly for publicity of some evil cause but also for the money that may be passed to their impoverished families. In fact, the result of their actions to date has been to increase the impoverishment of their families. Their own reward they believe misguidedly and selfishly is paradise.

Clearly, that money should be traced and halted. Better still would be to use that money to reduce the yawning and growing inequalities in the world. Most importantly, there must be an international fund that will pay a basic income to every young unemployed person to pursue education and skill training. That income must be conditional (and paid by electronic means to prevent fraud and corruption such as M-PESA) on attendance at an educational institution that specializes in giving youth the skills they need while giving them some money that can be used by their families to survive.

Spreading money in this way right across the world would create enough effective demand through building schools, alternative energy systems, planting food crops, mending houses, repairing roads etc. at a basic level – and then one can progress to higher and higher levels as well but that is another, and more expensive, story.

A calculation: the ILO finds that there are 73 million unemployed youth aged 15–24. Let's say 100 million and say we pay each one the sum of US$50 (what reportedly Al Shabaab pays their own murderers) for attending school and learning basic skills for six months which would lead to an annual sum of US$150 billion or only one quarter of the US annual 'defense' budget.

Let's start tomorrow on all of the above!

Role of the Death Trade Companies

I firmly believe that Corporate Responsibility is part of the everyday management of a responsible business and I expect all our employees to make it an integral part of all that they do – Mike Turner, CEO, BAE Systems, http://www.baesystems.com/CorporateResponsibility/

Can CSR contribute to reducing the spiralling military–industrial complex (MIC)? Yes, I think it can as I argue in the following section.

The problem

As noted above, the MIC dominates the main democracies' social, economic and environmental policies. The late Kenneth Galbraith wrote: 'Defence and weapons development are motivating forces in foreign policy. For some years, there has also been recognised corporate control of the Treasury. And of environmental policy.'

Anthony Sampson's famous book *The Arms Bazaar* (Bantam Books, New York, 1978) detailed the history of international arms merchants. Beginning with founders like Nobel and Krupp, Sampson worked forward through the post-war MIC to our contemporaries who have turned Lebanon (and now Bosnia) into arms marts and weapons laboratories. Along the way, Sampson detailed the subterfuge, bribery and power politics that inevitably shadow the arms trade. Sampson emphasized the difficulties of controlling this industry and noted that 'the ordinary citizen is right to lump the arms trade in with the slave trade, and be appalled at both'.

In my book *CSR and International Development* (Earthscan, London, 2006), I argued that the more we can hold corporations responsible for their actions, the less likely that large corporations like Halliburton, Bechtel or the Carlyle Group can benefit, and influence hugely, our political processes. Halliburton, which had US vice-president, Dick Cheney as one-time CEO, built the Guantanamo prison compound for terrorism suspects and donated $709,000 to political campaigns between 1999 and 2002. Bechtel, considered the largest contractor in the world, donated $1.3 million to political campaigns between 1999 and 2002 and is the earlier employer of former defense secretary Caspar Weinberger, former secretary of state George Schultz and former CIA director William Casey. The Carlyle Group had former UK prime minister John Major as Chairman of its European Group until 2004, and he served for many years as a consultant on energy matters.

The problem is the vicious circle whereby increased arms sales lead to increased wealth for the producers and, consequently, political power, leading to a thirst for war. Would the wars in Vietnam, Iraq, Afghanistan, Syria and Yemen have escalated so rapidly in the absence of the arms industry? Almost certainly not!

Closely related is the penchant for any bureaucracy to feed upon itself. Promotion in the armed forces depends on strictly observing the internal rules and following the leader unquestionably. Clearly, promotion is helped when an agency grows in size as invariably happens when war breaks out. Many believe it is not a coincidence that the war on terror was so aptly named. I do not believe in the conspiracy theory that 9/11 was aided and abetted by the military, although many in the military undoubtedly prospered because of it. Moreover, it is clear that the armed forces, and the companies that support them, are not reluctant to go to war and hence the need for close, and independent, democratic control. In the USA, the brain behind its foreign policy is the State Department with the brawn being in the Pentagon and relations have rarely been good between the two entities.

Not cheap either

None of the above comes on the cheap. Annually, around half the total US government discretionary expenditure was used for military purposes. Some sources believe that the overall expenditure of the misguided Iraq War will eventually end up at one trillion dollars (US$1000 billion) – note the US contribution to the UN is only around US$3 billion! What this means in foregone health care and educational services, not to say the loss to the reputation of the USA is incalculable.

We know that war in Africa has just about eaten up all foreign assistance and is a major factor behind the lack of development almost right across the continent – see BBC, 11 October, 2007 Wars in Africa wipe out aid gains. Can we again blame the MIC? Or is it just a case of there is a demand and someone has to fill it?

We know that not only is the USA the largest spender on the military but is also the leading arms supplier to the developing world with sales of US$10.3 billion as far back as 2006 followed by Russia (US$8.1 billion) and Britain (US$3.1 billion). The largest buyers were Pakistan (US$5.1 billion), India ($US3.5 billion), Saudi Arabia (US$3.2 billion) and Venezuela (US$3.1 billion). One might ask why a socialist president in Venezuela with no major armed or guerrilla conflict in his country chose to be so arms conscious? One might also ask why the arms that are sold continue to kill and maim long after their sell–buy date? Why can't landmines self-defuse after a period? Why does armour-piercing munition have to include nuclear material with a half-life of thousands of years?

The trade is not cheap in reputation either. Tony Blair, former UK prime minister, fell into its trap shortly before leaving office. At the time, Blair announced that an investigation by the Serious Fraud Office (SFO) into the circumstances of a major al-Yamamah arms deal agreed by the leading aerospace company British Aerospace (BAe) with Saudi Arabia in 1996 – which had long been surrounded by allegations of bribery – was being 'discontinued'. It was, he said, a tough decision, but one he had to take in the 'national interest'. The cancellation was designed to protect a subsequent, £10 billion agreement secured by BAe with Saudi Arabia for 72 Eurofighter jets. The Saudis had, it appeared, threatened to withdraw from the deal because of the SFO investigation.

The evolving, entangled story goes way beyond Britain, as Chris Floyd wrote: 'Slush funds, oil sheiks, prostitutes, Swiss banks, kickbacks, blackmail, bagmen, arms deals, war plans, climbdowns, big lies and Dick Cheney – it's a scandal that has it all, corruption and cowardice at the highest levels' (see 'War profits trump the rule of law', *Baltimore Sun*, 22 December 2006).

One may ask why is it that the arms trade has become so important to countries such as the UK which, otherwise, portray themselves as paragons of virtue in a corrupt world? Could not the UK live without the arms trade and develop alternative uses for its cutting-edge scientific expertise – global warming, for instance?

Is the defence industry capable of CSR?

There were some promising signs. For instance, the 2006 Corporate Responsibility Report of BAE Systems, part, as they state, 'of the everyday management of a responsible business'. Or is it a cynical strategy to gloss over the very unpleasant aspects of their trade? Certainly, BAEs 2006 report was a very professionally produced document that covered all the issues that a CSR report might be expected to contain.

But, following Charlton Heston, President of the National Rifle Association at the time of Michael Moore's brilliant documentary 'Bowling for Columbine', BAE seems to have a similar position to Heston who believes it is people that kill people not guns! BAE states in its CR report that 'Human nature creates conflict, not the defence industry'. There is not much doubt that the easy availability of guns in the USA leads to more injuries and deaths than in countries where arms are better controlled – 50 people were killed in 2005–2006 by guns in the UK, compared with the US figure for 2004 of 10,654, i.e. 200 times as many in a population, only five times as large! A similar conjecture applied to the arms trade would mean no arms, less conflict!

This brings me to another point. Given human vices – smoking is another area – should companies that cater to them, and make good profits, be banned? Or, should we accept such industries and work with them at least to be as socially responsible as possible? I take the latter stance, while being aware that a company is certainly not homogeneous, i.e. the CSR people in a company might just be accused of whitewashing while the real work gets done by the real believers. BAE wrote: 'We are proud to be part of the defence industry and see our role as providing national security and protection for sovereign governments while delivering to our investors. We recognise the serious nature of our business and know that we must operate at the highest level of responsibility.'

But maybe not all is gloom and doom as a report from the USA shows – Gov. Arnold Schwarzenegger signed a law that would require new semiautomatic handguns sold in the state to be equipped, starting in 2010, with microstamping technology, which imprints identifying markers on bullets as a weapon fires. With this technology, police can match bullet casings found at a crime scene to the gun that shot them. The potential benefit for crime-solving is enormous. In signing it, Mr. Schwarzenegger bucked not just his own party, but also the National Rifle Association which, true to form, waged an intense lobbying campaign urging a veto!

Is there a solution?

'Despite the snigger factor of "green bullets", there is no reason why BAE Systems, highly active in Saudi Arabia for instance, should be treated differently from any other large manufacturing company whose products have an environmental impact' – Rob Lake, Socially Responsible Investment Analyst (BAE Corporate Responsibility Report, 2006).

Money brings with it power, power corrupts and absolute power corrupts absolutely. Could the application of CSR break this stranglehold? CSR has been brought to prominence as much because of actions by NGOs as by the need for corporations to show that profits can be made responsibly. But when it comes to the arms trade, mainstream criticism has been muted. Certainly, if CSR had been as prominent in the USA before the preparation of the wars in Vietnam and Iraq, the wars would have been less likely, or even not have taken place. The relations between Halliburton, Bechtel, Carlyle and many other corporations in a CSR world would have been intensively examined. Stakeholders would have been held publicly accountable and socially irresponsible actions such as supporting war efforts for personal gain would have been stamped out. Naive? Perhaps. But right now, large corporations are more powerful than the UN, and also more powerful than many nation-states. Therefore, CSR is even more of an urgent issue than has ever been seen before. It's a tool that must be used wisely and my plea is to use it, certainly for impending catastrophes such as global warming, but also to control existing ones such as the seemingly uncontrollable MIC.

Concluding Remarks

So where next? I think we all agree that our economies must have a private sector. We know that we cannot regulate everything. Thus, social responsibility of our industries is key for the future. For instance, when former UN secretary general Kofi Annan launched the UN-backed Principles for Responsible Investment (PRI) in 2006, during the iconic opening bell ceremony at the New York Stock Exchange (NYSE), he was joined by executives from 11 institutions representing $4 trillion in assets. These founding PRI signatories understood that global threats being addressed by the UN – such as climate change, resource depletion, ecosystem destruction and water scarcity – also have the potential to threaten their own investment returns. For these globally significant investors, the challenge is to make investments that do not, over time, undermine the value of their entire portfolio.

Chapter Fourteen

OTHER BIG ISSUES CLIMATE CHANGE, CORRUPTION, HUMAN RIGHTS

Introduction

It is not possible to cover all the Big Issues of the day just in one book. There are so many and, I am sure, probably several that I have not covered. In this chapter, I shall cover, briefly and I am sure too briefly for many, issues that I have not touched upon so far.

Climate Change

In June 2020, Minnesota's Attorney General sued ExxonMobil, among others, for launching a 'campaign of deception', which deliberately tried to undermine the science supporting global warming. So what's behind these claims? And what links them to how the tobacco industry tried to dismiss the harms of smoking decades earlier?[1]

The most important issue facing humankind is undoubtedly climate change more even than global pandemics. Unfortunately, it is an issue that has been mostly ignored in the mainstream daily round of business and society until the November 2021 COP26 Summit in Glasgow. Why? The COVID-19 pandemic has proved that people are very diverse to taking measures that affect them even in the near future. That surely explains why half the population, and more in some countries considered advanced, such as France, Switzerland, UK, USA, Sweden, Spain, Italy, India, etc., simply refused to protect themselves with facemasks from the propagation of the COVID-19 disease via its main way of infecting them – through viral aerosols that hang in the air. The sight of Arctic glaciers breaking away into the sea gives rise to only a shrug for most people. On my daily run along a gorgeous beach, I seem to worry only about collecting plastic and placing in hard-to-find containers. That the weight of long-lasting plastics will, by 2050, outweigh the weight of fish in the sea is met by a vacant nod by most I people I pass by. A 10-metre rise in sea level within most people's lifetime and hurricanes that seem to occur more violently and frequently than ever before are met with a shrug since there have always been hurricanes.

An Oxfam report[2] has warned that at least 4.5 million children could die unless world leaders deliver additional funds to help poor countries fight the growing impact of climate change, rather than diverting it from existing aid promises. The report, 'Beyond Aid',

1. https://www.bbc.com/news/stories-53640382, accessed 29 September 2020.
2. Source: Oxfam, Chapter 44, http://tinyurl.com/yc5atwj

also warns that at least 75 million fewer children are likely to attend school and 8.6 million fewer people could have access to HIV/AIDS treatment if aid is diverted to help poor countries tackle climate change. Without at least $50 billion a year in addition to the 0.7 per cent of national income rich countries have already pledged as aid, progress towards achieving the SDGs could stall and then go into reverse.

What can the private sector do? A one key stakeholder is the environment, and not all is gloom and doom, as an article from the *Financial Times* (FT) noted,[3] 'Almost 1,000 multinationals have made Paris-aligned commitments' even though 'few have aligned their suppliers with those goals. The typical multinational's supply chain generates 5.5 times more emissions than its direct operations'.

And, as Martin Wolf noted after the COP26 Summit in a FT article[4] called 'Dancing on the edge of climate disaster', scepticism is fully justified when it comes to the COP26 outcomes. Wolf argues that it would be reasonable to conclude that COP26 was both a triumph, in that some steps were taken forward, and a disaster, in that they mostly fell far short of what is needed. Wolf's ominous warning is that '[i]t remains very doubtful whether our divided world can muster the will to tackle this challenge in the time left before the damage becomes unmanageable'.

He cites Climate Action Tracker[5] that has provided a useful summary of where we are: on current policies and actions, the world is set for 'a median increase in temperature of 2.7C above pre-industrial levels; with the targets for 2030 alone, this would fall to 2.4C; Full implementation of all submitted and binding targets would deliver 2.1C; and, finally, implementation of all announced targets would deliver 1.8C. Thus, if the world delivered everything it now indicates we would be close to the recommended ceiling of a rise of 1.5C'.

Martin Wolf insists that much can be contributed by the private sector and he cites a group known as the Glasgow Financial Alliance for Net Zero (GFANZ). Its aim, according to Mark Carney, the former governor of the Bank of England, is to 'build a financial system in which every decision made takes climate change into account'. GFANZ consists of the world's leading asset managers and banks, with total assets under management being $130 trillion. Wolf is adamant that the allocation of such resources towards the net zero objectives would make a huge difference. But, Carney noted, $100 trillion is the 'minimum amount of external finance needed for the sustainable energy drive over the next three decades'. This is daunting.

As noted in this book, it is not recommended that business does things they consider insufficiently profitable, after adjusting for risk. As Wolf notes, '[i]f they are to invest at the necessary scale, there must be carbon pricing, elimination of subsidies to fossil fuels, bans on internal combustion engines and mandatory climate-related financial

---

3. https://www.ft.com/content/936b4ab0-ac10-4860-a84f-02bfaa694b25, accessed 30 September 2020.
4. https://www.ft.com/content/6e2b366f-e139-4d69-bd4f-9254333bf316, accessed 28 November 2021.
5. https://climateactiontracker.org/publications/glasgows-2030-credibility-gap-net-zeros-lip-service-to-climate-action/, accessed 28 November 2021.

disclosures. But there must also be some way of getting vast amounts of private invest-ment into the climate transition in emerging and developing countries, apart from China'.

How could what Wolf proposes be carried out? One way, well known to readers here, is GFANZ call for the creation of 'country platforms', which would convene and align 'stakeholders - including national and international governments, businesses, NGOs, civil society organisations, donors and other development actors … to agree on and co-ordinate priorities'. A big and controversial issue will be risk-sharing. But a warning is that the public sector should not take all the risks and the private sector all the rewards from the energy transition.

Perhaps four additional areas over Wolf's list could be addressed relatively easily by all companies, especially those in the supply chain to big companies. First, use easily disposable containers and not long-lasting plastics. Second, ensure all packaging and waste materials are recyclable. Third, make use of renewable energy, such as solar, wind, tidal and geo-thermal energy, to the exclusion of coal, oil and nuclear. Fourth, minimize travel of employees when working from remote places is possible so as to reduce the use of mass transport and pollution from individual means such as cars and planes. Try and reduce but use tubes, buses, trains and boats, and use bicycles and walking as much as possible. All these latter trends can currently be seen accelerated by COVID-19 precautions and they will also lead to many opportunities, especially for small businesses.

Corruption

I have written that 'social and environmental benefits tend to be long term before impacting on stakeholder value' and that 'companies cannot simply put profitability on the same level as social and environmental considerations, as a company cannot survive by behaving in a socially or environmentally responsible manner whilst making losses'.[6] Quicker is to use trickery and unhappily, led by the ex-president of the USA, too many people succeed at it. In fact, corruption or bribery in business can be priced, according to the World Bank, to be at least globally about US$1 trillion per annum.

Corruption is a tough issue to deal with. As *The Economist* wrote,[7] '[t]rying to meas-ure corruption is a bit like surveying adultery. Those who indulge in it are unlikely to admit it'. Interestingly, this has led Transparency International (TI), when publishing their annual report (see also their data in Chapter 11 on National Social Responsibility) based upon surveying big companies, to ask a different question, namely: '[H]ow trans-parent are you?'. Their indicator measures three things. First, a company's internal rules and procedures to prevent corruption. Second, the transparency of its organiza-

6. Michael Hopkins, 'Corporate Social Responsibility: An Issues Paper', ILO Working Paper No 27, Geneva, May 2004, see https://www.ilo.org/legacy/english/integration/download/publicat/4_3_285_wcsdg-wp-27.pdf
7. https://www.economist.com/business/2012/07/14/measuring-mud?fsrc=rss

tional structure. Third, TI asks whether a firm publishes detailed financial information about its activities in every country where it operates, including how much it pays in taxes and royalties to each government.

Around the world just about every company has strict rules barring bribery. Shell, for instance, has zero tolerance for even miniscule levels of corruption. For instance, as I heard from a lecture on leadership by Globethics in October 2020, what would you do if a company of 400 employees asked 2 employees to work one weekend. Their cafeteria was stocked albeit closed. The two employees stole a chocolate bar and that was discovered on the Monday morning. The CEO was alerted and gave the two men a few days to see if they repaid the cafeteria. They did not. What would you do? Ignore the transgression because it was so small and any way they were working and were hungry. Or, give a warning to the employees and say they would be fired if they did that again. Or, most drastically, fire them. In the event they were fired. I would not have been so severe, unless the employees had already committed a transgression, I would have warned them and say not permitted at any level.

Frequently, it is the government employees who perpetrate the fraud. In Kenya, companies importing goods, asking for customs clearance, dealing with the tax authority or even with immigration to allow their workers to supervise their business operations are all asked for under the table payments. I have personally witnessed two such incidents in Kenya, refused to pay the bribe and suffered accordingly. In turn, that meant spending less time in their country, depriving the country of an expanding business and also advising potential investors of the situation. Some countries, such as China, take advantage to bribe and then gain property, land, fishing rights, etc.. Countries such as mine, the UK, which look at every financial transaction, don't allow the payment of bribes and I know a case that lost a half a billion-dollar wind energy investment as a result.

Thus, a company that is completely transparent may find it hard to win any more contracts from dodgy governments, which, alas, control a lot of the world's natural resources. For instance, Statoil, Norway's state-controlled oil-and-gas firm, was by far the best performer one year in a TI table, yet scored only 50 per cent on the transparency measure. More than a third of firms scored zero; the average was a meagre 4 per cent.

As the above-cited *Economist* article also noted, campaigners have long complained that money from oil and minerals props up predatory governments, and have lobbied firms to publish what they pay. Big Western miners and drillers have taken heed: the top five on TI's list are all involved in natural resources. Many firms, however, are reluctant to answer probing questions from Western busybodies: Gazprom, Russia's state-owned gas giant, scores zero on the first and third measures. And as oil exploration, development, refining and production increasingly move from well-known private companies, such as Shell, Total and BP, to state-owned companies, most rules are quickly broken and the oil business becomes even murkier than before.

Clearly, any TI calculation is open to challenge since TI's survey enquiry is based mainly on personal opinion from key informants, leading some to wonder whether Amazon, Google and Berkshire Hathaway deserve to be ranked near the bottom. Probably not. These firms may not disclose as much as TI would like to, but they are not usually in businesses where one is ever asked to bribe a cabinet minister to win a mining concession. TI does a good job of focusing attention on a serious problem. But like *The Economist*'s adultery survey, its results should be taken with a pinch of salt.

There have been new measures, especially by the EU, to look at uniform taxes on corporations. In fact, there has been an increased focus in the early days of the Biden government on international corporate taxation. In fact, one of my ILO colleagues, commenting on my earlier work, always chastised me by saying that CSR was simply about getting companies to pay their taxes[8]; in fact, the whole CSR/Sustainability area has expanded massively since then and my colleague might well be surprised at that!

Indeed, an anonymous reviewer commented that in addition to anti-corruption, two key big issues - taxation and ethics - are among the most important ones today. For example, in a very recent book on the 'main challenges in managing sustainable business', Arvidsson (2019)[9] said two of its five parts are devoted to 'anti-corruption and business ethics' (Part IV) and 'ethical taxation and tax transparency' (Part V) (the other parts being on sustainability reporting, sustainability assurance and sustainable finance).

The same reviewer cited Fleming and Zyglidopoulos's (2019)[10] idea that corporate corruption can be expanded to include activities considered as corporate crime, such as anti-competitive behaviour, illegal environmental damage, irresponsible working conditions, marketing and sale of unsafe products or tax evasion. That idea stems from a view of corporate corruption as encompassing not only situations in which the individuals in the organization benefit but also situations that aim at and result in benefits for the whole organization rather than specific individuals in it. The same reviewer thought that the definition of corruption could be further expanded to also include activities that do not conform to the definition of corporate crime. This is the case of corporate activities that are beneficial (actually or potentially) to the corporation while being detrimental to society as a whole, such as lobbying or the funding of political parties.

Such previous perspectives are not fundamentally different from the one underpinning Transparency International (TI) UK's proposal in their 2020 Annual Report of guidance on corporate anti-corruption reporting.[11] TI's approach has been that of identifying five key areas considered of a high risk of corporate corruption and providing guidance on disclosure pertaining to them. Besides reporting on anti-corruption programmes, Transparency International UK considers fundamental the reporting on the following:

---

8. Prof. Rolph Van Der Hoeven now of the Committee for Development Planning of the UN.

9. Susanne Arvidsson, *Challenges in Managing Sustainable Business* (Springer International Publishing Palgrave Macmillan, 2019).

10. Stelios Zyglidopoulos, Peter J. Fleming and Sandra Rothenberg, 'Overcompensation and the Escalation of Corruption in Organizations', *Journal of Business Ethics* 84, no. 1 (February 2009): 65–73.

11. https://www.transparency.org.uk/sites/default/files/pdf/publications/Transparency %20International%20UK%202020%20Annual%20Impact%20Report%20and %20Accounts.pdf, accessed 24 August 2021.

'The natural person who directly or indirectly ultimately owns or controls' the corporation (p.30) (beneficial ownership reporting).

'Fully consolidated subsidiaries and non-fully consolidated holdings' (p. 34) (organizational structure reporting).

'Financial data for countries in which the corporation operates, including payments to governments' (country-by-country reporting).

'Engagement in political activities, such as political contributions, lobbying'.

'The phenomenon of individuals moving "in either direction, between positions in the public and private sectors" (p. 46), usually called "revolving door"' (corporate political engagement reporting).

Readers here can see a whole chapter on the application of TI work to rank countries according to the TI index, as presented in Chapter 11.

Human Rights[12]

Corporations can violate human rights through their employment practices, or how their processes impact on workers, communities and the environment. Companies may also be implicated in abuses through their association with repressive governments or political authorities. Thus, companies may directly but also indirectly violate human rights (Amnesty, 2014[13]).

Despite increasing pressure upon nation-states to fulfil their duty to protect their inhabitants from harmful corporate activities, a substantial number of governments lack the ability or the willingness to ensure that human rights are adequately respected, especially when the issues at stake occur beyond their national territory (Ruggie, 2007[14]). Even today it remains difficult for states to sue corporations for human rights abuses outside their national territory.

Paying attention to human rights can present significant opportunities for corporations, such as a better reputation and brand image, which often translates into better sales and more investors; more secured licence to operate; improved employee recruitment, retention and motivation; and improved stakeholder relations. Also, NGOs monitor the CSR performance; multinationals and consumers are becoming more aware of the impact of corporations in human rights violations. For companies lacking internal motivation, there are growing external incentives for working on human rights such as the 11 points listed next.

---

12. This section has been summarized from Chap 9 in my book MJD Hopkins *CSR/Sustainability from the Margins to the Mainstream*, (Routledge, London, 2016 republished Taylor and Francis, London, 2017) on Business and Human Rights and largely written by Olga Lenzen and edited by myself.

13. Amnesty International (2014) *Injustice Incorporated: Corporate Abuses and the Human Right to Remedy*. March 7 London, UK Index Number: POL 30/001/2014.

14. J. Ruggie, *Human Rights Impact Assessments – Resolving Key Methodological Questions*, Report of the Special Representative of the Secretary-General, UN Document A/HRC/4/74, New York, 5 February 2007.

- Motivation of own employees
- Overall reputation
- Cost savings in risk management and legal claims
- Development human capital
- Improvement of stakeholder relations
- Licence to operate: acceptance and trust among all stakeholders
- Risk identification and management
- Improve access to capital
- Contribution to sustainable development
- Identification of business opportunities
- Contributing in peace-building processes in conflict zones

For a country there are also benefits to promoting human rights regarding companies. Respect for human rights in a country may directly attract Foreign Direct Investment (FDI), as the global investment market becomes increasingly diversified and the potential costs of human rights abuse continue to rise. Respect for human rights in a country may foster the development of human capital as more corporations seek out societies with a skilled, educated and productive workforce (Lindsey and Blanton[15] (2007)).

All companies, of all sizes and sectors, have the responsibility to respect human rights and to do no harm. It is the minimum requirement for all business in all situations. It exists independently from the state's duty to protect, that is, if a state does not live up to its duties, corporations still have the obligation to respect. In the Ruggie-led work under the auspices of the UN, states are urged to respect human rights such as those expressed in the Universal Declaration on Human Rights (UDHR), which was adopted by the UN General Assembly on 10 December 1948 as a result of the experience of the Second World War. Ruggie urges all companies to refer to those rights relevant for its activities and context and that all activities that touch human rights should be the subject of periodic review (Ruggie,[16] 2011).

Ruggie (2011) urges businesses to:

- have a policy commitment to meet their responsibility to respect human rights
- include a human rights *due diligence* process to help identify, prevent, mitigate and account for how to address the impacts on human rights
- implement processes to enable the remediation of adverse human rights impacts that they cause or to which they contribute.

---

15. S. Lindsey Blanton and R. G. Blanton, 'What Attracts Foreign Investors? An Examination of Human Rights and Foreign Direct Investment', *The Journal of Politics* 69, no. 1 (2007): 143–55.
16. J. Ruggie, 'Guiding Principles on Business and Human Rights: Implementing the United Nations 'Protect, Respect and Remedy' Framework', Report of the Special Representative of the Secretary-General on the Issue of Human Rights and Transnational Corporations and Other Business Enterprises, New York, 2011.

Due diligence is defined as the principle that, within a business context, a company is expected to ensure it operates in accordance with internationally agreed standards of fairness and reasonableness. Due diligence is an ongoing process and describes the steps a company must take to examine its human rights impacts. It entails procedures to make sure that a company does everything in its power to prevent complicity with human rights violations as follows:

- Assess any actual or potential adverse human rights impact with which they may be involved
- Integrate the findings from the impact assessments into the management system: in all relevant functions and processes, and take appropriate action
- Track effectiveness of the companies' actions, including asking feedback from affected stakeholders
- Communicate internally and externally.

The Human Rights Impact Analysis (HRIA) differs from other assessments in that it is framed by the International Bill of Rights. Ruggie states that the impact assessment of human rights can be included within broader risk-management systems, as long as it includes the risks of the rights holders and not only company risks.

Yet, clearly the guiding principles themselves will not offer an end to the problems regarding human rights and business. It will not stop incidents from occurring, and it will not solve the imbalance of power between a company and the people impacted by its activities. The principles do give a clear guidance on how states should innovate their judicial system. Unfortunately, that in itself will not speed up the legislative process, leaving the governance gap unresolved for many years to come. However, the expectations towards the operating systems of corporations are now comprehensively defined, at least in the richer countries. If due diligence processes become standardized and integrated into business practices, it is very likely that the occurrences of violations, their severity and the devastating impact they cause will be reduced, and the redress for victims will be improved.

Misinformation and Lack of Democracy[17]

Democracy under attack

The issue of the relation between the corporate sector and democracy is worth a book in itself! So, I shall restrict this chapter to a few remarks. First, of course, is that democracy comes in many guises although its key is being able to replace your government via a free and fair election. As I write, it does seem that democracies are backsliding amid the coronavirus pandemic as deaths rise to over one million. Brazil, India,

17. Based largely upon Adam Taylor, 'Democracies Are Backsliding amid the Coronavirus Pandemic', https://www.washingtonpost.com//world/2020/10/02/democracy-coronavirus-freedom-house Washington Post, 2 October 2020.

Poland, Hungary, USA and Venezuela, for instance, have all seen their democracies weaken and even the EU is suffering from COVID-19 uncertainty, and the creator of democracy, my country the UK, drawing back as BREXIT bites at the end of 2020. As noted in Chapter 11, democracies have struggled with the coronavirus, while the hardly democratic China is doing better than most democracies around the world, but, then, one democracy is starring, New Zealand, and even Germany is surviving well even as the ultraright up their presence amid their fascist tendencies. In poorer countries, some glimmers can be seen in Tunisia, which provided aid to refugees and minorities during the pandemic despite the country's economic devastation, and the country Georgia implemented 'strict but transparent' measures and has one of the world's lowest death rates. In parallel, its namesake the USA State of Georgia narrowly voted against the totalitarian Trump, providing additional breathing space for democracy in the USA.

Second, a report from Freedom House,[18] a nongovernmental, nonpartisan advocacy organization established in 1941, found that since the start of the pandemic, the state of democracy and human rights had worsened in at least 80 countries out of 192 nations surveyed. The report was based on an anonymous online survey of 398 experts and the work of Freedom House's own analysts. It presents a troubling paradox: the pandemic has made the case for political participation more urgent, while at the same time disrupting democratic institutions that enable that participation. In many cases, the virus has helped to trigger action over long-standing grievances - protesters in authoritarian Belarus, for example, were brought out by both a disputed election and a lacklustre and opaque pandemic response. Even in the USA, 71 million voted for anti-democratic President Trump in the 2020 presidential election. That number was the largest ever number of votes for anyone in a presidential election with fortunately the exception of the 76 million votes for the victor, Biden. Who these 71 million were will be the subject of intense debate in the next few years – my own suspicion is that the US election was indeed hacked but for the Republicans by the same people who hacked the 2016 election – Putin's Russia. I also suspect that China helped Biden, even though I have no evidence, but how did Biden win when all state institutions were blindfolded by Trump? A story still to be investigated and told. Third, the problem of weakening democracy is even more acute in developing nations or countries where democracy was already under threat. As a respondent to the Freedom House survey said of Turkey, the pandemic 'was used as an excuse for the already oppressive government to do things that it has long planned to do, but had not been able to'. In countries such as Egypt, Zimbabwe and Cambodia, governments were reported to be using emergency powers to crack down on political opposition. 'The judiciary has become a puppet of the executive branch', a respondent said of Serbia, noting that trials were 'conducted via video link, without the presence of defence attorneys'.

Fourth, over the past three decades, China has undergone a historic transformation. Once illegal, its private business sector now comprises 30 million businesses employing more than 200 million people and accounting for half of China's Gross Domestic

---

18. Taylor, 'Democracies Are Backsliding amid the Coronavirus Pandemic'

Product. Yet, despite the optimistic predictions of political observers and global business leaders, Tsai writes that 'the triumph of capitalism has not led to substantial democratic reforms. … Chinese entrepreneurs are not agitating for democracy. Most are working eighteen-hour days to stay in business, while others are saving for their one child's education or planning to leave the country. Many are Communist Party members … most entrepreneurs feel that the system generally works for them'.[19] Thus, Tsai reluctantly concludes that '[d]emocracy explodes the conventional wisdom about the relationship between economic liberalism and political freedom'.

Should the private sector care about democracy?

Of the many large companies, one can think of the big five in the USA – Apple, Amazon, Alphabet (Google), Microsoft and Facebook – the five most-valuable publicly traded companies on the S&P 500 with share value currently around $US5 trillion. Yet in September 2020, they all testified before the USA House Judiciary's antitrust sub-committee over possible anticompetitive behaviour![20] So, yes, they care since they all grew to their current massive size under democracy – of course, whether current issues will harm that state is something we hope will not happen.

But one should not expect too much from business to promote democracy, despite the strong move reported in this book towards the social responsibility of key stakeholders. Unfortunately, when it comes to government, business is happy when profits accelerate even in countries lacking democracy. Yet maybe, just maybe, there is light at the end of the pandemic tunnel, as argued by Jonathan Hopkin.[21] He writes that the 'catastrophic effects of war in the 1930s appear to have been important in the triumph of democratic capitalism in the 20th century. The spectre of war with communist nuclear powers also served to concentrate the minds of democratic policymakers afraid of revolutionary forces at home. The historian Walter Scheidel has gone as far as to argue that deeply unequal societies can be transformed only by what he calls the 'four horsemen of the apocalypse': war, revolution, state collapse and pandemics.

As the COVID-19 pandemic wreaks havoc across the globe, Jonathan Hopkin[22] concludes that 'broad acceptance of an increased role for government in managing the economy during the pandemic shows that the appetite for democratic capitalism remains'. I for one hope he is right.

---

19. Kellee Tsai, *Capitalism Without Democracy: The Private Sector in Contemporary China* (Cornell University Press, January 2007). DOI: 10.7591/9780801461897.

20. https://www.businessinsider.com.au/aapl-amzn-goog-fb-q2-earnings-big-tech-results-analysis-2020-7

21. Jonathan Hopkin in 'Anti-System Politics: The Crisis of Market Liberalism in Rich Democracies' (2020), see https://aeon.co/essays/postwar-prosperity-depended-on-a-truce-between-capitalism-and-democracy, accessed 11 October 2020.

22. Tax https://www.nytimes.com/2021/07/09/business/g20-global-minimum-tax.html?action=click&module=Top%20Stories&pgtype=Homepage, accessed 9 July 2021.

Chapter Fifteen

LEADERSHIP RESPONSIBILITY AND IMPLICATIONS

A leader is responsible when he or she is responsive to the needs, concerns and interests of those whom one aspires to lead

Christoph Stuckelberger and Jesse Mugambi[1]

Introduction

It is almost obvious to state that companies (and public institutions) should behave responsibly, especially in their leadership to ensure that issues of sustainability, ethics and the public interest are best addressed.[2] Of course, there are many examples of companies that state they will be responsible for their company and its actions but fall far short of that goal. Worse, these days, is that there are many leaders who lead but are not responsible however you define it.

Responsible leadership,[3] according to Marques and Gomez,

> deals with a broad spectrum of relationships, as it expands the focus of classic leadership theories – which are confined to leader-followers interactions – to the interfaces between leaders, on one hand, and various internal and external stakeholders, on the other hand. Consequently, responsible leadership explores concepts such as responsibility, ethics, sustainability, and stakeholders' interests, in order to understand the mutual influences amongst all those groups that are to some degree relevant to the organization. The study of responsible leadership sheds light on how institutions, companies, leaders, employees and individuals develop a more holistic, inclusive and responsible management approach in organizational settings.

The issue in the academic literature has been around for some time and has led to the issues of responsible management and responsible leadership mirroring Kotter's classical distinction between leadership and management (Kotter, 1990). Kotter claimed

---

1. Christoph Stuckelberger and Jesse Mugambi, *Responsible Leadership Global and Ethical Perspectives*, Globethics.net, Geneva, 2007.
2. *Source*: Institute of Responsible Leadership, https://responsible-leadership.org/, accessed 20 August 2020.
3. Tânia Marques and Jorge Gomes, "Responsible Leadership and/versus Responsible Management', in *Research Handbook of Responsible Management* (Edward Elgar Publishing Ltd, UK, December 2019).

that managing is about coping with complexity, whereas leading is about coping with change. Managers plan and prepare budgets; leaders set directions. Managers care about organizing and staffing, and controlling and problem solving; leaders worry about aligning and motivating people. Finally, managers do things right; leaders do the right thing. The two are not mutually exclusive; but rather they are complementary and both are needed in organizations and are closely linked to Corporate Social Responsibility.

Thomas Friedman[4] writes about leadership that '[i]f you show people respect, if you affirm their dignity, it is amazing what they will let you say to them or ask of them. Sometimes it just takes listening to them, but deep listening – not just waiting for them to stop talking. Because listening is the ultimate sign of respect'.

Yet George Monbiot in *The Guardian*[5] argued that 'political hucksters using aggression, lies and outrage to drown out reasoned argument' are becoming more and more successful, and he lists Donald Trump, Boris Johnson, Narendra Modi, Jair Bolsonaro, Scott Morrison, Rodrigo Duterte, Nicolás Maduro and Viktor Orbán, who have discovered that 'the digital age offers rich pickings. The anger and misunderstanding that social media generates, exacerbated by troll factories, bots and covertly funded political advertising, spill into real life'.

CSR/Sustainability takes place only, if not mainly, when there is an active leader/manager within the company who champions this approach. Szekely and Knirsch found[6] that it always takes a leader to 'transform a company into a sustainable, socially responsible enterprise. This individual needs to be both a good leader and a good manager. His/her sustainability work starts by carefully examining all the factors that determine the sustainability performance of his/her company and its suppliers. These factors can be internal (mainly managerial and organizational) or external (stakeholder's demands)'.

Then, there are at least three critical success factors that a company needs to fulfil to achieve sustainable performance. First leadership and vision, flexibility to change and openness for engagement. The link to corporate responsibility is heavily influenced by the full and honest commitment of management to sustainability and by the adoption of a management incentive scheme. The top management of a company needs to ensure the right messages are actually followed. A variety of management measures need to be taken and supported by top management, not only the establishment of management systems, but also the introduction of incentives and training on sustainability issues that drive performance on non-financial issues. These measures must also include product and process innovations that improve sustainability performance.

Second, there must be flexibility to change with key top managerial staff committed to the CSR/Sustainability objective, and companies must ensure that sustainability

---

4. *New York Times*, April 2020.
5. https://www.theguardian.com/commentisfree/2019/oct/03/demagogues-fury-violence-outrage-discourse, accessed 5 October 2019.
6. Francisco Szekely and Marianna Knirsch, 'Responsible Leadership and Corporate Social Responsibility', *European Management Journal* 23, no. 6 (December 2005): 628–47. DOI: 10.1016/j.emj.2005.10.009.

values and vision are not only integrated into business strategy, policies and culture, but also communicated to all employees: setting appropriate goals and targets, developing a coordinated approach, monitoring and evaluating progress and optimizing the process when necessary.

Third, openness coupled with strong stakeholder engagement. To develop a shared understanding of approaches and expectations, including the provision of external benchmarks, it is important to engage with key stakeholders in their own right and not only with investors with short-term financial interests. Stakeholder engagement means more than just entering into dialogue. It has to produce real learning effects that lead to product and process improvement or innovation. Engagement must be with internal and external stakeholders as well as with sectoral and multi-stakeholder initiatives that support the learning process and increase credibility, commitment and innovation.

How Does CSR Link to Responsible Leadership?

For the first time ever an influential body, the Business Roundtable, has rephrased the company rule book in August 2019 from maximizing shareholder value to maximizing stakeholder value, reported *The Financial Times*. Thus, the tide is beginning to change since the Business Roundtable is an influential US business group that is an association of chief executive officers (CEOs) representing the top corporations in the USA. It surprisingly and importantly amended its two decade-old declaration that 'corporations exist principally to serve their shareholders'.

The Financial Times also noted that for '40 or more years, corporate boardrooms had embraced the doctrine that economist Milton Friedman had laid out in a 1970 article with the blunt title The Social Responsibility of Business is to Increase its Profits. That approach was supercharged in the 1980s and 1990s by the ratcheting up of share-based executive rewards and arguably has led to a worsening distribution of income and rewarded rentiers of capitalism rather than its workers'.

The Roundtable further said: 'While each of our individual companies serves its own corporate purpose, we share a fundamental commitment to all of our stakeholders' – customers, employees, suppliers, communities and – last in the list – shareholders. Then, '[r]esponsible leaders in both the public and private sectors treat responsibly key stakeholders to ensure that issues of sustainability, ethics and the public interest are best addressed'.

Clearly, this is consistent with the goals of corporate social responsibility, and they state that 'the interests of major stakeholders such as clients, directors, owners, shareholders, employees, media, suppliers, environmental lobbyists, the community, citizens and future generations are variously taken into account'.

Years ago, in the mid-1990s, a senior British Airways (BA) employee told me that BA used my first book *The Planetary Bargain* to revise its company strategy. The results were difficult to observe and maybe should have been brought out across the company. I wasn't consulted, but it is worth noting that several decades later the BA September 2019 pilot's strike cost the BA tens of millions of dollars and further hurt their reputation. This despite the pilots, reportedly, having said they wanted to talk to BA about profit sharing. BA would have done well to at least show an openness to discussing it and extending it to all staff. This was thus a clear lack of stakeholder leadership by BA.

The goal of corporate social responsibility is to ensure that the interests of key stakeholders such as clients, directors, owners, shareholders, employees, media, suppliers, those representing the environment, the community and citizens are variously taken into account. Better still would be for each key stakeholder group to have a responsible leader to ensure the responsible treatment of stakeholders as well as vice versa.

Three further issues stem from these definitions. First, the golden rule where the leader is asked to treat his/her staff as he/she would wish to be treated himself or herself. Even better would be for the leader to imagine him/herself in the subservient role and then agree with the leadership taken.

A second issue is what is meant by a 'key' stakeholder? Clearly, not everyone can be key, so how best to choose? Graham Kenny[7] poses five questions and gives some examples that a responsible leader must address:

1. As often argued in this book, a key stakeholder has a fundamental impact on an organization or institution's performance. For instance, a manufacturer of frames for houses decided, on reflection, that a local council wasn't a key stakeholder. Though the council set regulations that the company had to follow, those rules didn't have much of an effect on sales or profits the way, for instance, customers did. But the company should listen since ignoring the rules set down would lead to legal expensive battles.

2. Then what do you really want a key stakeholder to do? For instance, members of a law firm's strategic-planning team knew they wanted three things: first, revenue from some key stakeholders such as clients; second, productivity and innovation from employees; and third, continued funding from partners. Yet they couldn't specify what they wanted from the community, so that relationship wasn't deemed key.

3. Is the relationship with your key stakeholders dynamic, and therefore you want it to grow? For instance, a company ran 17 retirement villages and had a relationship with current and potential residents. It wanted increased occupancy and more fees for the services used. The company's relationship with a university, by contrast, was static and operationally focused. It involved a fixed amount of research funding and co-branding each year. That's all that was needed. Though the co-branding generated broader awareness and may have indirectly yielded more residents and revenue, the university itself didn't achieve key stakeholder status.

4. Can you exist without or easily replace the key stakeholder? For instance, a professional services firm in HR that had taken out a loan initially listed the bank as a stakeholder. But ultimately that relationship didn't qualify as key, because the loan could be easily refinanced with another source.

---

7. Graham Kenny, 'Five Questions to Identify Key Stakeholders', *Harvard Business Review*, 6 March 2014.

5. Has the key stakeholder already been identified through another relationship? For instance, a government department involved in planning and infrastructure listed both employees and unions as key stakeholders. But this amounted to double counting: the unions represented employees' interests, and the organization's primary relationship was with its employees.

Kenny also noted how responsible leadership was important for employees, and he cited Krister Ungerboeck, CEO of Courageous Growth,

> who when he first became a business leader, thought that the CEO should be the smartest person in the organization. That mentality led him to doubt the capabilities of his team resulting in an unproductive work environment. But after getting honest feedback on an employee survey, he realized his leadership style wasn't working. When he finally realized that his leadership style left his workforce struggling to feel motivated, he made a 360-degree transformation. He realized that criticism is lazy leadership that will pump up the ego of the boss by making the employee feel inferior. Since that epiphany, Ungerboeck tried to do better by leading through encouragement and endorsing the employees' rights.

A further complication is when stakeholders get together to influence a company or institution. Such was the case with Greenpeace and Shell, when the former criticized the latter (in 1995) with wide press coverage for its plan to dump the Brent Spar Oil Rig into the North Sea. The combination of Greenpeace with the media – two important stakeholders that Shell had hitherto ignored – led to mass press coverage and an eventual decision for Shell to locate the rig elsewhere. This classic case eventually led to NGOs being more involved in Shell (and other oil company) operations than before.

Finally, and to confuse matters, if *all* stakeholders are key, there is a huge army of concerns that perhaps becomes too large since if everyone is important then, eventually, no-one is!

Better Performance with CSR and Good Responsible Leadership

Is there evidence to suggest that CSR/Sustainability leads to better performance in some way? According to Fan-chin Kung and Nicholas G. Rupp,[8] most academic research has found that companies that are engaged in corporate social responsibility experience greater stock returns due to establishing greater trust among its employees, customers and shareholders.

In my own experience, a truly responsible leader was the late Anita Roddick. She was one of, if not the, first to introduce CSR into a company and eventually she became known as the Queen of Green. I remember passing her shop in 1970 with my young baby son in Brighton. Her scruffy looking shop was selling strange looking oils and

---

8. https://www.intechopen.com/books/firm-value-theory-and-empirical-evidence/corporate -social-responsibility-and-firm-value-recent-developments, accessed 22 June 2021.

creams in, I found out later, urine specimen bottles containing all-natural cosmetics. I didn't enter the shop since at that time I shuddered at strange looking hippie type shops despite being relatively left wing and chair of the Labour Party in my small area East of Brighton. It was 20 years later when I addressed franchisers working for The Body Shop on CSR and found they were well ahead of me at least as far as green notions of products were concerned but also strong concerns for their staff and suppliers.

It was almost by accident that she started a revolution, and by the time she died in 2005 she had turned that first Body Shop into a global retailing phenomenon, the Starbucks of cosmetics with nearly 2,000 stores in 50 countries and revenue of $986 million in 2005. During her life she tirelessly campaigned for, at first, the environment and then to fair trade to human rights. Sadly, towards the end of her life she felt that CSR had failed and made a depressing video that, unfortunately, was widely shared. Yes, she was prescient about climate change and may well be depressed today as the globe warms and our leaders continue to be poor. That will change and thus that video, happily, did not destroy her legacy of a great responsible leader. She campaigned widely worldwide yet never forgot her humble roots and was a heroine to her employees. If she had been alive today, her company, now run by L'Oreal but with a good reputation for CSR, may well have reversed her last video's view.

But not all leaders are benevolent, and in business the Koch Brothers (now one, David, since Charles died in 2019) have a poor record on CSR. Their support for AFP (Americans For Prosperity based in Columbus, Ohio) with its focus on anti-union legislation is in part driven by the Kochs' libertarian embrace of free markets and limited government. AFP has recognized that to make lasting change in US politics, the Koch network would need to permanently weaken the organizations that support liberal candidates and causes – and above all, the labour movement. Reflecting on why conservatives failed to build power in earlier decades, AFP's national president, Tim Phillips, explained that the Democrats 'had the public employee unions … which have only gotten stronger, have only gotten better-funded, have only gotten better organized'. To succeed in electing conservative candidates and promoting right-leaning policy, then, AFP would need to hobble unions, especially those in the public sector that were powerful state-level allies of Democrats.

The members of AFP who helped brainstorm Walker's efforts knew that the legislation would impact union membership – and go far beyond it. Since the passage of the anti-union bill, public union membership rates in Wisconsin have plummeted by more than half, falling from around 50 per cent in 2011 to around 19 per cent by 2017. With fewer members and revenue, the political clout of the labour unions has fallen sharply. Campaign contributions by teachers' unions to state and local races have fallen by nearly 70 per cent.

The consequence: a profound and long-term decline in Democrats' chance of securing office in the state. As one Democratic operative explained to the *New York Times*: 'Maybe we can win high-profile races because Wisconsin still leans slightly Democratic, but at the level where Walker has produced the most profound change, it may prove very difficult to turn that around. That's where we pay the price'.

In presidential elections, Democrats lose around three percentage points after the passage of anti-union legislation, and turnout dips by around two points. So, while there are many factors that might explain Donald Trump's surprise win in Wisconsin in

2016 by a mere 23,000 votes, a weaker labour movement less able to turn out Democratic voters might have been one important contributor to Trump's victory.

Looking back at the transformation of Wisconsin since Walker's election, Phillips notes proudly that AFP's organization in the state now has more grassroots activists than the Wisconsin teachers' union has members.

'That's how you change a state,' Phillips bragged.

The two Koch brothers had vast resources to invest in politics, commanding over $50 billion each from their ownership of Koch Industries. That company, which the brothers inherited from their father, has grown under their leadership to become one of the largest privately held conglomerates in the USA, with activities spread across dozens of industries, including chemical manufacturing, energy production, paper production and ranching.

Although Charles and David have been committed libertarians for most of their lives, since the 1980s they have steadily ramped up their political involvement and by now have constructed a vast network of organizations that pool hundreds of millions of dollars from their own pockets and other wealthy donors each year in support of conservative idea generation, leadership training, election campaigning and policy advocacy.

Taken together, AFP's grassroots volunteers and staffing rival those of the Republican Party itself. However, AFP is not a free-standing political party – but instead is an extra-party organization that parallels and leverages Republican candidates and office holders. By providing resources to support GOP candidates and officials, and exerting leverage on them once elected, AFP has been able to pull the Republican Party to the far right on economic, tax and regulatory issues.

When the Tea Party burst on the scene in 2009, AFP-WI was heavily involved in promoting Tea Party events and activism. AFP-WI hosted a tax-day Tea Party rally in 2009, and made a point to include Tea Party speakers at AFP events and sign-up Tea Party participants as AFP grassroots activists. Yet it would be a mistake to think of the Tea Party as being simply an AstroTurf operation from the Kochs – AFP built on but did not create Wisconsin's Tea Parties.

Undoubtedly, however, AFP's biggest accomplishment has been the passage of new anti-labour bills, like Act 10, that will permanently weaken unions and the left's political power. 'We fight these battles on taxes and regulations, but really what we would like to see is to take the unions out at the knees, so they don't have the resources to fight these battles', one top AFP staffer has explained about his group's thinking.

With key anti-labour victories in states like Wisconsin, it makes sense why the Kochs are able to look past their squabbles with an unruly Trump presidency. Regardless of what happens in Washington, AFP and the Koch networks have already succeeded in shifting the political terrain of Wisconsin – and the nation from the states on up.[9]

---

9. Based on Alexander Hertel-Fernandez, Caroline Tervo, and Theda Skocpol, 'How the Koch Brothers Built the Most Powerful Right Wing Group You've Never Heard Of', cited in https://www.theguardian.com/us-news/2018/sep/26/koch-brothers-americans-for-prosperity-rightwing-political-group

Responsible Capitalism

The main point of CSR has been to promote a form of responsible capitalism. In some quarters, there is an increasing concern that capitalism itself is to blame for society ills. How true is that? In fact, capitalism has many definitions and forms and so I would like to be clear on what we mean by it. We have certainly moved on from the famous book *Das Capital* by Karl Marx written in 1867, which described capitalism critically and argued for its replacement by socialism. The latter led to the Russian revolution and the destruction of the Tsar and his family. But eventually socialism turned into communism and failure. People wanted the benefits of freedom and democracy that came from a mixed economy. Marx did not foresee the rise of trade unions that led to rises in the standard of living of workers and gave them a voice. Today, trade unions are seen as much as a constraint to prosperity rather than an enabling mechanism to promote prosperity for all. As we see in the France of today, trade unions have become very powerful. The Margaret Thatcher so-called revolution when she was Prime Minister of the UK over 1979–1990 sharply reduced the power of trade unions in the UK leading to both pluses and minuses for the UK economy. Today in the UK there is a continuing worry that capital and markets have alienated many in the UK as they have become dominated by large corporations. Strong implementation of CSR principles could possibly reverse that trend and hence the need for CSR in the UK, as well as elsewhere around the world.

Leaders Matter but Africa Needs More

Undoubtedly, Nelson Mandela was one of its stars, a remarkable leader. It was clearly highly regrettable that 27 years of his life were spent cooped up on Robben Island. Yet, coming out of prison without remorse, he showed the sympathetic, peaceful and understanding attitude that I have found myself among most Africans, especially in Kenya where I have spent a large part of the last two COVID-19-bound years.

There have been other superb leaders. One of my heroes was the huge success of 50 years of Habib Bourguiba (except toward the end of his Presidency as I documented in my Economist book on Tunisia[10], who while fighting the French managed to take Tunisia to where it is today – a reasonably well-educated and developed country that is one of the best hopes to resisting the forces of darkness in the Islamic world.

Even in Kenya, highly troubled by corruption, incursions by the forces of darkness and large-scale poverty, they had Jomo Kenyatta in post-independence. He was, as have been subsequent leaders, especially President Kibaki, a great believer in education and the result can be seen today with roads packed in the mornings and evenings with almost any form of transport taking Kenyan kids to school. The sight gladdens my heart. Yet the corruption in Kenya needs true leadership to stop. But its leadership has

---

10. Michael Hopkins: *Tunisia to 1993: Steering for Stability* Special report (Economist Intelligence Unit, London, UK,) 1989, ISBN 0850582415, 9780850582413.

failed it, and I think that its rescue must come from the grassroots, who, in turn, must refuse to pay even the smallest bribe.

There are green shoots in other parts of Africa, Nigeria, Botswana, Tanzania, Liberia, Ethiopia, Zambia and possibly Rwanda, although leadership skills have been mixed, especially in the past few years as COVID-19 has proved one step too far to many. What we see more of is the corrupt governments of Zimbabwe, Congo, Burundi, etc. Even my attempt to create one million jobs through basic education and skill formation with a basic income and thereby defeat the premise of Al Shabaab in Somalia has got nowhere. Such a massive investment in human skills needs leadership and vision, sadly lacking in that country as well as so many others.

I hear a rumour that President Obama is investing in land in Kenya so as to start a Foundation. That gives me great hope since Obama, of Kenyan origins, can be the visionary leader that Africa needs. And, yes, the new Mandela. Not with the power of a president but with the power of a superb role model with a warm sympathetic manner. We have seen the excellent work that President Carter has done in promoting democracy and the energy given by President Clinton to development through his Clinton Foundation. Socially responsible leaders matter. One doesn't have to be an ex-president – Gates has shown that – but it helps.

I am a great admirer of President Obama. A brilliant man, as shown by being the president of the Harvard Law Society at an early age, but also a caring man as shown by his successes as president of the USA – health care, withdrawal of troops, against the US gun lobby, climate change, fiscal responsibility, growing the US economy, negotiations with Iran and his attempt to close Guantanamo Bay. All done in the face of the most hostile Congress that any US president has ever had to deal with. It is so sad that gerrymandering in the USA has hurt its democracy and led to majorities of poor-quality Republicans in both houses. Gerrymandering?, whereby boundaries are redrawn so that reactionary states such as Wyoming (population 500,000) have the same number of Senate votes (two) as California (population 60,000,000). California should have 120 times the votes of Wyoming in the Senate based upon population but, in the powerful US Senate, has the same.

Yet, a huge glimmer of light did shine. Free of the constraints of a hostile US Congress, as of January 2017, Obama is starting to use the power of his words from his new African base (and no doubt many other bases) to drive human rights, democracy, education and, most importantly, socially responsible leadership right across Africa, if not the world!

Responsible Leadership in the New Era

There is no doubt that the private sector – small, medium and large sized – is mostly suffering deeply when, as I write, flights are cancelled, social distancing leads to places of entertainment closing and most forms of outside activities cancelled. Gradually, the richer countries are coming back to normal but the poor countries have really been left adrift. Few have, as I write, been able to obtain vaccines to cater to even 1 per cent of their populations. Former prime minister Gordon Brown of the UK is one of few who is advocating more, much more, in the area of international cooperation to help the poor countries, only to be rejected by the UK Prime Minister Boris Johnson, who is overseeing one of the largest reductions ever in UK foreign aid.

Just about all large private companies would have spent a small fortune today to have prevented today's current disaster. But what could they have done? Well, we saw Bill Gates' advocacy since 2015 against the dangers of pandemics, and we have seen Alibaba cofounder Jack Ma's offer to donate masks amid coronavirus to USA as well as poorer countries.

In a move that would have been unthinkable in Britain's largely publicly funded health sector before the COVID-19 crisis, the UK government has turned to the private sector to boost the availability of tests for key workers (FT 23 March 2020). Not before time as the UK was one of the worse hit in the developed countries, thanks to its incompetent Prime Minister Johnson.

Thus, there is even more need now, with the COVID-19 virus spreading, for a strong socially responsible leadership from both the private and the public sectors. As a guide let's look at the following stakeholders and see how a company can treat each one responsibly.

Board members – Provide advice and support to management and, especially in the case of CSR, it is often the independent directors who take a longer-term view and understand that a short-term focus on profit-making at any cost can ruin an organization's reputation and sustainability.

CEOs – Appoint task force to advise them on the main hits to the company and what to do. These are company profits, its reputation on what it does to the local community or country, how to cope with the pandemic among staff, business and likely futures.

All leaders – One of the key conundrums is can a leader treat a subordinate responsibly who he/she has to command? Yes, if the leader could, for one minute, put him/herself in the subordinates' position and think whether he/she would, if in that position, consider his/her boss, i.e. him/herself, to be responsible.

Shareholders – Keep investing if the company is helping reduce COVID-19 and also increasing its reputation that will lead to eventual increased profitability. Also do take a long-term view (greater than three months).

Managers – Respect the need for employees to observe social distancing, remain at home if not needed at work and have regular tele-conferencing meetings and discussions.

Employees – Keep management informed of issues and problems both at the workplace and at home, especially if working from home.

Suppliers – Ensure good contact and discuss any difficulties in the delivery of requested products and services.

Community – Work with key communities to ensure harmony, keep the company informed of problems and successes. Notify the company of any corrupt practices, and generate community leadership.

Government – Try and organize companies into groups that work together so as not to duplicate tasks and to ensure key issues are being addressed without waste so that all are on the same page.

Media and social media – Evidence-based journalism is vital in times of crisis. The last things that are needed are the false accusations of companies. Promote the good companies. Also messaging promoting responsible behaviour and social cohesion. Try and avoid false messaging.

The Environment – Probably the natural environment comes out the best as the urban areas reduce sharply pollution from CO_2, while lack of movement in forests and rural areas allows many species to recover.

Finally, when we have seen the results of my CSR rating app, which can be found on all mobile phones and my website www.csrfi.com, we find that most large private companies, if not all, have a higher CSR rating score than most public institutions, including such august bodies as the United Nations. More and more large companies are realizing that multi-stakeholder capitalism is more praiseworthy and, yes, more profitable than merely focusing upon shareholder value. In these times of suspicion and lack of confidence in most of our public sector leaders, that conclusion bodes well for the future of our society and planet.

Company Anti-COVID-19 Acts

The COVID-19 worldwide pandemic has thrown into prominence many of the arguments of this book. I had already argued that many (but not most) companies, and large corporations in particular did, after COVID-19, now see the need to widen their responsibilities to the big issues of the day. They had already been involved with trying to prevent global warming from reducing car exhaust emissions to substituting plastics with biodegradable plastics to creating alternative energy devices. The latter hurting the price of oil and leading to many oil-rich countries as well as companies to rethink their future strategies. The oil price will remain low for the foreseeable future unless new forms of use in the future age of conservation and low CO_2 emissions see a use for oil. In a previous article, I had shown that out of 55 single resource exporting countries only a handful had avoided the Dutch disease that helped to concentrate the distribution of income and price many business people in the export industry out of business as their domestic prices rise through exchange rate ballooning.

In an online conversation stimulated by one of my partner institution's, Globethics, I had two students from Kosovo: one the head of CSR, and her boss from the Raiffeisen Bank. New in their country to CSR, they asked how best their company could help their country through CSR. My response was:

1. Work with other companies to prevent duplication.
2. Work with the government and help them with management and priorities
3. Ensure you have a business case for what your own company does.

4. Down the road there will be much more communication through internet conferencing such as Zoom, Hangouts, Skype, etc., and much less travel. Already, less movement has led to improved environment.

5. But less movement has led to many business failures, especially small companies, even worse has been the poorer members of society who can't work, have no savings and are currently desperate. We have suggested a basic income to plug that gap – see, for instance, https://www.businessdailyafrica.com/analysis/columnists/Roll -out-basic-income-for-the-poor-in-slums/4259356-5530448-7r36bxz/index.html

Immediate CSR Advice to Governments in This Time of Post COVID-19[11]

CSR is normally applied to the private sector, and large corporations. But there is no reason why the methodology of CSR cannot be applied to other corporate entities such as the public sector. The basic structure of a CSR strategy is based, following my CR model, on the H-CSR-M,[12] which helps define key stakeholders of an institution and treating them with responsibility. In the time of COVID-19, one can imagine the key stakeholders to be the public at large, civil servants (especially the public health sector), the leadership, the private sector (especially health and the main pillars of the economy tourism and finance) and the vulnerable population.

Discussions between the government and each of the stakeholder groups, especially labour, are always ongoing and there are often cases of irresponsible behaviour on both sides. Clearly, during a pandemic there is a need to preserve employment, wages and look after the newly unemployed. But without the key player in the economy of many countries, especially tourism, everybody suffers.

It seems that a key issue is the social responsibility of individuals, especially now and especially to control and prevent new infections taking place. For tourists, they will now accept social distancing, the wearing of face masks and the avoidance of large groups. If the government made that clear to incoming tourists, there would be multiple benefits. Unfortunately, both governments approached ignored my advice. Consequently, tourism continues its collapse, airlines are in deficit and employment has plummeted.

Social Responsibility of Governments Not Great

CSR also applies to the public sector and governance. As many are aware, the tragedy of Brexit in my country is still unfolding, albeit almost forgotten, and even now the issues are not a priority for the British as they lurch towards complete disassociation from the EU by the end of 2020.[13] In times of crisis, such as with COVID-19, the steady

---

11. Based upon analysis by the World Economic Forum, https://www.weforum.org/agenda /2020/03/how-are-companies-responding-to-the-coronavirus-crisis-d15bed6137/, accessed 1 August 2020.

12. https://www.csrfi.com/hopkinscsrmodel, accessed 22 June 2021.

13. See Michael Hopkins, *'Brrrexit! Why England will be Left Out in the Cold: The UK Decides upon Perpetual Winter,* 'Kindle Edition, Amazon.com, January 2020.

hand of the UK would have been much appreciated in Europe as the disaster continues to rise. We even read that the British cannot get hold of products that may help them from the EU, and, of course, scientific links are gradually being broken.

Then, climate change is on everybody's list of concerns as potentially a crisis that could end civilization on our planet itself. Yet some public leaders wilfully destroy treaties, such as the Paris Agreement on Climate Change, for their own personal glorification as we saw, happily only temporarily, in the USA for instance. As CSR gets more and more popular, and encompasses all institutions not simply private ones, the link with basic income is clear since CSR simply cannot ignore the debate on basic income. My view, as expressed in Chapter 8, is that CSR should embrace a basic income for all poor but not to all, and certainly not to the very rich. Right now it is useful for the private sector and the government to come together to create and deliver a basic income to the most vulnerable right across the world. The other battle to be fought, and private sector CSR proponents have been weak on this, is the link to income distribution. It is in no-one's interest for a few to be barricaded in to protect their wealth, while the outside continues to fall behind.

Concluding Remarks

As can be seen, companies are involved in helping reduce the effects of COVID-19. Could they do more? Yes, there is no doubt that the private sector, who have to be very clear about what their products do and that they are non-injurious to people, could help the public sector enormously. It depends on the country. The rich countries have not come out so well with the exception of Australia, New Zealand, Eire, Switzerland, South Korea and Singapore. And most developing countries, from Ecuador to Yemen to Venezuela, are all over the place. Could companies help more? Rather difficult when the host country to many companies is behaving irresponsibly, as was the case with the USA's rejection of the World Health Organization (WHO). There is no doubt that a strong responsible leadership helps (responsible of course not what we saw in Russia with the awful and unnecessary Ukraine war), as seen in New Zealand, Canada and even in some developing countries such as Senegal. Kenya, from where I write, has seen impressive leadership with its leader wearing a mask in public. But resources, especially in virus testing, have been severely hampered. And hospitals struggle through lack of proper protective clothing, masks and ventilators.

Worse is the suffering of the poor in many countries, who have lost jobs and their livelihoods through curfews and social distancing. I have suggested the strong need for a basic income for the most distressed. But that has been slow-going process as resources needed are large and management is poor, and there is a huge space for the private sector to back such an initiative and lend its skills to implement as soon as possible.

To conclude, let me recite Thomas Friedman, who wrote 'if you show people respect, if you affirm their dignity, it is amazing what they will let you say to them or ask of them. Sometimes it just takes listening to them, but deep listening — not just waiting for them to stop talking. Because listening is the ultimate sign of respect'.

Chapter Sixteen

GENDER – WOMEN MAY NOT NEED CSR

Introduction

Emphasizing diversity, especially the increasing role of women, is part of a company's CSR. Increasingly, companies are looking at their level of diversity, especially that of gender. But such CSR may not be necessary because of evolution, as this chapter points out.

In fact, men have already started to become losers as far as the mainstreaming of women is concerned. That is due to the repression of women by men over the centuries, if not millennia, since women have toughened up in a myriad of ways.

In previous times, and still in many mainly poor countries today, the main role of women has traditionally been to produce children, a time-consuming endeavour. Then, for their employers, their childbearing absence would incur a significant cost. Women would often be absent for three months or more as they went through pregnancy and consumed their maternity leave even if they were allowed one.

In poor countries, the childbearing time is typically much longer – probably most of their lives, as mothers and then grandmothers. This has been mainly because of the absence or expense of contraception and the need to produce children and to look after the family when life expectancy is only up to 40 years, even today. Worse, in many poor countries, is forced intercourse leading to unwanted children. This has meant that poor women's lives were short – and often not so happy. Today, so much of that has started to change, especially in the richer countries. However, contraception is still a rarity for many poor women and many are not allowed early abortion when things go wrong. For instance, the rigid anti-abortion beliefs of the judges in the Supreme Court of the USA is likely to lead to continuing misery for many poor women who will also not be allowed contraception. I don't want to get into the issue of the importance of life and, of course, I don't object to life at any cost. But a foetus before the age of six weeks is hardly human and then consenting adults ought to decide, especially the woman involved.

Life Expectancy of Women Increased Significantly

The United Nations World Population Prospects 2015 report reveals that worldwide, the average life expectancy at birth over the period 2010–2015 was 71.5 years (68 years and 4 months for males, and 72 years and 8 months for females).

According to the UN's World Health Organization, Kenya, from where I write, has seen a dramatic change in life expectancy over the past 15 years. Statistics show that Kenyans now expect to live an average of 67 years, compared to 51 years at the start of the twenty-first century. And women in Kenya are likely to live nearly five years longer than men, WHO found. It puts the average span at 65 years for Kenyan males and 69 years for females.

As the *Daily Nation* of Kenya has reported, the reason has much to do in Kenya with rising levels of education, for both boys and girls. Concurrent with this has been the striking rise in standards of health, as the incidence of many previously debilitating diseases, both communicable and non-communicable, has been reduced, some dramatically so. These include malaria, measles, cholera, HIV/AIDS, polio, diarrhoea, respiratory infections, COVID-19 and strokes.

Increasingly, as a result of great efforts having been made on behalf of the girl child, girls are performing better than boys as far as education is concerned – to the point that many now worry that boys are being increasingly left behind. In 2018, for instance, Kenya's Certificate of Primary Examinations (KCPE) exam results showed that girls, who had for long been outperformed by boys, for the second year in a row edged out their male counterparts from the top positions.

Women in the Labour Market

In the labour market, women are also edging out males. According to the London *Financial Times*, investor behaviour is recognizing female contributions to the extent that there exists a correlation between gender diversity and high returns in public financial markets. And a recent report by the International Finance Corporation, 'Gender diversity yields an incremental alpha', found that funds with gender-balanced senior teams achieved 10–20 per cent higher returns than the unbalanced ones.

Then, in America's ongoing discussion on gender equality – I ignore as much as I can the fake news and false accusations – new research suggests that women's brains are about four years 'younger' than men of the same age, and that as they age, they remain mentally sharp for longer than if they were men.[1]

There are fears that technology is destroying jobs, although the evidence shows simply a change from one technology to another. More important is the worsening income distribution, as wages stagnate across the world after decades of minimal growth or even decline. The implications of this are dire for global political stability. We have seen that resentment of this unfortunate phenomenon among middle- and lower-class workers has given rise to populist leaders in both the USA and parts of Europe, leaders whose appeal tends to be racist and anti-immigration. It may well be that the increasing use of lower paid but highly qualified women is driving down the average wage.[2]

Companies are not sure how to handle all these changes in the labour market. For instance, the Union Bank of Switzerland (UBS) offers women six months of maternity leave at full salary, while new fathers are given only two weeks. Then the men's bonuses were not affected, but a reduction was applied to the annual bonuses of the women, followed by their incentive pay not being restored to its former level, even three years or more later.[3]

---

1. *Source*: https://patch.com/us/across-america/why-women-are-smarter-men
2. Source: https://www.forbes.com/sites/stevedenning/2018/07/26/how-to-fix-stagnant-wages-dump-the-worlds-dumbest-idea/#48656f8e1abc
3. *Source*: https://www.ft.com/content/2e72ddde-41bc-11e9-9bee-efab61506f44

In general, the working hours in Switzerland are long, at 42 hours, leading it to having the second highest rate of women working part-time in Europe. This is then coupled with women finding it difficult to access higher positions, with age discrimination on return to work and inadequate pensions at the end of a working life,[4] https://reconne ctingwithcommonsense.wordpress.com/2019/03/24/leadership-a-week-for-women/).

Finally, the United Nations has championed women's rights more and more in recent years. The UN promotes equal opportunities for access to employment and to positions of leadership and decision-making at all levels. It also works against the horrible practice of violence against women that occurs around the world far too often. However, as the following graphic shows, as of 2014, 143 out of 195 countries guarantee equality between women and men in their constitutions. Sadly, the UN is not a body that can make universal laws, as that is up to individual countries. So discrimination continues to exist, with many countries signing on to UN recommendations and then ignoring them.

Happily, the increasingly influential Sustainable Development Goals include Goal 5, which strives to 'achieve gender equality and empower all women and girls'.

So will all ships rise as the water supports movements towards gender equality? Or will, as I indeed suspect, men be the losers? As CSR/Sustainability becomes increasingly important, encouraging institutions and companies to treat all key stakeholders responsibly, women will undoubtedly see their positions improve. The previous poor treatment of women by men – by many but not all – will mean that men will lose some ground and that, probably, will be a big issue in the years and centuries to come.

Source: https://www.un.org/en/sections/issues-depth/gender-equality/

---

4. *Source*: Mary Mayenfisch, Leadership – A Week for Women, 24 March 2019 personal communication.

Chapter Seventeen

GOOD AND BAD CSR EXAMPLES

Introduction

In today's turbulent times, one can be very cynical about large private corporations and their social responsibility, but there are examples of exemplary behaviour as well as many of poor behaviour. For instance, the corporate world is not immune to caring about health issues, including pandemics. As noted previously, Bill Gates produced a famous eight-minute video[1] in 2015 on the need to do more to prepare for pandemics and he, famously, was ahead of his time as others still didn't realize the COVID-19 seriousness even as evidence of what to do mounted.

Gates, as in his own business, was prescient and warned then that a virus could affect millions of people. Taking the example of Ebola which saw over 10,000 deaths but was difficult to catch, he urged action to prevent a possible future easily transmitted virus that could affect the whole world. But, despite his wealth, fame and leadership with his own money, he was basically ignored.

I wonder why it is that people, such as Bill Gates, who see into the future with solid arguments about potential risky outcomes are ignored. Why do people only react when the disaster is on their doorstep?

Bill Gates did foresee the COVID-19 tragedy that unfolded across the world. In fact, what is worrying is that it always seems to take a crisis before anything much happens. I write now in the hope that all organizations can sit back and think seriously about their social responsibilities, work together and protect their customers as well as communities across the world.

US Chamber of Commerce

In the USA, the US Chamber of Commerce has come in for some criticism, ever since its anti-climate legislation stance led several companies, including Apple, PG&E Corp., Exelon Corp. and PNM Resources to announce they were quitting the chamber. It has since changed its stance and has now set up an institute for CSR, as I noted in the Preface. My own experience with the US Chamber was during 2009 when I was advising their corporate citizenship group on corporate work in emerging markets. My aim was to help the group increase the sustainability of projects and also to see how far I could go in widening the appeal of strategic CSR.

Today BCLC (Business Civic Leadership Center) is the US Chamber's resource and voice for businesses and their social and philanthropic interests. I noted today how far

---

1. https://youtu.be/6Af6b_wyiwI

BCLC has come along the CSR/Sustainability route, as there is now an institute of CSR in BCLC. They have adopted the multi-stakeholder view that I introduced and argued for at that time more than a decade ago.

The US Chamber, of course, made no bones about its support to business and reinforced that idea with its 'American Free Enterprise' project. On its website, it notes: 'While government efforts to stimulate the economy are considered useful in the short term, it's the free enterprise system that will grow our economy and create jobs over the long term.' It planned to accomplish this through a '20 Million Job Challenge that will highlight the state-specific jobs needed to meet this goal and encourage policymakers, business leaders, and the public to commit to supporting American free enterprise – the system that creates opportunity, encourages innovation, rewards hard work, and promotes growth'. On the surface, an emphasis on markets to resolve problems of low growth and high unemployment has been the conventional wisdom of most Western governments since the fall of the Berlin Wall – 40 years ago on the day I write this. Yet the phrase 'Free Enterprise' has been a code word for a reduced public sector, and lower taxes loved by the conservative side of society.

Again, nothing wrong with that until we understand the implications. Unadulterated free enterprise by banks, financial investment houses and the likes of Enron, WorldCom etc. just brought about the world economy to its knees in 2008. It was left to the public sector to introduce a strong dose of Keynesiam into the economies of the West (including China) to resurrect the economies of the West. The USA struggled with high unemployment because, as many commentators had argued, the stimulus package was too small and not job-focused enough.

The winds of change swept through the BCLC as well. Traditionally, they were more of a philanthropic, humanitarian assistance and development organization, but in the past two years they have begun to build relationships with NOAA, EPA, Forestry and various water and sustainability groups. They now state:

> Our members don't want to think just in terms of situational crises, but in terms of systemic approaches. They don't want to be called on just to respond to issues; increasingly, they want to be consulted in the planning process. They don't want to be asked just to financially support a cause or organization, they want to be able to leverage their employees skills and expertise, their products and services, and other assets.

Indeed, they now state that 'Companies are increasingly differentiating between assistance (charity, "giving away fish"), and development (investment, "teaching people how to fish"). They are thinking about how they interact with their external environment more strategically, holistically, and systemically'.

Levis[2]

Levis has always been big on CSR and insists that, as the well-known maker of denim jeans, it only wants investors focused on the long term. For instance, an investment in

---

2. Based upon Andrew Edgecliffe-Johnson, *Financial Times/ArcelorMittal Boldness in Business Awards*, 30 March 2020.

a laser process helped Levis cut out most of the chemicals whereby many of its workers had to scrub jeans with sandpaper for 20 minutes before finishing them with thousands of chemical brews to achieve the same distressed look. In fact, Levis has had a reputation for social responsibility that dates back to the nineteenth century. The man from whom Levi Strauss took its name was a gold rush-era merchant who, having commercialized a fellow immigrant's idea for denim overalls, gave away much of his fortune to fund local orphanages and university scholarships. His heirs burnished the reputation of Levi's for paternalism, continuing to pay workers after the 1906 San Francisco earthquake destroyed the company's factory, offering generous severance packages as America's garment industry moved overseas and spoke of the company as having a mission of 'profits through principles'.

Levis offers an unusual example of a company that has grappled for generations with a related challenge consuming its peers: how to stay focused on long-term value creation, even in the face of the fashion industry's short-term pressures.

For most of the company's history, the answer was family ownership, but in 1971 the need for capital and a desire to offer shares to employees persuaded the controlling Haas family to float a minority stake on the New York Stock Exchange. Just 14 years later, though, the family bought other investors out, explaining that being private again 'would allow management to focus its attention on the long term, rather than being concerned with the short term as a public company must be'.

The view that public markets are too trigger-happy has only gained in currency since then, with Warren Buffett among chief executives warning investors' desire for quarterly earnings guidance has led to an unhealthy obsession with short-term profits at the expense of sustainable growth. Prominent Silicon Valley investors are even backing a new Long-Term Stock Exchange that would give more voting power to the most patient investors.

Yet, in March 2019, Levi's decided to go back to Wall Street, offering a test case of whether other investors would share its founding family's focus on a horizon that stretches far beyond the next quarter. With more than 100 family shareholders, some wanting to cash out, there was 'a certain amount of inevitability' to a listing, said Chip Bergh, who is only the third chief executive Levi's has had from outside the family. If Levi's had stayed private as the family tree grew more branches, 'you [would] get to a point where you've got 250 shareholders and nobody holds more than 2 per cent. And how do you govern a company like that? It's impossible'.

To address concern in the company that its principles would be compromised by the public market's demands, the board first ensured the family's shares would have 10 times the voting rights of others. Dual-class shares have come under fire and the Council of Institutional Investors said the Levi's arrangement 'severely' limited accountability. But Bergh defended them as giving 'air cover' to manage for the long term.

According to a study by FCLTGlobal, a non-profit dedicated to encouraging long-term capitalism, companies that invest more than average, avoid excessive distributions to shareholders and steer clear of scandals perform best over the long run. A McKinsey Global Institute analysis similarly found that companies with a long-term view generate higher profits and shareholder returns.

Levi's scores well on both studies' metrics, but Bergh is adamant he is not just ticking boxes. When he became chief in 2011 after 28 years at Procter & Gamble, he recalled: 'I wanted Levi Strauss to be, and be seen as, the world's best apparel company, and among the best companies in any industry. That was the noble cause'. But Levi's had lost the lustre it enjoyed in the 1980s when Bergh had a pair of 501s swiped from a youth hostel. By 1999, having seen competitors erode its market lead, Fortune called the company a 'failed utopian management experiment'.

Bergh realized day-to-day discipline had to accompany a focus on the long term, telling his team 'profits through principles doesn't mean we're a non-profit organisation'. Its annual net income has almost tripled on his watch, from $135 million to $395 million.

In 1991, Levi's introduced its Terms of Engagement, a pioneering code of conduct for suppliers and has added requirements since then to improve workers' health, financial literacy and opportunities. In this, as in its support for sustainable cotton farming or its development of technology to cut water use in its manufacturing by almost 90 per cent, it has worked with NGOs and shared its insights with rivals for free.

Such efforts have not left it immune to criticism. Elizabeth Warren, the former Massachusetts senator and the then candidate for the 2020 Democratic US presidential nomination, derided Levi's for marketing an all-American brand while making most of its products abroad. It has also attracted controversy by intervening in some of America's most bitter political debates.

Its decisions to speak up on immigration and gun violence and to join other chief executives in urging the Trump administration to stay in the Paris Agreement on climate change have required little financial sacrifice. Still, Bergh defines such moves similarly as choosing 'the harder right over the easier wrong' – with the long view in mind.

In September 2020, he urged Congress to require gun buyers pass background checks. As a former army officer who has fired assault rifles (I might add that this author has also done that when a navy cadet but shall never use in anger), he said, 'the average American does not need to own one'. Many of his customers ardently disagreed, exposing Levi's to the risk of boycotts, but he expected the company to be vindicated in time. Levi's has also rallied other companies to back a bipartisan voter turnout initiative called Time to Vote.

Social Responsibility of Governments

Little is written about the social responsibility of governments which is surprising because it seems companies are held up to high standards, while CSR in the public sector lags behind in many instances. Then the tragedy of Brexit in my country, the UK, is still unfolding and I have argued elsewhere that it was one, if not the, worst decisions ever taken. Indeed, in times of crisis, such as with COVID-19, the steady hand of the UK would have been much appreciated in Europe.

Then climate change is on everybody's list of concerns as potentially a crisis that could end civilization on our planet itself. Yet some public leaders wilfully destroy treaties, such as the Paris Agreement on Climate Change, for their own personal glorification as we saw in the USA for instance. Now it is happily reversed under Biden leadership. But danger lurks now, as I write, from Russia where total lack of social responsibility exists in its summit in the Kremlin.

In the Western world, change is in the air as responsibility issues of financial corporations coupled with increased concern of energy issues, meaning sustainability has become the current watchword. Nearly two decades ago, the UK Government was one of the leaders in promoting CSR. It published a CSR report – a Government Update[3] – and appointed a minister for CSR. However, with the move towards 'Sustainability' and an eloquent spokesman, Jonathan Porritt, made Chair of the Government's Sustainable Development Commission, the balance has been towards the environment, carbon offsets and global warming. Nothing wrong with that but a Government suffering deep divisions because of an expense scandal was not best placed to promote CSR neither then nor now with the disastrous Brexit.[4]

Meanwhile, the EU contributed a fair amount of money for the CSR environment with, unfortunately, limited success. Its flagship project on 'stakeholder dialogue' led to much talk but little action.[5] While the Government of Nations, the United Nations, bravely launched its Global Compact at the turn of the century, only to discover that the 5,000 companies who signed up for its 10 principles wondered what they were doing there except to see and be seen?[6]

At one time the better known institution than the UN, the so-called 'rich man's club, the OECD, discussed CSR at its financial ministers meeting in Lecce in June 2009, in preparation for the July 2009 Italian G8 summit. Some progress in words when two newish components appeared – the finance minister's 'Lecce' declaration whereby new business conduct principles might lead to a revision of the largely ineffectual (to date) *OECD Guidelines for Multinational Enterprises* and that OECD Members, as well as Chile, Estonia, Israel and Slovenia, endorsed a 'Green Growth' Declaration. Although the *Financial Times* noted[7] that 'Preparatory talks on another agenda item – climate change – held by senior diplomats of the 16-nation Major Economies Forum late on Tuesday dropped a reference in the draft communiqué to the goal of halving greenhouse gas omissions by 2050'.

According to Forbes,[8] the business conduct principles in the *'Lecce Framework'* has the objectives of creating

a comprehensive framework, building on existing initiatives, to identify and fill regulatory gaps and foster the broad international consensus needed for rapid implementation. And it recognizes that there is a wide range of instruments, both existing and under development, which have a common thread related to propriety, integrity and transparency and classifies

---

3. See http://www.berr.gov.uk/files/file48771.pdf, accessed 15 July 2009.
4. Mihttps://www.amazon.com/Brrrexit-England-will-left-cold-ebook/dp/B0849ZLN7G
5. http://www.csreurope.org/pages/en/eu_and_stakeholder_dialogue.html, accessed 15 July 2009.
6. See Michael Hopkins http://bclc.chamberpost.com/category/globaldevelopment, accessed 23 November 2009.
7. *21 Financial Times*, 8 July 2009.
8. https://www.forbes.com/2009/06/13/g8-lecce-framework-markets-economy-full-text.html ?sh=7be1ea826a2b, accessed 23 June 2021.

them into five categories: corporate governance, market integrity, financial regulation and supervision, tax cooperation, and transparency of macroeconomic policy and data.

Nothing particularly new there – although the use of the word 'transparency' has been weakened from its normal euphemism of anti-corruption, to only mean the transparency of macroeconomic policy and data.

Perhaps more interesting, in the OECD preparatory meeting, was its mention of CSR for a rare moment, when they stated[9]:

> We consider that a renewed commitment to responsible business conduct will help to rebuild trust and confidence in markets. We firmly commit to the principles of propriety, integrity and transparency. Thus, we agree on the need to develop a set of common standards and processes regarding the conduct of international business and finance. For this purpose, we welcome the OECD work in relation to the Lecce Framework and a Global Charter for sustainable economic activity. We call on the OECD to strengthen its work on corporate governance and financial literacy. We will continue to promote corporate social responsibility and welcome further consultation on the up-dating of the OECD Guidelines for Multinational Enterprises to increase their relevance and clarify private sector responsibilities.

But how do countries measure up to social responsibility themselves? The index I created and discussed in Chapter 11[10] showed that, depressingly many, if not most, countries lack social responsibility. The key stakeholders of any nation-state are their citizens and their trading partners. Consequently, I defined National Social Responsibility as follows: a State that treats its citizens fairly, looks after their well-being and is respectful to foreigners – immigrants as well as their trading partners.

CSR: Hate Exxon Love Shell

Why is it that two large oil companies have such different approaches to CSR? One good (Shell) one bad (Exxon)? To elicit a response from both, I wrote an article a dozen years ago with the provocative title: Hate Exxon Love Shell! Interestingly, I had several responses from Exxon but none from Shell!

Background

In John Elkington's strangely named but influential advice book 'Cannibals with Forks', the idea was born that each company should account for their triple bottom line – social, economic and environmental. A sign of high visibility of Shell in these issues and the invisibility of ExxonMobil in the book was that Shell was referred to

---

9. https://www.oecd.org/investment/mne/43391277.pdf, accessed 23 June 2021.
10. http://www.mhcinternational.com/images/stories/national_social_responsibility_index .pdf, accessed 4 July 2009.

about 50 times while Exxon had no references whatsoever. Moreover, Exxon received a rocky reception from environmentalists opposed to its support at the time for President Bush's anti-global warming and anti-Kyoto treaty approach. As the *Financial Times* stated on 6 June 2002, ExxonMobil involvement in Bush's decision to end any pretence of US support for the Kyoto Protocol made it the environmentalists' most hated company. The word 'hate' also cropped up in a report by the UK *Sunday Telegraph* which reported that Exxon had 'committed the crime of opposing the Kyoto international pact on fighting global warming'. And, 'unlike BP and Shell, Exxon stalwartly refused to invest in renewable energy such as solar and wind power'. Unsurprisingly, its then CEO joined the Trump administration as Secretary of State but even his less than radical views couldn't survive the mindless onslaught of the failed dictator US president.

On the social front, Exxon has also been less visible than Shell. A major watershed for Shell was the Brent Spar incident in the mid-1990s where Shell had to take all the blame even though a little known fact was that this was a joint 50/50 venture between Shell and Exxon. Exxon 'ducked its head and left it to Shell to take the heat' while the Brent Spar conflict lasted.

The weight of the two companies on the world business market, let alone as oil majors, is huge. Exxon, based in the USA, is the world's largest non-governmental producer of oil and gas, and employs around 92,500 people in 200 countries (for more details, see www.exxonmobil.com). Shell, of similar size, is an oil major based partly in London and partly in The Hague and employs 115,000 people in 145 countries (see www.shell.com).

According to Mallen Baker, Shell was the first to produce a social report when Shell Canada produced its 'Progress Toward Sustainable Development' report in 1991 – just a few years after the Brundtland Report had more or less defined the term 'sustainable'. Mallen Baker also noted that the most obvious difference between this and a modern report is the rather light touch accorded to the 'social' side within the definition of sustainable development. Nevertheless, for a document produced well before the term 'corporate social responsibility' had entered any kind of common parlance it stands up remarkably well to the expectations of a modern audience.

Stung by the Brent Spar controversy (the abandoned attempt to ditch an oil rig in the deep waters of the Atlantic) and other well-known incidents such as the death of Ken Sara Wawa in Nigeria, Shell released a series of annual reports covering its ethical, social and environmental activities – the most recent of which was 'Meeting the Energy Challenge: The Shell Report 2002'.

Exxon's approach has been much lower profile, content to argue that there are sound scientific arguments against at least some aspects of the Kyoto Treaty. But Exxon's lower CSR profile might, indeed, reflect different concerns given that its homebase is in the USA and less subject to the perhaps more ferocious critics of Shell, in London and The Hague. According to Jon Birger, in comparison with other large European oil companies, ExxonMobil has apparently avoided major NGO and media scrutiny on CSR. The Birger report noted that ExxonMobil has kept a very low profile in its external communication on CSR issues. By promising little, there is actually a high level of association between what the company says and what it does.

The *Financial Times* (6 June 2002) reported that the company's critics include Mark Mansley, a former chief analyst at Chase Manhattan. His report said that ExxonMobil's opposition to the Kyoto Protocol, which called for cuts in greenhouse gas emissions, risks harming its shareholders. The report, which has a Foreword by Robert Monks, the corporate governance specialist, has as much to say about ExxonMobil's tone as about its views on global warming. 'The way in which you speak seems to create needless confrontation', Mr. Monks tells the company.

Yet another view of ExxonMobil's approach comes from Middlesex University Business Professor, Abby Ghobadian, who believes that differences and changes in CSR strategy may be due to company-specific factors such as organizational structure and learning capacity, leadership, corporate tradition, CSR reputation and so on. For example, since ExxonMobil has not been the wrong side of serious CSR transgressions, it has apparently fewer incentives to change course, as compared to European companies. ExxonMobil's organizational structure and the organizational changes in the wake of Exxon's merger with Mobil merger could, therefore, also have consequences for company society relationships.

But does Exxon ignore CSR issues?

ExxonMobil has deliberately allowed BP and Shell 'to seize the moral high ground' on CSR issues. As already noted, the company has chosen to keep a low profile on 'macro' CSR issues while implementing social programmes at a 'micro' community level. ExxonMobil claims that it contributes to social welfare worldwide by efficient production of energy and chemicals, community outreach programmes and high performance on SHE (Safety, Health & Environment – stepped up in the wake of the Exxon Valdez incident). The company has not changed this policy, but it did add human rights to its portfolio of corporate responsibilities. While this new element has not led to any significant changes in corporate principles and procedures, ExxonMobil's involvement with the World Bank in the Chad-Cameroon pipeline project indicated change in how to develop projects in extremely poor countries.

In 2002, ExxonMobil responded to the widening CSR agenda by publishing the report Corporate Citizenship in a Changing World. The aim of this report was to take stock of the company's responsibility through its involvement in society. One section discussed commitments to governments, communities and societies. As in the case of environmental publications and official statements, the section in question is amazingly sparse in clear commitments in contrast to the European oil majors and considering the size and importance of the company. The report does not signal any significant change in ExxonMobil's CSR strategy. Micro CSR issues related to communities and neighbours represent the main focus in the report. On the other hand, ExxonMobil has included a commitment on human rights. ExxonMobil condemns the violation of human rights in any form.

ExxonMobil has taken a clear stance on corruption and bribery. The company argues that fraudulent practices, bribery and dubious accounting methods could contaminate the whole organization leading to an acceptance of such practices. ExxonMobil's Standards of Business Conduct on ethics states:

Employees must understand that the Corporation does care how results are obtained, not just that they are obtained. Employees must be encouraged to tell higher manager all that they are doing, to record all transactions accurately in their books and records, and to be honest and forthcoming with the Corporations internal and external auditors. The Corporation expects employees to report suspected violations of law or ExxonMobil policies to company management.

Sustainability reports compared

Shell has produced sustainability reports for a number of years. Definitions and concepts aside, what would I expect, at minimum, to find in a report on CSR? At the very least, one would hope for (1) a top level statement from the CEO or equivalent on CSR; (2) some commentary about the policies and/or values of the business; (3) a review of the company's stakeholder engagement; (4) an analysis of what are the key social and environmental issues for the company with narrative on how the company is responding; (5) data showing performance in each of these areas; and (6) an independent assessment of replies.

How do the most recent sustainability report of Shell and the corporate citizenship report of ExxonMobil stand up to my six criteria? The results are shown in Table 17.1 and I have used a scale that reads 1 = Nothing, 2 = Poor, 3 = Neither poor nor good, 4 = Good and 5 = Very Good.

From the table, it can be seen that Shell has an overall score bordering on very good (to my mind it could do more on social indicators and governance issues). Exxon performs just a little bit better than poor due to its main focus upon environmental issues (and even there its views are found wanting as discussed above) and little information on social issues; it only addresses two stakeholder groups other than the environment (the community and its own workforce); indicators are scanty and no independent assessment is provided. Exxon could draw many lessons from the Shell report should it so wish, especially the innovative 'Tell Shell' which provides frank and sometimes discordant views to those Shell would wish. However, the report neither provides any cost of their 'social' involvement nor their corresponding 'benefits'. I didn't include the latter in the table since few companies have done such an exercise.

Table 17.1 Comparing Shell and Exxon Reports of 2002

	The Shell Report 2002	ExxonMobil: Corporate Citizenship Report 2002
1. Top-level statement by CEO	5	5
2. Commentary on policies/values	4	2
3. Review of stakeholder engagement	4	3
4. Analysis of key social and environmental issues	5	2
5. Data showing performance for each stakeholder group and issue	5	2
6. Independent Assessment	5	1
Average Score	4.7	2.5

Shareholder value

What does the above tell us about the two companies? Strong, usually negative, words are used when discussing the social responsibility of Exxon. While Shell is considered a model corporate citizen. My scores above and those calculated with my online CSR assessor CRITICS show that Exxon is a long way behind Shell, but is not as bad as many believe. Moreover, cynics might argue that Shell is doing a disservice to its shareholders in fussing (and spending) about its social responsibility while the more 'hard-nosed' penurious approach of Exxon is more beneficial.

Thus, one hypothesis is that Shell's extra (but unreported) costs compared with ExxonMobil should reduce the shareholder value of the company simply because all this extra 'non-business' effort detracts from the company's main focus of creating profits. An alternative hypothesis – I called this the j-curve hypothesis – is that care and attention given to main concerns of stakeholders in a socially responsible manner would eventually lead to increased shareholder value. I have not been able to measure this so far, given available data, but one measure is the share (stock in the USA) price performance of the companies' respective shares over a reasonable period. Drawing from information readily available on each of the two companies websites for the share price of each company in the USA (on the NYSE) over a five-year period, 1999–2003, I saw that both charts showed that their share price varied from around $30 to $45 (ExxonMobil) and $40 to $65 (Royal Dutch Shell), and that the fluctuations were pretty much the same over the period.

This rough and ready method allows us to reject the first hypothesis above but not necessarily to accept the second hypothesis. Nevertheless, it does appear that a more socially responsible approach does not negatively affect share price over and above other factors and hence there is little reason not to behave in a socially responsible manner. Indeed, given that the future is unknown, the CSR approach is a risk aversion approach that may as well be followed since it could help reduce future problems while, at the same time, does not injure share price. Moreover, this view is backed up by the fact that a shareholders' resolution calling on ExxonMobil to take renewable energy more seriously picked up 20 per cent of the vote in 2002 – more than double the 2001 level. More worrying to ExxonMobil should be the quality of the opposition. Pat Mulva, vice-president for investor relations, said supporters of the resolution appeared to have been swayed by Institutional Shareholder Services, which advises institutional investors. ISS backed the resolution after opposing similar motions in the past two years.

So, can my section title be justified? As the arguments in this section show, both the words 'hate' and 'love' are too strong since, clearly, Exxon is not as bad as all that, while Shell is not quite as perfect as some would have us believe. Clearly, Exxon's poor reputation has a lot to do with its cautious approach to CSR coupled with its obvious support for the then President Bush's anti-environmentalist views and Trump's total nihilism. But should Shell revert to a more minimalist position on the social front given that Exxon has managed to survive with its own parsimonious approach? Only time will tell but my view is Exxon's position will eventually weigh negatively on its share price, while my money goes on Shell!

Chapter Eighteen

CSR COVERS SUSTAINABLE PHILANTHROPY AND SOCIAL ENTERPRISE[1]

Introduction

CSR is sustainable in that CSR actions become part and parcel of the way in which a company carries out its business. Its links to the bottom line of a company must be clearly laid out simply because, if it does not contribute to the bottom line, it will eventually be rejected by hard-nosed directors and shareholders. Normally, philanthropy is more whimsical as it simply depends on the whims of the company directors at a particular time. Many NGOs receive their funds from corporations and carry out excellent work. However, like Heineken beer, most NGOs carry out programmes that others (mainly government programmes) can't reach.

According to Wikipedia, philanthropy means the 'love of humanity' and 'private initiatives, for the public good, focusing on quality of life'. Further, philanthropy has distinguishing characteristics separate from charity; Wikipedia states that 'not all charity is philanthropy, or vice versa, though there is a recognized degree of overlap in practice. A difference commonly cited is that charity aims to relieve the pain of a particular social problem, whereas philanthropy attempts to address the root cause of the problem – the difference between the proverbial gift of a fish to a hungry person, versus teaching them how to fish'. Curiously, Wikipedia doesn't cover sustainable philanthropy.[2]

However, Wikipedia does elaborate the corporate social responsibility (CSR) and sustainability point of view when it states that 'the definition also serves to contrast philanthropy with business endeavours, which are private initiatives for private good,

---

1. Based on Michael Hopkins, 'CSR and Sustainable Development in Practice – Examples from Bangladesh, Sri Lanka and South Africa', Fifth Annual Forum on Business Ethics and Corporate Social Responsibility in a Global Economy: Corporate and Stakeholder Responsibility. Theory and Practice, Milan, 22–23 May 2008. Published in POLITEIA: RIVISTA DI ETICA E SCELTE PUBBLICHE Anno XXV – N. 93 – 2009 Corporate and Stakeholder Responsibility. Theory and Practice Edited by Emilio D'Orazio (Milan, Italy). Revised after presentation by the author to a Sustainable Philanthropy course given in Tblisi, Georgia, on 4 July 2019 hosted by the EU and the Center for Strategic Research and Development of Georgia.
2. https://en.wikipedia.org/wiki/Philanthropy, accessed 21 July 2019.

e.g. focusing on material gain, and with government endeavours, which are public initiatives for public good, e.g. focusing on provision of public services'.

But philanthropic interventions by NGOs tend to be based on a scatter gun approach and are spotty. They can intervene wherever they like. Governments, on the other hand, have to intervene everywhere or nowhere. Better, much better, for a company to assist a government in making its contributions either nationally, or internationally, which would be more efficient and appropriate. This then ensures widespread and even coverage. There is a new dimension as discussed later, and briefly in this chapter, of introducing social enterprise aspects to NGO work.

But what about all those good causes? I can see that my words will irk many readers who may accuse me of undermining good people and good causes. But this is not my point; I want sustainable actions that do not depend on the whims of, albeit, good-natured people. But, what about all those charities that depend on companies for financial support? Should these be stopped? Obviously, this is unreasonable and many hundreds of millions would suffer if corporations suddenly stopped contributing to charitable organizations.

Yet, there is a structural problem here. Governments mainly encourage charitable giving, often through tax breaks, since it takes the responsibility away from them. Governments are also corporations and must act in a socially responsible manner. My suggestion is that charitable giving is phased out over a long term, say 10 years, so that both existing charitable organizations and governments can adjust. Corporations can help in this transition period not only with managerial and technical advice but with cash too.

Michael Porter Gets It Wrong

Corporations have always been involved in philanthropy. One of the leading thinkers in corporate strategy even believes that CSR is simply philanthropy. Michael Porter wrote, "Corporate philanthropy – or corporate social responsibility – is becoming an ever more important field for business. Today's companies ought to invest in corporate social responsibility as part of their business strategy to become more competitive'.[3] However, as will be seen in this chapter, Michael Porter was not on the right track. When even an internationally respected management guru mentions philanthropy and CSR as being the same, it is hardly surprising that business leaders, academics and politicians confuse them. CSR is not the same as corporate philanthropy.

As noted in this and my other books,[4] CSR is a system-wide concept that touches all the stakeholders of a corporation. CSR, as defined here, does not concentrate on only one stakeholder, whereas philanthropy, 'the practice of performing charitable or

---

3. https://hbr.org/2002/12/the-competitive-advantage-of-corporate-philanthropy, accessed 9 August 2019.
4. Over 100,000 reads according to Researchgate.com over the past two years. See https://www .researchgate.net/profile/Michael_Hopkins5

benevolent actions' does. Most, if not all, philanthropy is devoted to items that governments should be doing (health grants to developing countries, help to the handicapped and drugs for HIV/AIDS, for example). And their failure should not be the preserve of corporations. However, since government is one of the stakeholders of a corporation, there is nothing to stop corporations from offering their management and technical skills to government to improve or introduce programmes to help vulnerable groups. Corporations exist to make profits. There is nothing wrong with that; only the way profits are made is the concern of CSR practitioners. Philanthropy does little or nothing to help companies make profits, while all CSR activities are linked, in general, to improving a company's bottom line.

CSR Is Before Profit

One of the confusions over defining and acting upon CSR, according to Professors Young-Chul Kang and Donna Wood of the Katz School of Business in the USA, results from a flawed assumption that CSR is an after-profit obligation. This means that if companies are not profitable they do not have to behave responsibly! They say that 'in the extreme, if all firms are affected by severe economic turmoil or are run by lazy, short-sighted managers, then societies would have no choice but to accept pollution, discrimination, dangerous working conditions, child labour, etc'.

Embedding socially responsible principles in corporate management is what the two authors call a 'before-profit' obligation. They cite corporations that embody these ideas and see the trend accelerating. For instance, in 1950, Sears' CEO listed four parties to any business in order of importance as 'customers, employees, community and stockholders'. For him, profit was a 'by-product of success in satisfying responsibly the legitimate needs and expectations of the corporations' primary stakeholder group'. By the 1980s, Levis even repurchased its stock in the public market under the rationale that stockholder's interests might limit the firm's effort to be a socially responsible organization. And, Migros, of Switzerland, funds its cultural and social programmes not by profits, but by gross sales, so that profitability does not influence the firm's level of involvement.

CSR Is Sustainable, Philanthropy Is Not

CSR is sustainable in that CSR actions become part and parcel of the way in which a company carries out its business. Its links to the bottom line of a company must be clearly laid out simply because, if it does not contribute to the bottom line, it will eventually be rejected by hard-nosed directors and shareholders.

Is Sponsorship Philanthropy?

Corporate sponsorship is different from corporate philanthropy. Sponsorship is a business tool used by companies as part of their communication, advertising or public relations (PR) budgets to associate the corporation's products and services with dynamic images for their customers' consumption. Sponsorship usually requires a service, or action, in return for financial support, and so this frequently has clear marketing benefits and is therefore directly linked to a company's bottom line. Sometimes, this may indeed be for good causes, such as supporting UNICEF to associate the company's products with reducing child labour around the world. Philanthropy does not necessarily ask for a definite service or action in return, and it is certainly not usually based on a business relationship or partnership. On a personal level, this is like responding favourably to the postal requests made by major charities. Yet the line between philanthropy and sponsorship is difficult to draw, and there are many grey areas – but better to have a clear sponsorship potential than a fuzzy charitable action that is more than likely to be unsustainable.

In the end, a company that is philanthropically generous but is not aware of, or engaged in, its broader CSR role will not be in business for very long. In this I agree fully with one point of Michael Porter: 'If companies are just being good and donating a lot of money to social initiatives then they will be wasting shareholders' money. That is not sustainable in the long run, and shareholders will quickly lose interest'.

As you know dear reader, CSR/Sustainability is essentially about treating key stakeholders responsibly, leading to the issue that philanthropy is not, in general, sustainable. One definition of sustainable is that after an initial investment will the project continue and even grow in the future? This latter view is nicely encapsulated by a banker from UBS (a lecturer on my University of Geneva course) who told me that 'we provide an investment sum into philanthropy but we get no return on our investment and not only that but we also lose all our capital!'

Happily, some philanthropic projects are sustainable as will be shown in the rest of this chapter with a methodology that can be applied to almost any development project. The methodology works for NGOs, government and private companies that are seeking to increase the well-being of disadvantaged people through development acts. It doesn't work so well for NGOs that are advocates for a cause such as Greenpeace or Human Rights Watch, with laudable objectives, but often difficult to get a return on investment without straight donor funding.

The 3-M Approach to Sustainable Projects

I suggest that any socio-economic development project should have at least three components – what I have called the 3M approach to development.[5] These are:

A *micro* component that demonstrates the viability of the project at the ground level and
    better if it has plans for replication.
A *meso* component that works to enhance governance such as improving the efficiency
    of local government institutions which will eventually bear responsibility for the
    micro project.

---

5. First used by Michael Hopkins when he was senior evaluator for the UNDP over 1995 to 2007, the UN adopted the framework for a time but as often happens once the advocate (the author) moves on, the concept fades and today not sure what model, if any, is used.

A *macro* component that works to improve overall government or institutional policy which touches the meso and micro parts of the project.

Let me give an example. In Iasi in Romania, in June 2019, I was approached by a smartly dressed schoolgirl carrying a bucket and a folder. She was asking for a contribution to a charity she supported which provided homes and supervision for orphans and other abandoned children. The children were as young as a few months old and stayed until they were 21. Thus the charity provided meals, supervision, education, health and, in general, life. Few would consider such a charity doing anything but a wonderful job. My contribution was not money but advice. Did you think to ask the children once they were adults, say 16, to sign a contract with the charity to promise 10 per cent (say) of their future salary to give to the charity? After all without the charity, they would probably not be in such good shape and eventually valuable members of the labour force with decent incomes. Of course, some would not pay, nor be able to but many would especially if reinforced with regular annual meetings of the alumni. Another benefit of such contracts is that the charity could then show many promises of future income to a bank that could lend on a concessional basis assuming the process had worked. Clearly proof would have to be provided. In fact, each time I meet, in a shopping mall or wherever, someone collecting money for a similar charity –in two shopping malls in Kenya I found similar ventures – I gave similar advice. I know that in one year the same people will be asking for money in the same location for the same charity. But ideas do take root, and my specula-tion is that one of the people I meet will mention such a possibility at one of their focus group meetings. I do leave my name and a precis of my idea and I shall check every time I meet the collectors, some of whom are of course recipients of the charity. Of course, not all the money eventually collected will probably be enough, but the experience helps the charity to start thinking about how they can be sustainable and not dependent on handouts.

What are the macro, meso and micro (I call 3-M) implications? If the charity is successful, then others may copy – replication and hence a movement toward policy and policy is the link between a macro idea (such as ending poverty), the means to do so (meso) and the actual project (micro). Now you can say that looking after under-priv-ileged children should be a government (public) responsibility and I agree. However, governments especially in poorer countries or parts thereof (e.g. Alabama in USA) don't or can't afford such an investment. But they can encourage the sort of move to a social enterprise that I have just described.

I was recently asked (July 2019) to give a lecture, funded by the EU, to companies in Tblisi, Georgia, on strategic philanthropy. In fact, most of my talk and discussion was on sustainable philanthropy and my arguments are written up here. Archie Carroll, one of the founders of CSR, describes strategic philanthropy[6] as the approach by which cor-porate or business giving and other philanthropic endeavours of a firm are designed in

---

6. Strategic Philanthropy. see https://www.researchgate.net/publication/327100647_Strategic _Philanthropy, accessed 7 August 2019.

such a way that the donation 'best fits with the firm's overall mission, goals, and values'. Indeed, strategic philanthropy is not simply altruistic as in the UBS example cited earlier but is also intended to help both the company and the society. Then the argument is that it is more difficult to judge what activities to choose since for many companies the business case for, say, something like the orphan giving case discussed previously is clearly a good thing to do but not easy to fit into a corporate model. Possibly something a company would do for a poor community in which it has located a manufacturing facility and where it seeks the goodwill of the local population. Consequently, strategic philanthropy would be better helped if it had a strong social enterprise component and that is where companies have strength.

Other questions were asked of me, such as 'How to be more strategic about giving – developing a strategic plan for the company's charitable and philanthropic activities?' Not easy since, as mentioned above, what is the business case for a company? Is it not enough that the company pays its taxes and is happy that the government will use such revenue wisely in the best interest of its subjects? Well one does not have to be much of a cynic to conclude that is somewhat far-fetched. To this end, I have suggested that companies issue a Charter on how best they can contribute to the big issues of the day as discussed in Chapter 3.

Two further questions lead to a similar response: (1) How to define focus areas for philanthropic programme? (2) How to plan philanthropic programmes with the view of a larger purpose to achieve more significant social impact?

These questions lead to the main question raised and that is, How to align philanthropic programmes with business goals in order to produce simultaneous social and economic gains? To which, as noted above, there is no easy answer but the 3-M approach would help radically change most philanthropic approaches!

India, Philanthropy and CSR

There is great interest in CSR in India, as I mentioned in Chapter 12, particularly since the publication of CSR rules in Indian company law went into force a few years ago. As also noted above, CSR is a multi-stakeholder initiative, and in turn, also forms the basis of the EU, ISO26000 and GRI definitions.

In India, CSR has meant[7] CSR projects, and large companies with profits over a certain amount are compelled to spend 2 per cent of these on CSR projects. They are also invited to set up CSR committees within their company – leading, according to some estimates, to about 16,000 companies using 48,000 board members.

---

7. Working with India CSR colleagues during COVID times has led to India revising its view of CSR. I am grateful to Harsha Mukerjee, CEO of the International Institute of Corporate Sustainability and Responsibility (IICSR) for working with me to help promote that change see https://iicsr.com/team/knowledge-advisors/

For some large companies such as Tata or Infosys, compliance is easy since they already partake in many so-called CSR projects. The company law lists the project areas where companies are invited to create CSR projects and are displayed in the table below.[8]

India CSR Rules Schedule 7

---

(1) In Schedule VII, for items (i) to (x) and the entries relating thereto, the following items and entries shall be substituted, namely:-

   (i) eradicating hunger, poverty and malnutrition, promoting preventive health care and sanitation and making available safe drinking water;

  (ii) promoting education, including special education, and employment enhancing vocation skills especially among children, women, elderly and the differently abled and livelihood enhancement projects;

 (iii) promoting gender equality, empowering women, setting up homes and hostels for women and orphans, setting up old age homes, day care centres and such other facilities for senior citizens and measures for reducing inequalities faced by socially and economically backward groups;

 (iv) ensuring environmental sustainability, ecological balance, protection of flora and fauna, animal welfare, agroforestry, conservation of natural resources and maintaining quality of soil, air and water;

  (v) protection of national heritage, art and culture including restoration of buildings and sites of historical importance and works of art; setting up public libraries; promotion and development of traditional arts and handicrafts;

 (vi) measures for the benefit of armed forces veterans, war widows and their dependents;

(vii) training to promote rural sports, nationally recognized sports, paralympic sports and Olympic sports;

(viii) contribution to the Prime Minister's National Relief Fund or any other fund set up by the Central Government for socioeconomic development and relief and Welfare of the Scheduled Castes, the Scheduled Tribes, other backward classes, minorities women;

 (ix) contributions or funds provided to technology incubators located within academic institutions which are approved by the central government;

  (x) rural development projects

Normally lists like those above are more familiar in UN or government planning documents and are essentially for guidance to the public sector. Sometimes such plans also include incentives for the private sector to be involved in executing the programmes. But the new company law in India is unique across the world – nearest parallels are probably in Mauritius and Nigeria.

The law has led to great interest in CSR around India and raised the profile of companies and their role in Indian society. I think raising the level of this interest is a very good thing but I wish it had been handled very differently. Clearly, many believe that given India's high level of poverty which some estimates put at 60 per cent of the population, large companies should contribute to development.

---

8. *Source*: https://taxguru.in/company-law/csr-provisions-schedule-vii-companies-act-2013.html

However, there are a number of questions and implied objections:

1. Is it not the job of the government to invest in development projects? Using tax revenue to invest in such things as the Prime Minister's National Relief Fund or rural development projects or measure for armed forces veterans? Or at least to provide the incentives for the private sector to be involved such as tax breaks, incentive systems, foundations, social funds, tax subsidies (such as a basic income), micro-credit institutions, and so on?

2. If the private sector is much better at such things as promoting education, gender equality, or setting up old age homes, why does the government not raise taxes on corporate profits and then allocate the revenue to so-called CSR projects using the private sector through a bid and tendering system?

3. Will the emphasis on CSR projects actually hurt CSR in India? This is my main worry, since companies caught in the CSR profit net will feel that they need do no more on CSR and will avoid multi-stakeholder systematic CSR? This could mean India being behind companies around the world that have adopted full-fledged CSR. In Mauritius, a similar tax of 1 per cent on profits allocated to government chosen NGOs had led to the phrase 'CSR' being considered by companies as a dirty word!

4. Without Indian companies adopting CSR frameworks that are not required under the new law – – such as GRI G4 sustainability reporting, SA8000 labour conditions, fair-trade production of their exports and UN Human Rights Principles for Companies – will these actions lead to less exports? And will Indian consumers, as in many countries, prefer to pay a premium for fairly produced products from companies that have a full-fledged CSR system? Or will the same old exploitations of labour, shoddy products and environmentally unsound policies continue? Not by all companies it must be said since many large companies have adopted, as I mentioned above, system wide CSR policies that are both up to international standards and are actually beneficial to the company itself (see my book *The Planetary Bargain* on such a system-wide approach or a shorter free version on my website – 'A Strategic Approach to CSR'.[9])

5. Should not any CSR project be closely aligned with the business case of the company involved in the new law? If this is not the case, then the new CSR law is simply introducing a new tax.

6. Will investment in the new CSR projects be sustainable, i.e. once the initial investment is done will the projects look after themselves?

---

9. *Original Source*: Michael Hopkins (MHCi), *A Planetary Bargain: Corporate Social Responsibility Comes of Age* (Macmillan, 1998; updated and re-printed by Earthscan, 2003 and also re-printed by Routledge, UK, 2010. Updated to emphasize materiality on 2 October 2014). Also updated in Michael Hopkins, *CSR/Sustainability – From the Margins to the Mainstream: A Text Book* (Sheffield: Greenleaf, 2016). The definition was further updated on 1 January 2017 with clause 6, thanks to Siemens and Bob Munro for edits.

7. How will the government ensure that the companies involved don't all choose the same projects? In an exercise in our workshops, involving groups choosing projects for Tata, many opted for bio toilets, a great need in India, but could such an investment simply lead to a huge surplus of bio toilets while other key problems are ignored?

The above issues were discussed, and participants carried out a number of interactive case studies in groups in the workshops held over the 10 days when I was in India in October 2013 and again in March 2019. Most companies I spoke with, except the very largest, were rather bemused by the new laws and were asking for guidance on what to do next. Although, now nearly a decade later, the discussion continues and now widens to encompass some of my own views of multi-stakeholder treatment.[10]

So huge possibilities for new consulting and advisory services. But was that the real intention of the government? Certainly not, since to be fair they are seriously interested in reducing poverty and many Indian intellectuals have been writing what to do about that for many years. Perhaps, it is time to turn back to listen to these intellectuals and come up with laws that actually do help to reduce poverty in India while not punishing large companies? Rather use large companies' management expertise, which they have in great abundance and, as many civil servants would admit, strikingly lacking in public institutions in general.

What Is Social Impact and How to Measure the Impact of Philanthropic programmes[11]?

There is no easy way to measure social impact. Often one needs a socio-economic survey taken before the intervention has taken place and again after a certain time has passed. Then one needs a control group of similar characteristics where the measures have not been applied. For small interventions, such sophistication is rarely done and simpler techniques must be used. Below I suggest using a simple rating scale that, albeit not as scientific as the foregoing, does provide a rapid answer as will be seen in the case studies that follow its presentation.

Nevertheless, the Rockefeller Foundation has produced a set of guidelines that provide more sophistication than my own methodology which I found attractive. That is because as an evaluator of UNDP (UN Development Programme) projects and programmes over 1995 to 2007, I saw the same techniques being used. It is never too clear what is meant by a programme (also called a programme approach by the UNDP) and a project – the best distinction is that a programme is a collection of projects

---

10. Drawn from http://www.csrfi.com/wp-content/uploads/2014/06/The-new-India-CSR -rules_Help-or-hindrance-to-India.pdf, accessed 16 February 2018.
11. This section draws upon Melissa Berman, CEO, Rockefeller Philanthropy Advisors https:// www.verenigingvanfondsen.nl/viewer/file.aspx?fileinfoID=331, accessed 4 July 2019.

while a programme is a theme such as an anti-poverty programme for a country as a whole. Even then, the programme's projects need to be evaluated through the techniques presented here. Five main steps are recommended by the Rockefeller team which I have amended slightly:

Step 1: Be clear on what you are trying to assess
         Did the funds obtained get used in the way they were intended? If the agency committed to training 100 women as health aides in 18 months, say, how many were trained in that time? Were there any attempts to make sustainable changes?

Step 2: Measuring effectiveness: Make sure indicators are chosen to match the assessment
         Two aspects are useful: (a) evaluation and (b) systems thinking.
         a. Evaluation
             Ensure that the goals are set as well as the outcomes, then check the actual outcomes with the goals, such as the number of teachers trained, the number of students who got eye examinations, the number of performances and the number of acres conserved.
             The project may be ongoing and as such you will be looking at evaluating the process more than the results.
             Using a control group is a more rigorous method of evaluation and seeks to document results by measuring the target population against a comparable group that did not participate in the programme and sometimes compares the effect on participants before and after the programme. For example, health programmes may compare participants who were carefully matched on most characteristics but who take part in different (or no) programmes to reduce weight and increase exercise. This methodology requires considerable sophistication, resources and a large research base for findings to be statistically valid.
         b. Systems thinking
             For a given problem, there are many aspects. For instance, the fate of children in poor neighbourhoods will change only if their entire environment changes. Thus the whole system needs to be considered so as to end the generational cycle of poverty by addressing the needs of the community at all levels – home, school and neighbourhood.

Step 3: Deciding on a level of assessment
         For instance, a grant is given to build a school in India. Among the things to assess are:
         Is the construction completed on budget and on time?
         Does the school have the right facilities for the target population?
         Does it have qualified teachers?
         Are students attending?

Are students making academic progress?

Are students going on to higher education?

Are students getting better jobs than they would have otherwise?

Are their lives better?

Is their community better overall as a result?

Each of these questions deals with the issue of impact at a different level – and generally implies a different time frame.

Step 4:   Understand challenges in assessing impact

Nonprofits do have a bottom line: They have financial results and tax returns. The real difference between 'investing' in a nonprofit or in a for-profit is that when we invest in a company, we only look for results at the company level. In the nonprofit sector, we are often looking at how the non-profit can deliver programmes that will bring about sustainable change in the community or even the world. Clearly, no grant of $50,000 (or even $1,000,000) will, alone, solve women's health problems in Haiti. In fact, it's likely that funding health organizations alone may not end disease in Haiti: The inability to access clean water and sanitation, poor nutrition, benefits, inadequate transportation, poverty and ill-treatment of women are complex, interwoven factors that result in poor health for women. Grants can, however, provide important relief as the society rebuilds or works to make services more available.

Another factor that makes assessment difficult is the huge range in time horizons among philanthropic endeavours. Only for some vaccinations do the treatment and cure happens simultaneously. Medical research can take decades. Most social challenges – poverty, lack of human rights or ethnic conflict – have time horizons that in some cases may have no real endpoint. But donors can hope to see progress and certainly benefits to individual communities and organizations.

Does this mean that donors should walk away from thinking about impact at the system level? Not at all. Without considering the broader context, donors run the risk of funding 'successful' programmes that make no real difference in addressing the problem they are seeking to solve.

Step 5:   Build a partnership

Donors and grantees should, ideally, reach a respectful agreement before a grant is made about what kind of assessment can be provided, by whom, and at whose cost. What is the grantee responsible for? What will the donor do? What might a third party be engaged to do? Who pays? Are there existing reporting methods that will work for the donor? Could the donor partner with other funders on a common approach?

Reporting is a necessary evil that no one likes and often seems to get in the way of focusing on the project activity at hand. Yet accountability is required since no one likes to provide grants for poor results. The rule should be to make reporting not intrusive but timely depending on the project.

Social Enterprise[12]

The reality is that the old NGO model simply cannot be sustained in a time of shrinking government funding and increased call for efficiency and impact in international development. It is time to realize that NGOs need to become more independent from governments, financially resilient and accountable for their activities.[13]

Most NGOs have two huge problems. First, they are partial in that their activities (in general) only cover a part of the problem they tackle – micro-credit, education, health provision, entrepreneurial start-ups, and so on. They are confined either to few geographical areas or to a part of the issue such as female primary education. Often NGOs simply do the work that governments cannot afford to do. Second, at the end of every project cycle they look for funding in grant form. In fact, probably most NGOs spend half their time (and therefore resources) looking for donors.

Of course, many NGOs – we can think of Medecin Sans Frontieres, International Red Cross, Amnesty International, Transparency International, Greenpeace and WWF – are either advocacy organizations or performing tasks across countries that national governments can't do.

But many, if not most, NGOs are supported by external funds and basically stop once the funds dry up. Many governments from the rich world support NGOs through their aid budgets as well as through support coming from philanthropic donors. But the former is starting to dry up as 'populism' or 'illiberalism' starts to make people more selfish. The latter is also under examination as philanthropists start to examine socially responsible investments. As UBS recently noted, an investment in a socially responsible activity could lead to modest returns and one's capital preserved. Philanthropy means that all money invested is totally lost and the return on investment is zero. Clearly, an alternative that leads to sustainability through money-earning activities that may also make a profit is highly attractive. That is why the notion of a Sustainable Social Enterprise (SSE) has risen so quickly and is becoming popular around the world.

Most entities such as an institution are systems and therefore a systems approach is very helpful in ensuring that the various bits and pieces fit together in a whole, where each person knows their responsibility – also known as Performance Management.

Chris Meyer[14] suggests six key steps that are needed to take an NGO into being a fully fledged SSE. Briefly, these are:

1. Cut down to (bare) essentials
   • Decide what you are good at and cut down everything else.
2. Get help – but not too much

12. Based on 'Transition from a Donor Dependent NGO to a Sustainable Social Enterprise', unpublished, by Michael Hopkins, Bob Munro, Martin van Straaten, Nairobi, December 2017.
13. See Chris Meyer, September 2014 in Devex, https://www.devex.com/news/from-ngo-to-social-business-why-and-how-84259
14. In Devex, https://www.devex.com/news/from-ngo-to-social-business-why-and-how-84259

- Make sure one or two consultants are there to help with the development of business plans for each business unit, working with, not just for, the board and managers.

3. Build a business plan – a real one
   - Setting out your values and ambitions and spelling out the external forces influencing the organizations do not count. And yet, the business plans of many NGOs are just that.
   - A real business plan addresses the six operational areas of any organization: activities, structure, communication, HR, finance and support infrastructure.

4. Accept the casualties
   - Be clear in your communication and expectations from each staff member. Ask them if they really understand the need for and the path of the change. Ask them if they think they have the skills, tenacity and motivation to see it though.

5. Give profit-and-loss skill and responsibility
   - Giving people the skills and responsibility to run their own profit and loss creates better results and increases satisfaction of most managers.
   - Profit is not a dirty word in the development-and-aid sector, and once everyone understands that a reasonable surplus actually ensures sustainability and independence from donors, most managers support it enthusiastically.

6. Move toward 'open development'
   - Ensure that transparency and accountability are central to the process.

Putting all these steps together provides a plan to look at all aspects of the NGO and identify parts of the system that need to be preserved under existing rules. That means those that are key to the NGO's activities, but are not easily turned into profit centres, must be financed by other profit centres or by direct grants. Then to look at areas that can be expanded or created to become revenue earners. I look next at an NGO in the slums of Nairobi that was set up by my friend and colleague Bob Munro 30 years ago, and his NGO MYSA (Mathare Youth and Sports Association) is an example of change from NGO to SSE, and that is also where I have been involved as an adviser on that change.[15]

One day, Bob Munro went to a part of one of the poorest slums in Africa with one million people and saw three youths kicking a can around in the midst of rubbish. He asked them why they didn't clear up the rubbish – not our problem was the reply. He then promised them a new football if they cleared up the rubbish in three days. They did. He did. MYSA was founded under the vision of Bob Munro:

You do something for me and I'll do something for you.

MYSA was founded and registered as a self-help youth sports and community development project in 1987 and was first based in Mathare – one of Africa's largest and poorest

---

15. www.mysakenya.org accessed May 2020. I was privileged to be invited to chair the MYSA Board's Annual Meeting on 9 December 2021 via Zoom but based in Nairobi.

slums. There around half a million people live and call home. They largely live in mud huts with no clean water, electricity or sanitation. When you grow up in a place like this, it can be hard to be optimistic about your future.

Today over 30,000 youth on 2,052 teams take part in the MYSA sports, slum cleanup, AIDS prevention, leadership training, jailed kids, photography, music and other community development activities. Another 10,000 youth from eight countries participate in a similar sport and development project initiated by MYSA in 1999 in the Kakuma refugee camp in northwest Kenya.

Sport is combined with community outreach and development activities. To give young people the skills and confidence they need to aim higher, achieve more and improve their lives, MYSA is run by the youth and for the youth who take part in its activities and gives the youth an opportunity to dream of a brighter future.

Today, there are 30,098 (20,107 boys and 9,991 girls) football teams in 234 leagues across MYSA's 16 zones. But MYSA is more than football; apart from goals, teams earn points from taking part in other activities off the pitch, like community cleanups, participating in HIV/AIDS awareness sessions and volunteering as a referee or a coach for other teams. Participation in such activities earn extra points, which could be the difference between a team winning the league or being relegated

Since then:

- MYSA has been a global pioneer on sport for development and peace for three decades
- But MYSA has also been donor dependent during those three decades
- MYSA is now committed to a new and trailblazing transition into an SSE
- MYSA's transition is anchored by its new performance management approach
- MUFC/MYSA was nominated for the Nobel Peace Prize:

A team from the slums of Nairobi has been nominated for the Nobel Peace Prize. The Mathare United Football Club (MUFC) and the Mathare Youth Sports Association (MYSA) are among the 165 nominees alongside such disparate hopefuls as Bono and the Pope ... In return for the facilities and organization, the players keep their neighbourhood clean, plant trees and attend AIDS, pregnancy and drug-awareness classes. There are scholarships too for photography, music and drama. Teams get points for their work as well as their football.

'The Pope, Bono and Mathare United FC', The Observer *(UK)*,
October 5, 2003

In the deep mire of poverty that is Mathare, a giant rotting shanty town of Nairobi, the Mathare Youth Sports Association (MYSA) has tapped the enormous passion for the game to create a unique programme of football coaching and social and personal development. Founded in 1987, MYSA has become Africa's largest youth organization ... Participation and coaching is linked to voluntary public service. The senior team, Mathare United (MUFC), built on this huge foundation ... gained national league status and then won two of three Kenyan Cup finals in the next four years. The message has not been lost on aid agencies elsewhere who have sought to use football as an instrument of post-conflict reconciliation in Liberia and Sierra Leone'.

BBC documentary on MUFC Scoops 2009 Foreign Press Award.[16]

MYSA's 'most successful failure' is Moses Muturi who lost the goalkeeper competition for the 1992 MYSA U16 team for the Eco-Youth Tournament in Brazil. He then refocused on his studies, graduated at the top of his class at the University of Nairobi, won a Rhodes scholarship to Oxford University, qualified as an actuary, worked for Deloitte in London and South Africa and is now Head of Actuarial Services at CfC Life in Kenya. In 2011, Moses became the first MYSA alumnus to join the MYSA board of trustees.

How is MYSA being changed into a SSE?

The work started in 2015 and is aimed to be completed by 2020. Already MYSA has created profit-making social enterprise centres in:

- Training/consultancy services on sport for development and peace
- MYSA fitness centres
- MYSA sports cafés

Planned income generating activities include:

- Sports hall rental for external functions (e.g. weddings, meetings, etc.)
- Playing field/stadium rental
- Branded products
- Physiotherapy clinic(s)
- Borehole water sales

Much of MYSA was already a social enterprise, but it provided its services for free. For instance, MYSA has trained many professionals including professional soccer players such as Wanyama at Tottenhem Hotspur in the English Premier League. Yet it got no return on its training investment. Today, each entrant into the MYSA complex is asked to sign a form that requires them to give 1 per cent of their revenue to MYSA should their income exceed a certain level.

As in all things in life, there are no quick fixes. Yet MYSA already has been replicated in over 300 NGOs around the world. The next step is to create a sustainable MYSA that is 75 per cent free of grants and also works with other NGOs, governments, donors and international organizations to bring the dream of development to young kids around the world while remembering that:

You do something for me and I'll do something for you.

---

16. https://www.sportencommun.org/wp-content/uploads/2020/09/200909-mysapresentation-executive-summaries.pdf

Concluding Remarks

It is worth noting that the issue of sustainability was not a high priority in any of the projects overseen by British American Tobacco (BAT) when I evaluated their development programmes almost two decades ago. Then, as now, a major fault of the evaluations is that the same evaluator is rarely employed again to check on the accuracy of his/her observations and this institutional memory is lacking. Do any of the projects I evaluated then still exist today? We don't know but hope those judged more sustainable will still be in operation.

The issue of social enterprise is a move towards sustainable philanthropy. Not every project can be sustainable, but many are life-saving projects that need to be done irrespective of sustainability criteria, and many others are advocacy projects where donations are essential to keep the issue alive (for instance, Human Rights Watch, Médecins Sans Frontières, etc.). The theme of this chapter is that each project (or programme) should be looked at in terms of any viability to make the project more sustainable even if complete (100 per cent) sustainability is not possible. In conclusion, here are some actions that could be considered:

- Companies should abandon all philanthropy which is outside of a CSR framework.
- Companies should work hand-in-hand with governments to promote economic and social development.
- Governments should help those people who cannot be helped to help themselves through a subsidy. They should look after vulnerable groups and not just await the whim of corporate philanthropy: if a charity fails because a company fails, then this is a disaster for all the vulnerable groups and people concerned.

The need to address questions of low living standards, exploitation, poverty, unemployment and how to promote human development through the SDGs, in general, has been almost entirely the preserve of governments. Corporations have entered the field of helping communities through philanthropy. But whatever the sources the author argues that sustainable philanthropy should be the objective for all institutions involved in project support whatever part of the globe they are from and wherever they invest.

Chapter Nineteen

CONCLUSION: NEXT STEPS
AND FOR WHOM?

Introduction

Where is CSR going? The issue of responsible business and behaviour has taken a huge leap forward because of the pandemic and the growing realization that climate change may rapidly become another huge global disaster. Responsibility now touches every part of business, and personal responsibility has become essential to self-protect against the coronavirus. And, as noted in this book, the social responsibility of governments is high on the agenda even as so many populist leaders are crushing dissent from Russia to Myanamar. It is not clear what direction the public sector will go, and many worry that the Trump fiasco could be the start not the end of mafia-like domination. Then, whatever CSR is called, there is no doubt that the issue of sustainability, and sustainable investment in particular, are key new areas. In 2020, my Swiss bank already proposed a sustainable portfolio for me, which was surprising given that the Swiss are notoriously hard-nosed and tough to change.

But many activists expect rapid change from companies, and they are concerned that exploitation is not a thing of the past but a continuing issue. On the other hand, if you watched the television series *Mad Men*, with its depiction of early 1960s corporate mores compared with today, it is clear that corporate mores have changed profoundly. In the series, the men are casually sexist, everyone smokes and drinks on the job, health care is an afterthought, and environmental consciousness is nonexistent. It is clear that much has changed since then.

Companies are starting to realize that ethics, stakeholder relationships and external conditions affect their competitive position. They realize that the more they build up their internal ethical culture, the more productive and dedicated their employee teams become. The more they actively manage their stakeholder relationships, the more they leverage their business ecosystem. The more they actively engage with their external environment, the more effective their internal resources become.

Over the next few years, I would submit that concepts like 'social capital', 'stakeholder relationship management', 'sustainable enterprise' and 'sustainable development' are going to become much more mainstream and widespread and that there will be a transformation in the management of the private sector. And as the theme of this book suggests, companies will be more aware of the big issues of the day and will probably *all* do something, whether it is something as small as using less plastics or it is something as major as investments in sustainability and stakeholder dialogue. These ideas will also be exchanged between the public and private sectors in ways hard to envisage today.

But if social capital management and stakeholder relationship management would seem to place CSR in more of a brand/reputation/marketing/communications/legal continuum, the assistance, recovery and development challenges that we are seeing seem to be pulling CSR in a more strategic planning and operational direction.

Enough of Theory

What happens when these ideas are transformed into a strategic framework to enhance the competitive advantage of a company while preserving the values of CSR?

My company MHC International Ltd. worked out such a strategy for the oil company Addax Petroleum (AP) a few years back. The following steps were identified.

1. Report on where the key overall CSR trends are heading, including any legal requirements.
2. Provide benchmark examples of CSR and assess CSR trends. To draw upon other oil companies such as Premier Oil, consolidate who have won awards for their CSR approach.
3. Analyse AP's record in the light of GRI reporting guidelines and act accordingly.
4. Identify AP's existing CSR activities and projects to date with a view to identifying the competitive advantage.
5. Use MHC International's H-CSR-M to judge their sustainability.
6. Identify, according to the stakeholder model of CSR, key activities that AP could do, while bearing in mind (and identifying, at least qualitatively) the costs and benefits of additional CSR activities.
7. Identify and interview key stakeholders as a precursor to future, fully fledged stakeholder dialogues. Note that Premier Oil, for instance, has as its stakeholders 'owners and investors, management, employees, customers, suppliers, government, joint venture partners and the local community'. Also note that the process of stakeholder dialogue is more important for company performance than simply reporting on it.
8. Interview only a selection of stakeholders in each category but attach importance to investors, suppliers and employees in the first instance. At this stage, a fully fledged stakeholder dialogue will not be carried out but will be something for the future (see the next section).
9. Make use of the industry standard key performance indicators (KPIs) (for social, economic and environmental issues), as suggested by GRI, and suggest which ones are most appropriate for AP.
10. Provide data for as many KPIs as possible in the short term and suggest methodologies for calculating those currently missing over the long term.
11. Work out key next steps and alternatives towards establishing a fully fledged CSR strategy for AP over a period of three years into the future.

CSR Projects: The Next Step Forward or Backwards?

In the past decade, CSR has turned into many forms. At one end of the spectrum, it is used to emphasize corporate philanthropy where we often hear of 'CSR projects'. This notion can be found in some developed countries such as the USA but is mainly found in emerging markets across the world and is intended to increase the sustainability of such projects. This latter issue was discussed at length in the previous chapter where it was noted that CSR is far wider than a narrow project-centred view. Clearly, at the other end of the spectrum many large corporations now have a much broader view of CSR where the concept is at the core of a company's business strategy.

Moreover, the collapse of firms such as Enron, Lehman Brothers and General Motors, all of whom suffered from poor strategic models, shows that new business strategy models are essential. And, as argued here, a key message is that CSR is becoming the core of business activity. It is fast becoming acknowledged that a strategic stakeholder model of engagement with the business environment means that the potential for avoiding disasters and increasing success and innovation can be increased. CSR is obviously not a panacea for all ills, but more and more companies are seeing that it can enhance their competitive advantage.

Big Issues: What Next?

pure, stateless, market capitalism, a sort of international bourgeois anarchism … (or) a planned socialism uncontaminated by private profit-seeking. Both are bankrupt. The future, like the present and the past, belongs to mixed economies in which public and private are braided together in one way or another.
Eric Hobsbawm, *The Guardian*, London, April, 2009

The responsibility of companies, corporations and institutions to their stakeholders is probably more important today than ever before. This is because the lack of responsibility in so many of our largest companies in recent years has thrown the whole issue of market freedom into question. Even the limited version of responsibility, beloved to Milton Friedman, where the only responsibility of companies is to their shareholders, has been undermined by COVID, the crash and then rise of shares in the past two decades, bonds, titles and, in some cases, the total loss of pension funds.

As our politicians and press speculate about the future model of our economies, and 'more of the same, but better' remedies emanate from various bodies such as the April 2009 G20 World Leader's Conference in London, questions remain: Where are we? Should we follow either a socialist (aka communist) or a market (aka capitalist) agenda? Currently, a third way of responsibility with a mix of socialist and market principles is attractive as Eric Hobsbawm has argued (cited above).

Yet companies have lurched against responsibility as exemplified by their seeming move to embrace 'corporate sustainability' or 'corporate citizenship'. This is aided and abetted by the 'think-tanks' of change such as the consultancy *SustainAbility* or *The Global Reporting Initiative* neither of whom suggest system-wide definitions. If either embraces the tenets of system theory and strategic CSR,[1] then perhaps we should worry less. But it does appear that those who embrace the last two corporate buzz words have lurched either toward more environmentalism (sustainability) or more community involvement either at home or abroad (citizenship).

Now there is nothing wrong with being concerned with either of the latter two issues. A strategic approach to CSR includes both of these as part of its overall systems approach. So has CSR been rejected too soon?

CSR Rejected?

Curiously, the increased need for 'responsibility' comes at a time of a perceived tiredness with the concept of CSR. The rush into CSR in the 1990s was led mainly by environmentalists who had seen a useful concept to use in a world that eagerly and continually searches for new concepts. Further, when CSR is defined as 'treating the stakeholders of a company in an ethically responsible manner', it provides a powerful systems tool to managing a company.

But the problem with CSR has not been about what it means, when carefully defined, but the combination of words. Of course, corporations are responsible, some would argue,[2] because they could not otherwise survive – an irresponsible company would soon have its wings clipped. Yet, many companies have had their wings clipped because of irresponsible behaviour (Shell, Nike, Gap, Exxon, BP, Parmalat, Fanny Mae, etc.) and some have been disembowelled (Enron, Bear Sterns, Lehman Brothers, Worldcom, etc).

Perhaps the problem is the word 'social' as companies may believe that this means socialism through the backdoor? Clearly, on first sight, it seems to exclude economics and the environment. But then, do not economics faculties in our universities come under the heading of social science? And can we deal with environmental problems without their social and economic roots? Of course not!

I think we would all love a 'new' term that describes all that succinctly. CSR has survived because it, as I define it, has concentrated minds on all key stakeholders and how they are treated by a company or entity. Yet, when people start saying goodbye to concepts without defining them, as many have done with CSR recently (e.g. the overly dramatic 'death' of CSR in the *Financial Times* and an earlier critical piece in *The Economist*, subsequently reversed), perhaps these concepts have more mileage left in them. For instance, many have predicted the 'death' of GDP as a concept because the growth it purports to measure does not capture such things as 'intangible' assets, environmental protection and so on.

---

1. Strategic CSR consists of the principles, processes and products that cover treating the key stakeholders of a corporate body in a responsible manner. The aim is to behave as responsibly as possible while preserving the profitability or survival of the corporate body. This is covered in detail in my book *The Planetary Bargain: CSR Matters* (Earthscan, London, 2003).
2. E.g. Bo Ekman of the Tallberg Foundation, personal communication, 3 April 2009.

Companies, or at least some of them, are now delighted that new terms allow them to forget the stakeholder model that covers such knotty issues as corporate governance, employee layoffs, supply chain standards, customer concerns, corruption and so on and allow them to concentrate on such things as 'corporate sustainability' (i.e. long-term environmental issues) or 'corporate responsibility' (which is what they do already).

A VP of Unilever, who looks after these issues, confirmed what I suspected: that many companies switched too quickly over to 'sustainability' issues and ignored the social and economic ones and he felt that a re-alignment towards 'social responsibility' was sorely needed.[3]

A truly independent and forward thinking advisory company can best serve companies by not being a slave to them and giving them a 'get out of jail for free' card, but to help them honestly and critically to deal with all their stakeholders so that the 'responsibility' crisis of the present, and the future, can be avoided and their reputation and business model be reinforced.

Evidence

Corporate & Social Responsibility is part of the fabric of our business – it informs, influences and drives our operations and our commitment to the well-being of the world. We see our responsibility falling into two categories: we have a 'sphere of control' where we can ensure that we run our operations in the safest and most responsible way we can; there is also a 'sphere of influence' where we seek to take a lead in key areas, such as climate change and development, to enable change and help achieve a positive outcome.

www.bp.com

Corporate social responsibility is generally considered conducting business activities in a responsible manner. At General Motors, CSR is the attempt to balance environmental and social aspects of our business with the economic aspects of our business.

www.gm.com

So much for theory. If we look at the websites of the 10 largest corporations in the Fortune 500 list, what do we find a decade ago? Surprisingly, as Table 19.1 illustrates, 'sustainability' did not appear as often as one might have expected nor did 'corporate citizenship'. The term 'responsibility' appeared in five out of the 10, and 'social' responsibility in three out of the 10. A headline writer might well capitalize 'CSR still dominant term in 30% of world's largest corporations!' or, even better to support my case 'CSR not dead as 50% of top corporations focus on their 'responsibilities.' Alternatively we might also get 'No mention of CSR in 50% of top corporate websites', depending on the orientation of the imaginary journal. Today the picture has improved and we find that one of our poorest CSR companies a decade ago, Walmart, has accelerated its CSR initiatives since CEO Doug McMillon took the reins in 2014.[4]

---

3. Private communication, 9 April 2009.
4. https://footwearnews.com/2020/business/retail/walmart-corporate-social-responsibility-2020-1202915258/, accessed 25 June 2021.

Table 19.1 Largest Ten Corporations in Fortune 500 (2008 Revenues)

Company	Dominant Concept Used	Items on 'CSR' from Search
Wal-Mart	Sustainability	0
ExxonMobil	Corporate citizenship	0
Royal Dutch Shell	Responsible energy, sustainability	0 after 2006
BP	CSR	25
Toyota	None in particular	3
Chevron	Corporate responsibility	0 after 2006
ING Group	Corporate responsibility	0 after 2004
Total	Environment and society	19
General Motors	Environment and social responsibility	20
Conoco Phillips	Social responsibility	4

What Could Be the Next Evolution of CSR?

There is little doubt that the lack of responsibility in markets has led to the increasingly frequent financial turmoil and recession in most international markets. The private sector has taken a huge blow, even more due to COVID, but there is agreement that no one wants too much control by governments – although the exact division of public and privately provided goods is one of the greatest economic dates of today. CSR does provide many of the elements of a solution but its ideas were largely ignored by many of the big financial players to date and has led to increased public sector involvement in the governance of corporations. As Thomas Friedman noted in the *New York Times*:[5] 'This financial meltdown involved a broad national breakdown in personal responsibility, government regulation and financial ethics....That's how we got here — a near total breakdown of responsibility at every link in our financial chain, and now we either bail out the people who brought us here or risk a total systemic crash'.

However, if you adhere to the theories of Adam Smith you may disagree about a larger role for the public sector. Smith argued more than 200 years ago that the general welfare was better served by people pursuing their enlightened self-interest than by misguided attempts to serve society.

So has CSR been rejected too soon? This may be so and the trend does seem to be along this path. On the other hand, the financial crisis which is still with us will demand increased responsibility. So look out for sustainable corporate responsibility or even a new CSR – corporate sustainable responsibility – or some such phrase!

What Can We Expect From Corporations? What Will Be Their Role?

According to my company's mail bag, CSR is still attracting interest across all markets – from China to Pakistan to Nigeria to Brazil – each with differing rationales. In

---

5. Thomas Friedman, 'All Fall Down', *New York Times*, Op-Ed, 25 November 2008.

a poll conducted by *The Economist's* Intelligence Unit of 566 US based respondents at the end of 2008, 74 per cent said that CSR can help increase profits. In fact, CSR is not expensive, although the respondents did think that financial philanthropy would be reduced over the coming year.

An example illustrates simple, but powerful, applications of CSR. When the three CEOs of Ford, Chrysler and GM came to Washington, DC, at the end of 2008 to plead for a $US25bn bail out of their companies, the Senate committee was scandalized that the three CEOs each flew in their private jets from Chicago to DC. At a time of recession, socially responsible CEOs would, at least, have shared the same jet or, better still, travelled commercially!

In 2021, therefore, where will CSR be going? First, the industry in the recession and those coming out of COVID will take a hard look at all their programmes. They will have to look, hard and rapidly, at the business case for CSR. Second, given the lack of responsibility among Western sub-prime holders, banks and financial institutions, there will be a new move toward responsibility. Third, great hope arose over the election of Biden and despite increasing criticism of lack of action, his actions are still likely to increase, and encourage, the need for national, corporate, public and personal responsibility.

So what next for CSR? I suggest six points:

First, CSR can help. A major stakeholder of a firm is its employees. CSR does not imply that downsizing should be prevented, which would be absurd. What it does imply is that companies must make an effort to organize layoffs in a socially responsible manner. This could include early warning, counselling, re-training, temporary financial assistance, and so on. The tendency of US companies, for instance, to give immediate notice is both distressing and can be counter-productive once re-hiring starts again. There is no doubt that there is an unequal power between companies and employees. A company can recover; it has its own institutions such as banks that are willing to keep it going through hard times. A redundant employee has none of these advantages and is in a very weak position once he or she leaves the confines of an institution.

Second, CSR urges transparency of operations through socially responsible reporting of activities such as informing shareholders and staff about off-balance sheet holding of debts. Enron, for instance, may well have been in much better shape today if it had behaved in a socially responsible manner. Even though Enron was a lavish donor, Simon Caulkin of *The Observer* (3 February 2002) regarded its CSR as a 'fig leaf' and 'of a piece with Enron's overall strategy'. In fact, CSR is an overall strategy for systematic management of all of a company's stakeholders and should not be confined to its PR department!

Third, CSR has not been given as much prominence, especially in the USA, simply because of the legal framework under which most corporations operate. Robert Hinkley argues,[6] for the

---

6. Robert Hinkley, 'How Corporate Law Inhibits Social Responsibility', *Business Ethics,* January 2002.

USA, that the law, in its current form, actually inhibits executives and corporations from being socially responsible because the law baldly states that the purpose of the corporation is to make money for its shareholders. Any deviation from that could leave the corporation open to a lawsuit. So Hinkley suggests simply adding a phrase on CSR to corporate law so as to enhance CSR. Law, he advocates, would then read something like:

> Directors and officers have a duty to make money for shareholders, but not at the expense of the environment, human rights, the public safety, the communities in which the corporation operates or the dignity of its employees.

Fourth, CSR has a positive impact on the intangible assets of a company, and investing in CSR is not simply a cost but also a market opportunity. Assets such as reputation and knowledge networks can turn into a source of market value and competitive advantage.

Fifth, CSR has a long-term effect on improving a company's bottom line. There is a positive link between social and financial performance especially when looking at the increased relevance of intangible assets such as reputation and knowledge networks. These turn into a source of market value and competitive advantage. As Warren Buffet said, 'reputation takes years to obtain yet can be ruined in a minute'.

Sixth, social responsibility is not confined to corporations. Institutions that have a major impact on the way we live are also expected to behave in a socially and personally responsible manner – NGOs and public institutions. Thus, for organizations caught in financial storms or off course due to the buffetings of the markets, CSR will, more and more, become part of their strategic planning. A true stakeholder focus crystallized around reworked values is crucial for these difficult times and will help responsible companies eventually sail into calmer, safer waters.

Some commentators are trying to return us to the hopelessly out-of-date Milton Friedman view of business but the conclusion remains, that social responsibility has been, is and will continue to be crucial to the future prosperity and integrity of our businesses.

Can, therefore, we call it what we like but still mean a robust strategic and systems approach to social responsibility? Perhaps a better expression will surface but so far none of the contenders – sustainability, citizenship, business and society, ethical business – have stuck long enough to focus minds. CSR is not dead, simply there is a 'dearth of CSR'! And, happily, companies will now, governments, NGOs and individuals[7] be involved as part of their CSR with many of the big issues of the day!

---

7. With personal responsibility.

ANNEX: THE CHARTER APPLIED:
THE CASE OF NESTLÉ[1]

'For a long time, corporate social responsibility was a buzzword marketing tool, walled off within an organization', said Alan Fleischmann, president of Laurel Strategies, an executive advisory firm. 'Now it has to be central for the C.E.O., part of their everyday responsibility and leadership'.

Chief executives face a constellation of pressures, and speaking up can create considerable uncertainty. Customers can be offended, colleagues can feel isolated and relations with lawmakers can suffer. Words and actions can backfire, resulting in public relations disasters. All this as a chief executive is expected to constantly grow sales.[2]

'We all feel unsettled. I feel I have an even bigger responsibility as a business leader now to step into the political discussion', said the head of Starbucks[3].

Preamble

I have noted that Nestlé's focus upon shared value has led to a greater involvement in some of the great issues of the day. Yet the world stumbles from crisis to crisis such as the beginning of Islamophobia, UK shuddering under the influence of a perceived EU blindness, fears of a nuclear war in the Korean Peninsula and the ascendance of centralized power as democracy seems to have faltered.

Nestlé writes: We as other companies were given tremendous power after the Fall of the Berlin Wall to conduct business more or less as we wished. Yet we are aware that many longer-term events could severely affect our bottom line as the global crises may well swing out of control.

So what could the private sector, and companies in particular, do more? Nestlé thinks that business could help the debate and thereby help themselves through addressing the key society issues that affect them. We are happy, therefore, through a new 'Charter' for companies to re-examine our role from focusing upon key stakeholders to enter the wider policy discourse and to address the main questions in the Charter.

---

1. Draft done for Nestlé by Michael Hopkins to test his idea of a Charter for Companies on the Big Issues of the Day. Based on the Nestlé website and various documents. Note it has been discussed with Nestlé, but they are *not* responsible for any of the above content at the current time. They expressed interest but felt it was not the right time for them as of September 2017, possibly later.
2. https://www.nytimes.com/2017/08/19/business/moral-voice-ceos.html?hp&action=click &pgtype=Homepage&clickSource=story-heading&module=second-column-region&region =top-news&WT.nav=top-news
3. https://www.ft.com/content/ca33669a-8335-11e7-94e2-c5b903247afd, August 20 2017.

Each company has been invited to write an annual statement on how they see their concerns and potential influence on society. In this way, we hope that Nestlé can be part of the democratic process to try and improve the societies in which we operate and, eventually of course, to ensure sustainability in our own enterprises.

What We Are Already Doing

Every day, we touch the lives of billions of people: from the farmers who grow our ingredients and the families who enjoy our products; to the communities where we live and work; and the natural environment upon which we all depend.

Our work focuses on three areas and is supported by these 42 commitments[4]:

Caring for water

- Work to achieve water efficiency and sustainability across our operations
- Advocate for effective water policies and stewardship
- Treat the water we discharge effectively
- Engage with suppliers, especially those in agriculture
- Raise awareness on water conservation, and improve access to water and sanitation across our value chain

Acting on climate change

- Provide climate change leadership
- Promote transparency and proactive, long-term engagement in climate policy

Safeguarding the environment

- Reduce food loss and waste
- Improve the environmental performance of our packaging
- Assess and optimize the environmental impact of our products
- Provide meaningful and accurate environmental information and dialogue
- Preserve natural capital, including forests

Our focus areas are firmly embedded in our purpose. Individuals and families, our communities and the planet as a whole are interconnected, and our efforts in each of these areas are supported through our original 42 public commitments (now extended to 50):

We publish these commitments to hold ourselves publicly accountable for our performance. We report annually to show progress. During 2016, we conducted an extensive internal review of our commitments and, in line with our ambitions, we introduced

---

4. http://www.nestle.com/csv/what-is-csv/commitments

some new commitments to go further and deeper than previously. All 42 commitments are directly aligned with our business and the majority are now supported by objectives towards 2020.

Nutrition, health and wellness

- 1. Launch more nutritious foods and beverages, especially for mothers-to-be, new mothers and children
- 2. Further decrease sugars, sodium and saturated fat
- 3. Increase vegetables, fibre-rich grains, pulses, nuts and seeds in our foods and beverages
- 4. Address undernutrition through micronutrient fortification
- 5. Simplify our ingredients list and remove artificial colours
- 6. Support breastfeeding and protect it by continuing to implement an industry-leading policy to market breast-milk substitutes responsibly
- 7. Empower parents, caregivers and teachers to foster healthy behaviours in children
- 8. Market to children only choices that help them achieve a nutritious diet
- 9. Inspire people to choose water to lead healthier lives
- 10. Leverage our marketing efforts to promote healthy cooking, eating and lifestyles
- 11. Apply and explain nutrition information on packs, at point of sale and online
- 12. Offer guidance on portions for our products
- 13. Partner for promoting healthy food environments
- 14. Build and share nutrition knowledge from the first 1,000 days through to healthy ageing
- 15. Build biomedical science leading to health-promoting products, personalized nutrition and digital solutions

Rural development

- 16. Roll out of rural development baseline assessments to understand the needs of farmers
- 17. Improve farm economics among the farmers who supply us
- 18. Improve food availability and dietary diversity among the farmers who supply us
- 19. Implement responsible sourcing in our supply chain and promote animal welfare
- 20. Roll out the *Nestlé Cocoa Plan* with cocoa farmers
- 21. Continuously improve our green coffee supply chain

Water

- 22. Work to achieve water efficiency and sustainability across our operations
- 23. Advocate for effective water policies and stewardship
- 24. Treat the water we discharge effectively

- 25. Engage with suppliers, especially those in agriculture
- 26. Raise awareness on water conservation and improve access to water and sanitation across our value chain

Environmental sustainability

- 27. Provide climate change leadership
- 28. Promote transparency and proactive, long-term engagement in climate policy
- 29. Reduce food loss and waste
- 30. Improve the environmental performance of our packaging
- 31. Assess and optimize the environmental impact of our products
- 32. Provide meaningful and accurate environmental information and dialogue
- 33. Preserve natural capital, including forests

Additional commitments as of 2016

Human rights and compliance

- 34. Assess and address human rights impacts across our business activities
- 35. Improve workers' livelihoods and protect children in our agricultural supply chain
- 36. Enhance a culture of integrity across the organization
- 37. Provide effective grievance mechanisms to employees and stakeholders

Our people

- 38. Enhance gender balance in our workforce and empower women across the entire value chain
- 39. Roll out the ***Global Youth Initiative*** across all our operations
- 40. Provide training on ***Corporate Business Principles***, Nutrition and Environmental Sustainability
- 41. Ensure that all Nestlé employees are covered by a certified safety and health management system
- 42. Advocate for healthy workplaces and healthier employees

These commitments will in term enable us to meet our three ambitions for 2030 in line with the timescale of the Sustainable Development Goals (SDGs).

To date Nestlé has:

For individuals and families: Helped 50 million children to lead healthier lives
For our communities: Helped to improve 30 million livelihoods in communities directly connected to our business activities
For the planet: Striven for zero environmental impact in our operations

What Are the Key Big Issues that Affect Your Company or Institution Directly?

The basic motto of our work is enhancing quality of life and contributing to a healthier future for all.

Paul Bulcke[5] when CEO emphasized shared values as a way to intersect with society and Nestlé's 330,000 members of staff. Trust is both a brand and a product. The company behaves as a citizen with the same sense of responsibility both within and outside the company.

As the world's largest food and beverages company, Nestlé can shape sustainable consumption and steward resources for future generations. We focus our efforts on reducing water use across our operations, using sustainably managed and renewable resources and working towards our goal of zero waste.

As such we are also concerned that society moves to improving the quality of life of its peoples, including disadvantaged groups around the world. We are therefore against anything that degrades the quality of life of people, especially their food, water, education and health.

We are a large company, so just about all global issues affect our business in some way. For instance, just about all the big issues of the day are of importance to us in some way, as we have listed in Table A.1.

From Table A.1 (see also SDG list in Table A.2), it can be seen that the SDGs link to most of the big issues listed above. The exceptions are anti-terrorism, anti-racism, immigration, cybernetic control, robotics and jobs, anti-corruption, youth alienation and defence (military) issues.

What We Do Already to Address These Issues

Table A.1 shows that we are active in many of the 'big issue' areas.

Table A.2 shows many of our efforts on the SDGs.

We admit, however, that many of our activities cover mainly our own internal operations and closely linked stakeholders in our supply chain.

Our work to expand our efforts to the bigger issues of society as listed in Table A.1 do identify that we have more to do outside our company on:

- anti-terrorism
- anti-racism
- immigration
- cybernetic control
- robotics and jobs
- anti-corruption
- youth alienation
- defence (military) issues

---

5. Chairman and former CEO of Nestlé in https://www.youtube.com/watch?v=I3LkvWfHwcw &feature=youtu.beas, recorded in February 2016.

Table A.1 Nestlé and the Big Issues of the Day, Including SDG Activity

List of Issues	Not of Interest	Can't Do Much	Can Do a Little	A Concern	A Major Concern	SDG?	Nestlé 50 Commitments
1. Democratic participation (human rights, freedom of the press, rule of law, freedom of association, gender equality)					X	5, 16	43–46*, 47* [*partially not globally]
2. Poverty (both relative and absolute) and income distribution				X		1, 10, 11, 12	
3. Illiteracy			X			4	
4. Appropriate education, skills and human capital				X		4	
5. Ethical treatment of stakeholders					X	16, 17	16–20, 44, 46
6. Work for the social good with other companies					X	8, 9	
7. Climate change					X	6, 7, 13, 14, 15	27–42
8. Anti-terrorism				X			
9. Anti-racism				X			
10. Immigration, including international migration and refugees		X					
11. Cybernetic control					X		
12. Robotics and jobs				X			
14. Health and life expectancy					X	3	1–15, 49, 50
15. Anti-corruption				X			45*
16. Quality of jobs and unemployment and underemployment			X			8	
17. Youth alienation			X				48*
18. Hunger, water and famine					X	2	16–21, 22–26, 27–42
19. Defence (military, terrorist, drug industrial complexes)	X	X	X	X	X	X	
20. Others – please add	X	X	X	X	X	X	

Table A.2 Nestlé and the SDGs

SDG Goal	Meaning	Nestle's Involvement?
1. Poverty	End poverty in all its forms everywhere	Pay living wage, reach out to families and communities
2. Food	End hunger, achieve food security and improved nutrition and promote sustainable agriculture	New methods of sustainable crops and products
3. Health	Ensure healthy lives and promote well-being for all at all ages	Work with public health sectors to develop cheaper and more appropriate products
4. Education	Ensure inclusive and equitable quality education and promote lifelong learning opportunities for all	Work with public sector to ensure supply of appropriate skills and education
5. Women	Achieve gender equality and empower all women and girls	Gender equality in companies
6. Water	Ensure availability and sustainable management of water and sanitation for all	Nestle has shown the way with big push on clean and available water
7. Energy	Ensure access to affordable, reliable, sustainable and clean energy for all	Government to provide incentives and adequate tax and pricing structure to mobilize alternative energy private sector
8. Economy	Promote sustained, inclusive and sustainable economic growth, full and productive employment and decent work for all	Private sector led
9. Infrastructure	Build resilient infrastructure, promote inclusive and sustainable industrialization and foster innovation	Sustainable construction to lead to many new companies
10. Inequality	Reduce inequality within and among countries	Accept fairer tax regimes
11. Habitation	Make cities and human settlements inclusive, safe, resilient and sustainable	New technologies for construction will lead to more new companies and innovation
12. Consumption	Ensure sustainable consumption and production patterns	Major efforts required by retailers and supply chains
13. Climate	Take urgent action to combat climate change and its impacts	Needs massive private sector innovation

(Continued)

Table A.2 (Continued)

SDG Goal	Meaning	Nestle's Involvement?
14. Marine ecosystems	Conserve and sustainably use the oceans, seas and marine resources for sustainable development	Shipping and fishing industries to innovate and then expand rapidly
15. Ecosystems	Protect, restore and promote sustainable use of terrestrial ecosystems, sustainably manage forests, combat desertification and halt and reverse land degradation and halt biodiversity loss	Millions of new products and companies required government incentives
16. Institutions	Promote peaceful and inclusive societies for sustainable development, provide access to justice for all and build effective, accountable and inclusive institutions at all levels	Companies to respect local laws, weed out corruption and benefit through enhanced reputation
17. Sustainability	Strengthen the means of implementation and revitalize the global partnership for sustainable development	Huge opportunities for public–private partnerships in sustainability agendas

We, as a company, shall be exploring how we can contribute in improving societies across the world in these major issues of our time. We intend to publish our efforts in our Annual Charter on Big Issues on 16th Nov each year.

If you need further information on the Charter, check out[6] Michael Hopkins web page.

---

6. https://www.csrfi.com/csr-charter

INDEX

CPSIA information can be obtained
at www.ICGtesting.com
Printed in the USA
JSHW030652310522
26496JS00011B/13